Wandering at Ease
in the *Zhuangzi*

Edited by Roger T. Ames

STATE UNIVERSITY OF NEW YORK PRESS

Published by
State University of New York Press, Albany

The cover image is a detail from "Chung K'uei [Zhong Kui] The Demon-Queller" by Kung K'ai [Kong Kai] of the Song dynasty, and is reproduced courtesy of the Freer Gallery of Art, Smithsonian Institution, Washington, D.C. Accession # 3.84 Chung K'uei.

Printed in the United States of America

For information, address State University of New York Press, State University Plaza, Albany, N.Y., 12246

Production by Cathleen Collins
Marketing by Dana Yanulavich

Library of Congress Cataloging in Publication Data

Wandering at ease in the Zhuangzi / edited by Roger T. Ames.
    p. cm. — (SUNY series in Chinese philosophy and culture)
    Includes bibliographical references and index.
    ISBN 0-7914-3921-6 (alk. paper). — ISBN 0-7914-3922-4 (pb : alk. paper)
    1. Chuang-tzu. Nan-hua ching. I. Ames, Roger T., 1947–
II. Series.
BL1900.C576W34 1998
299′.51482—dc21
                                      97-43323
                                        CIP

10 9 8 7 6 5 4 3 2 1

For our teacher Yang Yu-wei 楊有維
with affection and respect.

As it is recorded: "Understand continuity
thoroughly and all things will be done; win them
over without prejudice and the demons and spirits
will submit." (*Zhuangzi*)

Contents

Introduction   1

1. What Is the Reason of Failure or Success? The Fisherman's Song Goes Deep into the River: Fishermen in the *Zhuangzi*
KIRILL OLE THOMPSON   15

2. Just Say No to "No Self" in *Zhuangzi*
CHRIS JOCHIM   35

3. Between Chen and Cai: *Zhuangzi* and the *Analects*
JOHN MAKEHAM   75

4. How to Interpret Chapter 16 of the *Zhuangzi*: "Repairers of Nature (*Shan Xing*)"
HENRY G. SKAJA   101

5. Living Beyond the Bounds: Henry Miller and the Quest for Daoist Realization
RANDALL P. PEERENBOOM   125

6. On Hui Shi
LISA RAPHALS   143

7. Transformational Humor in the *Zhuangzi*
JAMES D. SELLMANN   163

8. Cook Ding's Life on the Whetstone: Contingency, Action, and Inertia in the *Zhuangzi*
WILLIAM A. CALLAHAN   175

9. On the *Zhenren*
DANIEL COYLE   197

10. A Meditation on Friendship
     BRIAN LUNDBERG   211

11. Knowing in the *Zhuangzi*: "From Here, on the Bridge, over the
     River Hao"
     ROGER T. AMES   219

     About the Contributors   231

     Index   235

Introduction

Master Zhuang (fourth century B.C.E.), also known as Zhuangzi 莊子 or Zhuang Zhou 莊周, is generally associated with the Daoist text named for him, the *Zhuangzi*. Scholarly consensus, encouraged by the recent research of scholars such as Guan Feng 關鋒, Lo Genze 羅根澤, A. C. Graham, and Harold Roth, regards the thirty-three chapters of this text to be composite—the product of several if not many hands. As such, the text contains passages that offer different and even at times conflicting interpretations of basic Daoist tenets. The opening seven "inner chapters" are traditionally thought to be the literary product of Master Zhuang himself, while the remaining "outer" and "miscellaneous" chapters are taken to be later elaborations and commentary by members of what retrospectively can be called a Master Zhuang school, or perhaps better, lineage (*jia* 家).

The *Zhuangzi* as a philosophical text is for the most part addressed to the project of personal realization, and only derivatively concerned about social and political order. As one of the finest pieces of literature in the classical Chinese corpus, the *Zhuangzi* is itself an object lesson in marshalling every trope and literary device available to provide rhetorically charged flashes of insight into the most creative way to live one's life in the world.

Philosophical Daoism is often called "Lao-Zhuang" philosophy, referring directly to the two central and most influential texts, the *Daodejing* 道德經 (sometimes also called *Laozi* 老子) and the *Zhuangzi*. The former like the *Zhuangzi* is composite, probably compiled in the fourth and third centuries B.C.E. and edited into its present form sometime between 250 and 150 B.C.E. Beyond these two texts, we might include the syncretic *Huainanzi* (c. 140 B.C.E.) and the *Liezi*, reconstituted around the fourth century C.E., as part of the traditional Daoist corpus.

The difference between the *Daodejing* and the *Zhuangzi* tends to be one of emphasis rather than substance. As a text, the *Zhuangzi* focuses on personal spirituality and insight, while the *Daodejing* is more concerned with the social and political consequences of this heightened state of awareness.

1

The consummate human being in *Zhuangzi* is the "Authentic Person" (*zhenren* 真人), and consummate "ethical" concerns have to do with the quality of one's contributions to the ethos or total character of one's world. Institutions and conventions—generally associated with Confucianism—are regarded as nothing more than artificial structures established by human beings as an apparatus for giving expression to the accommodation, contribution, and enjoyment that constitute the fabric of an integrated human existence. The *Zhuangzi*'s quarrel is not with these conventions per se, but with any overriding concern for and attachment to these abstracted rules of conduct at the expense of the expression of one's own particular genuineness—one's self-disclosure (*ziran* 自然). When we say "self-disclosure," we must bear in mind that "self" is not the superordinated agent "self" familiar in some modern Western philosophers, but is always "in context," a particular "focus" (*de* 德) in the ongoing "field" of experience (*dao* 道) that is sponsored by, and ultimately reflects in itself, the full consequence of existence. One's self-disclosure impresses itself on and conditions *dao*, just as *dao* conditions the expression of one's particularity.

To the extent that Daoism is normative and prescriptive (and it certainly is), it is so not by articulating rules to follow or asserting the existence of some underlying moral principle, but by describing the conduct of the achieved human being—the Authentic Person (*zhenren*)—as a recommended object of emulation. The model for this human ideal, in turn, is the orderly, elegant, and harmonious processes of nature. Throughout the philosophical Daoist corpus, there is a "grand" analogy established in the shared vocabulary used to describe the conduct of the achieved human being on the one hand, and the harmony achieved in the mutual accommodations of natural phenomena on the other.

Although the Daoists on occasion use the term "sage" (*shengren* 聖人) for the consummate human exemplar, it is interesting that they also create, or at least popularize, a new technical expression—the *zhenren*. The common translation of *zhenren*—"True Man" or "Real Man"—belies the fact that etymologically *zhen* implies both "authenticity" and "transformation." That is, whatever the human exemplar might be, he or she is one who is able to express personal integrity and uniqueness in the context of a transforming world.

The choice of "authentic" to translate *zhen* is calculated. With the same root as "author," it captures the primacy given to the creative contribution of the particular person. It further registers this contribution as what is most fundamentally "real" and "true." It is because of the primacy of the "authorship" of the "authentic person" in creating human order that "there must be the Authentic Person before there can be authentic knowledge." This claim made at the beginning of *Zhuangzi* 6 suggests that a "knower" does not simply cognize a preexisting reality. Zhuangzi challenges the notions of discrete agency and the "objectivity" of knowledge—the independence of the world known, from the knower. Knowledge is always proximate as the condition of an experience rather than of an isolated experiencer. Situation has primacy, and agency is an abstraction from it. Knowledge is thus a tracing out and mapping of the productive patterns (*li* 理) of one's environs in such a manner as to enable one to move efficaciously and without obstruction.

Thus, "knowers" participate actively in the "realization" of their worlds through their own "self-disclosure" (*ziran*). "Knowing" for the Daoist, in addition to being cognitive, is profoundly experiential and performative—a "making real." It is precisely because the Authentic Person must "author" the world to "know," or better, to "realize" it, that this term *zhen* has at once metaphysical and epistemological significance: *zhen* as what is "authentic" is both what is "real," and what is "true."

There is need for further refinement. As we have suggested, the "self" of "self-disclosure" (*ziran*), is always "in context." It is an individuated focus in the ecological process of existence that is dependent upon and ultimately reflects in itself, the full consequence of nature. The Authentic Person has an interdependence and mutuality with all environing conditions such that one's own disclosure and *their* disclosures are mutually entailing. The Authentic Person is both transforming and transformed in that, as one's contribution impresses itself on and conditions *dao*, so *dao* conditions the expression of one's own insistent particularity.

We can make this profile of the consummate exemplar more concrete by referring to the texts. The *Daodejing* is primarily a *political* treatise. As such, it is the portrait of the ruler who, emulating the regularity of nature, sets broad political and social conditions for the pursuit of personal realization. The sage-ruler is thus referred to as the "model of the world" under whose organization the people are at leisure to pursue their own realization.

The concerns of the *Zhuangzi* are somewhat different. Instead of focusing on the sage-ruler and the manifestation of his personal enlightenment in the appropriate government of the state, the *Zhuangzi* concerns itself more with the realization of the particular person, assuming perhaps that enlightened government is simply a natural extension of the enlightened person. The most salient features of this enlightened person—the Authentic Person—that can be abstracted from the Daoist texts are the following. First, the Authentic Person through modelling human conduct on the rhythm and cadence of natural change, is able to realize an integration and continuity with the process of change as a whole. A recognition of the mutuality one shares with one's environments leads to a reconciliation of opposites: a transcending of the self/other distinction and freedom from the desires, attachments, and dichotomous values that are generated from the notion of a discrete self (that is, a reconciliation of "this/that," "good/bad," "right/wrong," "life/death," and so on).

This "deconstruction of polar opposites" is pervasive in the Daoist literature, and can be illustrated in the androgynous ideal of the *Daodejing*. In chapter 28, it describes "one who knows masculinity and yet preserves femininity" as "the river gorge of the world" to which all repair. Another example of this deconstruction of polar opposites is the *daode* 道德 or "field-focus" relationship. As we have seen, *de* as a focus in *dao* is a unique particular with its own integrity and character. But when viewed as a perspective on *dao* that entails all of its environing conditions as integral to itself, the focus/field distinction is deconstructed. *Zhuangzi* 1, "Wandering at Ease," observes that "if you look at things in terms of how they differ, the gap between liver and gall is as great as the distance from Chu to Yue; if you look at them in terms of their sameness, everything is continuous."

Among the *Zhuangzi's* central concerns is maximizing human creativity. Creativity can be compromised, however, where one attempts to express one's unique particularity in a "dis-integrative" way that fails to accommodate the mutuality and interdependence of other things. This diminution in creativity can be brought about either by interpreting one's environment reductionistically through one's own fixed conceptual structures and values, thereby impoverishing context in service to oneself, or by allowing oneself to be shaped wholly by context without contributing one's own uniqueness, thereby abnegating oneself in service to context. To be fully integrative, individuals must overcome the sense of discreteness and discontinuity with their environment, and they must contribute personally and creatively to the emerging pattern and regularity of existence called *dao*.

Throughout the *Zhuangzi*, there is considerable discussion of "overcoming one's discreteness" (*wu sang wo* 吾喪我) through "nonassertive action" (*wuwei* 無為) that is free of coercion, "nonprincipled knowing" (*wuzhi* 無知) that is free of fixed conceptual patterns and precedents, and "objectless desire" that is free of attachments (*wuyu* 無欲). This cultivation of the interdependence of self and context has the effect of making the "Authentic Person" different from others in the quality of the relationships that are developed. The Authentic Person's activity is characterized by flexibility, efficacy, and noncontentiousness—one collaborates with one's social and natural environments, serving as frictionless ground for their self-disclosure, and they reciprocally for one's own. Because one has an identity with the whole process, one is calm and imperturbable. One exists beyond the plethora of disintegrative dualisms—self and other, creator and creature, life and death, reality and appearance—and achieves immortality not by escape to some more "real" world, but by coming to realize and to celebrate the mutually entailing identity of oneself and one's world.

To turn to Daoist moral philosophy—an appropriate way of living in the world—"ethics" would refer to "ethos" in the classical sense of "character." It would involve not simply moral judgments, but the total character of the person in his or her social and natural environments. This total character is the changing lineaments of habit and disposition that include not only what might be deemed "good" or "moral" but the full complement of the qualities that constitute the personal, social, and natural fabric of one's existence. Thus, no clear separation between ethics, social, and political philosophy, and environmental philosophy, exists in this tradition. Importantly, in the emergent, ecological cosmology of Daoism, the ethos is always experienced and interpreted from some particular perspective. Appealing to the vocabulary of Daoism itself, this then is the basis of the polar and correlative relationship between *dao* 道 as environment or field, and *de* 德 as individuated particular, or focus. *Dao* is the defining conditions—the context or environment—for the particular *de*. Given that one of the core Daoist texts—the *Daodejing*, or "Classic of *Dao* and *De*"—takes its name from these two terms, an exploration of Daoist philosophy might well begin from a closer examination of *dao* and *de*, and of their relationship.

There is a potential problem in using "ethos" as an equivalent for *dao*. *Dao* is perhaps most frequently translated as the "Way." "Ethos" quite adequately captures the determinate and intelligible order of our various environments—the "way" or "mode" of existence. However, *dao* is not only the "how," but also the "what." That is to say, *dao* is ontologically categorial: it is both the perceived order of the cosmos, and the energy of *qi* in which this order is expressed. The myriad things are perturbations of hylozoistic energies that coordinate themselves to constitute the harmonious regularity that is *dao*. *Dao* produces the myriad things, and the myriad things are constitutive of *dao*.

More also can be said about *de* as particular perspectives or foci on the ethos we call *dao*. *De* is frequently translated as "virtue" in the sense of "potency," "capacities," "strength," or "influence." If we think of particular phenomena in relationship to their environments, they register varying degrees of impact on the character of their contexts as a function of their own particular potencies. *De* is the full range of the ways and the qualitative degrees by which a phenomenon alters and contributes to the character of its world. Having said this, it must be clear that any "ethical" judgments in the narrow sense are going to be derived from aesthetic sensibilities—the intensity, integrity, and appropriateness that one detail has for its environing elements as interpreted from some particular perspective.

Daoism has often been construed as an anarchic critique on the constraining conventionalism of Confucian morality. It has frequently been characterized in terms of passivity, femininity, quietism, spirituality—a doctrine embraced by artists, recluses, and religious mystics. Confucianism, by contrast, has been cast in the language of moral precepts, virtues, imperial edicts, and regulative methods—a doctrine embodied in and administered by the state official. This difference has been articulated through a plethora of distinctions: feminine versus masculine, heterodox versus orthodox, mystical versus mundane, anarchy versus top-down regulatory government, other-worldliness versus this-worldliness, rebellion versus political authority, nature versus culture, personal creativity versus social responsibility, and so on.

Recalling familiar assumptions about gender traits that have promoted a sexist reductionism in our own culture, the injudicious application of this *yin-yang*-like contrast to Daoism and Confucianism tends to impoverish our appreciation of the richness and complexity of these two traditions. Used in a heavy-handed way, this distinction can potentially obfuscate the fundamental wholeness of both the Confucian and Daoist visions of meaningful human existence by imposing an unwarranted conservatism on classical Confucianism, and an unjustified radicalism on Daoism.

How then should the Daoist critique on Confucianism be understood? There is a common ground shared by the teachings of classical Confucianism and Daoism in the advocacy of self-cultivation. In general terms, both see life as an art rather than a science. Both express a "this-worldly" concern for the concrete details of immediate existence rather than exercising their minds in the service of grand abstractions and ideals. Both acknowledge the uniqueness, importance, and primacy of the particular person and the person's contribution to the world, while at the same time stressing the ecological interrelatedness and interdependence of this person with his context.

Wherein do they differ, then? For the Daoists, the Confucian penchant for reading the "constant *dao* 常道" myopically as the "human *dao*" is to experience the world at a level that generates a dichotomy between the natural and human worlds. The argument against the Confucian seems to be that the Confucians do not take the ecological sensibility far enough, defining self-cultivation in purely human terms. It is the focused concern for the overcoming of discreteness by a spiritual extension and integration in the human world that gives classical Confucianism its sociopolitical and practical orientation. But from the Daoist perspective, "overcoming discreteness" is not simply to redefine the limits of one's concerns and responsibilities within the confines of the human sphere. This only results in an extended "discreteness" with the same kind of limitations and attachments that one is seeking to transcend. That is, instead of *personally* being "dis-integrated" with the world, it is the human being *as a species* that is disintegrated. The Daoists do not reject human society and culture as such; rather, they reject the notion that human experience occurs in a vacuum, and that the whole process of existence can be reduced to human values and purposes. They reject the pathetic fallacy implicit in the early Confucian religiohumanism that gives the human being special status in the world, a status that ultimately serves to "dis-integrate" even an integrated social world from nature as a whole. The Daoist, observing that the human being has a natural as well as a social environment, insists that the Confucian model for self-cultivation be opened up from sociopolitical order to cosmic order, from the emulation of only human exemplars to the emulation of natural order broadly.

The consummate person in Daoism is characterized by a seeming indifference to worldly conditions, reflective supposedly of the relative and arbitrary nature of value judgments. This attitude is frequently misunderstood. It is sometimes construed as a passivity, a quietism, and a resignation, when it is perhaps better seen as a relaxation of conventional value judgments through an attitude of tolerance and accommodation. It is certainly not the case that Daoism eschews value judgments. This point can be made through a further discussion of what perhaps is Daoism's central normative concept, *wuwei* 無為.

Dao has been described as an emerging pattern of relatedness perceived from the perspective of an irreducibly participatory *de*, or particular. The perceived order is an achievement, not a given. Because *dao* is an emergent, "bottom-up" order rather than something imposed, any interpretation of *dao* that would reduce it to preexisting laws or principles that discipline the natural world in some necessary way would be problematic. This being the case, the question is: What is the optimal relationship between *de* and *dao*, between a particular and its environing conditions? The Daoist response is the self-dispositioning of particulars into relationships that allow the fullest degree of self-disclosure and development. In the Daoist literature, this most appropriate action is perhaps most often described as *wuwei*, formularistically translated "nonaction." Those translators who seek to avoid the passive and quietistic implications of the translation, "nonaction," generally render it as "not acting willfully," "acting naturally," or "nonassertive activity." Of course, any attempt to thus define *wuwei* as "natural action" and to distinguish it from "unnatural action" (*youwei* 有為) will give rise to the perennial question that haunts most interpretations of Daoism: If all is *dao*, and *dao* is natural, what is the source, the conditions, and the ontological status of unnatural activity?

To answer this question, we might want to consider the philologically similar term, "anarchy," as a more appropriate translation of *wuwei*, describing as it does the negation of the authoritarian determination of one thing by another. *Wuwei*, then, is the negation of that kind of "making" or "doing" that requires that a particular sacrifice its own integrity in acting on behalf of something "other," a negation of that kind of engagement that makes something false to itself.

The sympathy between *anarchy* and *wuwei* that lies in their common reference to activity performed in the absence of coercively determinative constraints would certainly recommend "anarchy" as a translation for *wuwei*. But there is also an important difference. Anarchy describes the fundamental relationship between a particular thing and a determinative principle—an *archē*. Because the *archē* is an "originative beginning"—that which determines without itself being determined—there is an ontological disparity between the *archē* and the particular that makes their relationship dualistic. *Wuwei*, by contrast, does not describe the dualistic relationship between independent principle and dependent particular, but the interdependent relationship that obtains between two particulars. In human terms, the personal integrity that must be sustained in the project of self-disclosure requires an awareness that uncoordinated action between oneself and the elements of one's environment not only deprives environing particulars of their possibilities, but further, impoverishes one's own possibilities. *Wuwei* describes a productively creative relatedness. *Wuwei* activity "characterizes"—that is, produces the character or ethos of—an aesthetically contrived composition. There is no ideal, no closed perfectedness. Ongoing creative achievement itself provides novel possibilities for a richer creativity. *Wuwei* activity is thus fundamentally qualitative: an aesthetic category and only derivatively, an ethical one. The distinction between *wuwei* and *youwei* activity is not made by appeal to some fixed principle or standard. But because there is no invariable structure to provide a science of "correct" relatedness, this does not mean that there is no basis for making value judgments. *Wuwei* can be evaluated on aesthetic grounds, allowing that some relationships are more productively *wuwei* than others. Some relationships are more successful than others in maximizing the creative possibilities of oneself in one's environments.

This classical Daoist aesthetic, while articulated in these early texts with inimitable flavor and imagination, was, like most philosophical anarchisms, too intangible and impractical to ever be a serious contender as a formal structure for social and political order. In the early years of the Han dynasty there was an attempt in the *Huainanzi* to encourage the Daoist sense of ethos by tempering the lofty ideals with a functional practicability. It appropriates a syncretic political framework as a compromise for promoting a kind of practicable Daoism—an anarchism within expedient bounds. While historically the *Huainanzi* fell on deaf ears, it helped to set a pattern for the Daoist contribution to Chinese culture across the sweep of history. Over and over again, in the currency of anecdote and metaphor, identifiably Daoist sensibilities would be expressed by inspiring a range of theoretical structures and social grammars, from military strategies to the dialectical progress of distinctively Chinese schools of Buddhism to the constantly changing face of poetics and art. It can certainly be argued that the richest models of Confucianism, represented as the convergence of Daoism, Buddhism, and Confucianism itself, were an attempt to integrate the Confucian concerns with human community with the broader Daoist commitment to an ecologically sensitive humanity.

Early Daoism has had an incalculable influence on the development of Chinese philosophy and culture broadly. Second in influence only to the Confucian school, the classical Daoist philosophers in many ways have been construed as both a critique on, and a complement to, the more conservative, regulatory precepts of their Confucian rivals. And when Buddhism entered China in the second century C.E., Buddhist adepts appropriated many of the ideas and vocabularies of indigenous Daoism as a sympathetic language through which to express a fundamentally foreign system of thought. In so doing, they made Buddhist ideas more palatable to the Chinese audience, but at the same time, also set Buddhism on a course of irrevocable sinicization.

Turning now to the specific contributions to this anthology on the *Zhuangzi*, in the course of Kirill Thompson's examination of the fisherman image in the *Zhuangzi*, he has the occasion to reflect on the cosmological significance of recurrent Daoist metaphors: the rivers, the fish, and water itself. The fisherman, communing with sea and sky, is living a life that both celebrates and defers to the dynamic continuity obtaining among "the myriad things"—the *wanwu* 萬物. Thompson then lets the text itself speak, rehearsing the various anecdotes in the *Zhuangzi* text that recount the experiences of the fisherman, anecdotes that include Zhuang Zhou himself angling on the Pu River. The fishermen, contemplating the vast expanse of the sea, are repeatedly transformed by their growing understanding of the natural and spontaneous interconnectedness of things. Moreover, the image of the fisherman highlights the concentration immanence and practicality of the sage.

The centerpiece of the discussion is "The Old Fisherman" chapter in which the Daoist *zhenren* 真人—the "Authentic" or Perfect Man—serves Confucius discomfiture, setting up a contrast between the natural and the contrived, the tranquil and the agitated, the sincere and the artificial, the free-spirited and the constricted. Having traced the fisherman motif through the *Zhuangzi* and established its value, Thompson then turns to the aesthetic traditions of China—its paintings and poetry—to recount how frequently the representation of this motif recurs, invariably aspiring to capture and elaborate upon the meaning invested in it by the early Daoist philosophers.

The essay by Chris Jochim is a sustained argument against anachronistically imposing a modern, culturally specific conception of "self," or alternatively and derivatively, a specifically Buddhist conception of "no-self," on the *Zhuangzi*. He begins by establishing the parameters of the superordinated "self" as it has emerged in the history of Western philosophy, and underscoring the complexity of the problem, remarks on how this modern concept has, as a response to Western literature, insinuated itself into contemporary Chinese philosophical reflection. Having surveyed some of the most prominent English and Chinese examples of the interpretative literature that claim that one first has a self and then forgets it, loses it, transforms it, or that self is, in a Buddhist sense, illusory, Jochim concludes that a way of thinking about oneself, either as a hypostatized individuated and isolated agent, or as a Buddhist "no-self," has distorted our understanding of a third position that holds a very different image. He argues for a holistic notion of "person" entailed by the use of *shen* 身 that resists bifurcation into self/body, mental/physical, inner/outer, spiritual/mundane, and importantly, singular/plural kinds of dichotomies. Similarly, he takes *xin* 心, heart-mind, to refer to the functional role of the *xin* as thinking and feeling rather than as decontextualizing it either as a physical organ or a mental faculty. Returning to *ji* 己—conventionally rendered "self"—he reinterprets it as bad habits and behaviors—a kind of egoism. And *wangwo* 忘我 (or mutatis mutandis, *sangwo* 喪我 or *shiwo* 失我) become the reflexive "forgetting oneself" as opposed to the objectifying "forgetting *the* self." As a strategy for overcoming the hypostatization of "self," Jochim concludes by bringing in a fresh look at what has been called "the flow experience," a radically situated sense of being in the world that is reminiscent in some ways of the notion of person as it played in Homeric Greece long before the invention of the unitary "self."

In John Makeham contribution, "Between Chen and Cai: *Zhuangzi* and the *Analects*," he continues to develop his investigation into traditional assumptions concerning the historical vintage of the Confucian *Analects* as a text, and the commentarial tradition that supports it. Beginning from the observation that Confucius is the most frequently cited person in the entire *Zhuangzi*, the question emerges: Is this portrait of Confucius consistent with the record preserved in the received *Analects*, or is it invariably a distortion of this text? Focusing the analysis on two contiguous passages in the *Analects* 15/1 and 2 that recount the adversity that Confucius encountered on his journey from the state of Chen to Cai, Makeham accomplishes several things.

First, Makeham demonstrates how versions of this particular story are used throughout the early corpus (and even in a single text—it is referenced seven times in *Zhuangzi* alone) to score a variety of often competing and sometimes even contradictory philosophical points, prompting the astute student of these texts to read for a rhetorical rather than a logical coherence. Different compilations appropriate some variation on a theme in service to their own particular program. A careful reading of these related yet disparate passages provides us with some insight into how the classical texts are compiled, and how continuity and novelty are expressed in them.

Secondly, given Makeham's misgivings about the tradition that claims that the *Analects* was compiled early—he dates its emergence as a fixed text to 150–140 B.C.E.—there is no compelling reason to believe that the version found in the received *Analects* is unquestionably authoritative. And thirdly, contrary to expectations, the *Zhuangzi*'s "Yielding the Throne" elaboration on this particular Confucius story is demonstrably closer in philosophical import to the *Analects* than either the *Mencius* or *Xunzi* versions, which, in fact, are markedly different.

Henry Skaja focuses on some problematic, seemingly "Confucian" passages in the "Repairers of Nature" chapter of *Zhuangzi*. Question: How are we to explain the presence of decidedly Confucian themes—the derivation of Confucian social virtues from the *dao* 道, and the limitations imposed upon the human experience by *ming* 命, conventionally understood as "fate" or "destiny"—in a chapter attributed in the tradition to a Daoist thinker?

By appeal to the social philosophy of John Dewey, Skaja mounts an argument that a social application of the Daoist notion of *wuwei* 無為—"nonassertive activity"—does not contradict the basic impulse of the Confucian worldview that communal harmony is achieved through deference and collaboration. In fact, argues Skaja, the nonhermetic side of the Daoist tradition, and the author of this *Zhuangzi* chapter specifically, share with the Mencian wing of classical Confucianism, at least as it has been interpreted by A. C. Graham, a commitment to a fundamentally social and cooperative understanding of the human being.

By challenging the appropriateness of the conventional heavily deterministic translation of *ming* as "fate" or "destiny" in the case of the *Mencius*, and instead reading it as "that which happens" in a negotiation between one's nature (*xingming* 性命) and the times (*shiming* 時命), Skaja is able to resolve a second interpretive difficulty.

In spite of the real philosophical differences between the *Mencius* and "Repairers of Nature"—for example, a stronger pro-active and deliberate attitude toward personal cultivation in the *Mencius*, and a celebration of historical worthies —there is enough "Daoism" in the *Mencius* and enough social commitment in Daoism, to locate this chapter somewhere in between.

In "Living Beyond the Bounds: Henry Miller and the Quest for Daoist Realization," Randy Peerenboom provides this volume with a comparison between Miller and the *Zhuangzi* "sage" that, at first blush, seems unlikely. In this comparison, he probes the perennial tension in the human experience between "living beyond the bounds" with the freedom to pursue personal fulfillment on one's own terms, and "living within the bounds" set by acknowledging one's social responsibilities, a tension that animates the *Zhuangzi* and perhaps two contemporary Daoists, Henry Miller and Yang Yu-wei.

Peerenboom rehearses both the life, and the autonovel recreated "life," of Henry Miller, provoking us the readers of this essay to resource our own familiarity with the *Zhuangzi* to establish pertinent links. The most obvious and persistent association is perhaps, a cultivated and irreverent nonconformity, certainly expressed differently, but then such personal uniqueness too is consistent with the premises of the Daoist text.

Whether or not the reader is ultimately persuaded that the life and escapades of Henry Miller is a Daoist life, or that the oeuvre of Miller taken in its own historical moment is a Daoistic intervention, Peerenboom, in invoking this concrete and dramatic example, is successful in challenging us to test the bounds of our own interpretative imagination. If Miller is at all a hard sell, the candid and wholly affectionate "Zhong Kui the Demon-Queller" (see cover) image of Yang Yu-wei that leaps to life in his "coda" is a masterpiece for anyone who knows and loves this extraordinary teacher, walking as he does straight out of the pages of the *Zhuangzi* onto the streets of Taipei.

One of the most mysterious and intriguing characters in the *Zhuangzi* miscellany is the sophistical Hui Shi. Lisa Raphals brings some light, and perhaps even more shadow, to this philosophical phantom by generating four competing profiles and valorizations of Hui Shi from the *Zhuangzi* and the extant third century B.C.E. literature: the sympathetic sophist of the *Zhuangzi*, the maladroit sophist of the *Lüshi chunqiu*, the dangerous heterodox philosopher of the *Xunzi*, and the skilful analogist of the *Han Feizi*. Raphals then traces these images of Hui Shi through documents dating from the second and first centuries B.C.E.—*Hanshi waizhuan* and *Huainanzi*, and *Shuo yuan* and *Zhanguo ce*, respectively—suggesting that a positive appreciation of Hui Shi might be linked to the degree of humor found in these disparate texts.

James Sellmann celebrates the way in which humor functions in the *Zhuangzi* as a liberating and transformative trope, challenging conventional wisdom while at the same time pointing to a myriad of alternative perspectives. In imitation of the ever transforming nature of human experience in the world, irony undermines certitude by always entailing the negation of whatever might be posited as true and enduring.

But laughter is more than just a literary device for the *Zhuangzi*; it teaches us how to live and how to die. Humor, in revealing the correlation between seeming disjunction and enjoyment, creates the optimal attitude for entertaining our life experience, awakening us to the sometimes concealed continuities that exist among the events of our own lives, located within the unfolding of our natural, social, and cultural environments. By contextualizing our processional existence in the world around us, we are able to generate a kind of living syntax that makes our experiences meaningful.

Beginning from the familiar story of Cook Ding, William Callahan explores "contingency, action, and inertia" in the *Zhuangzi*. The problematic that he sets for himself is: How does decision-making and the consequent action (and inertia) proceed in a Zhuangzian world when conventional approaches—the "usual"—are no longer efficacious? This requires Callahan to develop an understanding of the liberating technique of "illumination" (*ming* 明)—a conceptual rendering of the various images of the whetstone of nature (*tianni* 天倪), and the potter's wheel of nature (*tianjun* 天均) within the cosmos, and the axis of *dao*s (*daoshu* 道樞) beyond it. These devices within the cosmos enable one to interchange and accumulate the available alternatives within the context of the problem, and to harmonize them as contingent approaches to resolution within a specific situation. Beyond the cosmos, it provides one with an inert posture from whence to entertain the limitless possibilities that converge at the axis of *dao*s.

There is no absolute answer, no ultimate ground, no transcendent "reason" that will provide us with certitude. Rather, there is only the untrammeled person's search for the alternatives available within any particular situation that provides one with the opportunity to get the most out of those specific circumstances.

In the Daoist literature, it would seem that a new term—*zhenren* 真人—is being coined to denote what Callahan has called the "untrammeled person." Danny Coyle brings this expression under scrutiny, looking to define *zhenren* both by appeal to etymological evidence, and by a careful reading of those passages in the *Zhuangzi* where it first occurs. Given that *zhen* and *zhenren* are new terms, many of the occurrences that we find in the *Zhuangzi* are intended to provide a definition of them. Coyle, having established an interpretive context and a working definition for *zhenren*, turns to the "Great Ancestral Teacher" chapter, arguably the philosophical heart of the *Zhuangzi*, as a touchstone to test these insights. It is from the sustained rhymed excursus in this chapter devoted entirely to the *zhenren* that we derive our best insights into what is being invested in this neologism.

After all, it is the rhyme and rhapsody that is Zhuangzi's "reason." The undulating and pulsating rhythm of these passages, evoking an "image" of the effective continuities that dissolve all dichotomies to make the *zhenren*'s passage in the world "one," provide a better explanation of the untrammeled style of the *zhenren*—coming and going—than any conceptual analysis ever could. And the cosmic dimensions of the *zhenren*, liberated through imagination to frolic across and beyond those categories that otherwise confine the particular human experience, invest the term *zhenren* with a profoundly religious content. Like Nietzsche's *Übermensch*, Zhuangzi's *zhenren* is the meaning of the world.

Drawing his images from the same "Great Ancestral Teacher" chapter, Brian Lundberg appeals to the concrete representations of Zhuangzi's *zhenren* to breath life into this model of personal realization. As a corrective on the familiar portrait of the Daoist sage as a hermit communing with nature, Lundberg insists that human transactions are also celebrated in the *Zhuangzi*. It is not the *zhenren* alone, but rather the *zhenren* in the company of like friends that reveals a true awareness of the continuity that obtains among people, and then by extension, among the things of this world. There is a line between personal communication, the formation of community, and ecstatic communion—a standing out of oneself—that is played out in the enjoyment that the Daoist exemplars find in their relationships in the world.

Zhuangzi is profoundly aware that the greatest challenge to a person's appreciation of the interdependence of things, and explicitly, to friendship, is the prospect of death—a cold experience that we each must face alone. Not so, says the *Zhuangzi*, refusing to see the transformation entailed by personal death to be different in kind from the transformations that we experience throughout our lives. The central theme of "The Great Ancestral Teacher" is overcoming the fear of death by understanding it as that dimension of experience that enables us to relish life. That is, life tells us that this experience called "death" must be anticipated within the context of the shifting physicality and the dynamic network of thoughts and feelings that locates us resolutely within the company of familiar friends and a familiar world.

Finally, Roger Ames explores a single Zhuangzian anecdote that finds Zhuangzi and Hui Shi on the bridge over the river Hao. What is at issue in this familiar story is what the Daoist thinks it means to know the world around one. Whereas Hui Shi, representing a recessive analytical position in the classical tradition, argues that knowing lies with the subject of knowledge, Zhuangzi insists that knowledge belongs to situations, and only derivatively, to abstracted agents.

There is much in this essay that recalls the insights of the other authors in this same volume: Kirill Thompson's reflections on the scope of Daoist continuity, extending as it does, beyond the human world to the world of nature; Randy

Peerenboom's portrait of the wild and antinomian instincts of the liberated Daoist demon-queller—maybe Henry Miller, but surely Yang Yu-wei; Lisa Raphal's multivalent portrayals of Zhuangzi's intellectual nemesis, Hui Shi; Chris Jochim's concern over the familiar interpretive problem of commentators insinuating a culturally alien, essentialized "self" into the *Zhuangzi* text; William Callahan's emphasis on the kind of decision-making that kicks in when "usual" circumstances become "unusual," a form of decision-making that is grounded in an appreciation of the full range of alternatives that factor into any particular situation; the porous line that John Makeham discovers in comparing Daoist and Confucian commentary on a Confucian text; James Sellmann's celebration of Daoist humor as not only an instrument of liberation, but as a literary device that creates the Daoist appreciation of continuities within disjunctions; relatedly, Danny Coyle's rhetorical reading of the *zhenren* thematic, where the presentation itself creates the image and rhythm of the attuned person; Hank Skaja's rehabilitation of the social dimensions of Daoist thought via John Dewey—and Brian Lundberg's "friendship" theme as an initial relationality for the would-be Daoist adept.

Together the essays in this volume reflect an overlapping and sometimes coherent interpretation of *Zhuangzi* that respects the bottomlessness of one of the world's great achievements in philosophical literature.

The Editor wishes to thank Lawrence C. Becker, Editor of the *Encyclopedia of Ethics* (New York: Garland Publishing, 1992), for permission to adapt portions of my entries on Chuang Tzu, Lao Tzu, and Taoist Ethics for the Introduction to this anthology.

The cover is a detail from "Chung K'uei [Zhong Kui] The Demon-Queller" by Kung K'ai [Kong Kai] of the Song dynasty, courtesy of the Freer Gallery of Art, Smithsonian Institution, Washington D.C. During the early Tang dynasty, Zhong Kui, an able physician, took the civil examinations to advance his career in government service. Having performed brilliantly in the examinations and compared by the examiners to the wisest of the ancients, he achieved first rank among the examinees, only to be cruelly cheated of the opportunity he had earned by a capricious court. In defiance of this injustice, he stood before the emperor and took his own life by smashing his head against a palace pillar.

In China, cultural heroes become deities, and Zhong Kui is worshiped for his abilities as a physician to exorcise the malignant demons that roam the earth, pressing them to make wine and mincing them to make demon jelly.

Roger T. Ames
University of Hawai'i

1

"What Is the Reason of Failure or Success? The Fisherman's Song Goes Deep into the River"

Fishermen in the Zhuangzi

KIRILL OLE THOMPSON

> Make few your needs, lessen your desires, and then you may get along even without rations. You will ford the rivers and drift out upon the sea. Gaze all you may—you cannot see its farthest shore; journey on and on—you will never see where it ends. Those who come to see you off will all turn back from the shore and go home, while you move ever farther out into the distance.... [R]id yourself of hardship, ... cast off your cares, and ... wander alone with the Way to the Land of Great Silence.
> —*Zhuangzi*, "The Mountain Tree"

A variety of fishermen appear in the *Zhuangzi*,[1] ostensibly because they can utter (or non-utter) spontaneous Daoist insights[2] and conjure up vivid impressions of Daoist cultivation and realization in the mind of the reader.[3] The fishermen thus portrayed suit Zhuangzi's philosophic purposes because, (1) their cultivation is not an artificial regimen, nor is it ascendant in nature—it consists in the very process of their apprenticeship and work as fishermen and proceeds as a gradual deepening of their experience of rivers, lakes, and seas; (2) their realization and insight occur out of their daily interaction with and contemplation of rivers, lakes, and seas—their realization arises spontaneously through their direct experience of these waters, as limpid manifestations of *dao*.

Zhuangzi's portrayals of fishermen have moved generations of readers. Chinese poets and painters have felt inspired to recast their images again and again down through the centuries.[4] Despite the philosophic and cultural importance of the fishermen in the *Zhuangzi*, this topic rarely has been singled out for consideration in the scholarship to date.[5]

Given the pristine nature of the subject, we shall embark on an exploration of fishermen in the *Zhuangzi* organized around a set of guiding questions, rather than advancing a focused argument. Questions we shall entertain below include: What is the source of the power and attraction of the image of fishermen in their element as portrayed in the *Zhuangzi*? What levels of realization do Zhuangzi's fisherman display? And how have these fishermen been recast in traditional Chinese poetry and art? What sorts of realization do the later fishermen display?

By exploring such questions, we may open the way to an understanding of the fisherman figure as a representative of the man of *dao* 道 for Zhuangzi and Chinese poets and painters.

FISHERMAN IN THEIR ELEMENT

What distinguishes fishermen from most people is that they lead their lives on the water. They spend hours, days, months, even years, on the water, working on the water, probing the shallows, plumbing the depths, contemplating the water, meditating on the water, sometimes gaining realizations and insights thereby. What, then, is it about the waters of rivers, lakes, and seas that bestows realization and insight on those who are attuned to them and contemplate them for extended periods?

The *Laozi* and the *Zhuangzi* offer some clues.[6] A "practical" text, the *Laozi* presents several guiding statements about water as "close to *dao*" and as a good exemplar of features and functions of *dao*. The *Zhuangzi*, a more "imaginative" work, on the other hand, opens with a myth in which the northern sea figures as a dark, mysterious realm.

The *Laozi* reads:

> That which is best is similar to water.
> Water benefits ten thousand things and does not oppose them.
> It is always at rest in humble places that people dislike.
> Thus, it is close to *dao*. (ch. 8)

> Water is the softest and meekest thing in the world.
> Yet it is best able to overcome that which is strong and solid.
> This is the truth that cannot be changed. (ch. 78)

Thus, by contemplating the beneficent passivity, the recessive humility, the resilient softness of water, the student of *dao* will grasp certain salient features of *dao* and nonaction as "enlightened conduct."

The water metaphor is implicitly at work throughout the *Laozi*. The following passage, for example, implies the relevance of water as a metaphor that highlights hidden, generally unnoticed features of life and conduct accentuated in Daoism:

> The meekest in the world
> Penetrates the strongest in the world,
> As nothingness enters into that-which-has-no-opening.
> Hence, I am aware of the value of non-action
> And of the value of teaching with no-words.
> As for the value of non-action,
> Nothing in the world can match it. (ch. 43)

By contrast, the *Zhuangzi* opens with an invocation of dark, mysterious oceanic depths in describing the immensity and range of the primordial Kun fish that suddenly transforms into the great Peng bird:

> In the northern darkness there is a fish, and his name is Kun. The Kun is so huge I don't know how many thousand *li* he measures. He changes and becomes a bird whose name is Peng. The back of Peng measures I don't know how many thousand *li* across and, when he rises up and flies off, his wings are like clouds all over the sky. When the sea begins to move, this bird sets off for the southern darkness, which is the Lake of Heaven.[7]

Sea and sky, the respective elements of Kun and Peng, represent yin and yang poles of *qi* 氣, the flowing fluid substratum of the cosmos and all phenomena. Primal yin and yang *qi* impulses, movements, formations, and distributions shape the world, and thus body forth primal patterns of *dao* creativity. Zhuangzi's expression "northern darkness" signifies the yin-pole of the world, whence the yang-*qi* and the *qi* of incipient phenomena begin to emerge. Zhuangzi elsewhere qualifies the expression "darkness" as "mysterious darkness," to describe the realm where phenomena—mental as well as physical—originate, the realm where they are yet-to-begin-to-exist.[8]

In Chinese culture, fish symbolize fertility, strength, prosperity, freedom, and joy; fish are also regarded as supernatural since they can survive in seemingly uninhabitable depths and move freely in any direction.[9] Hence, the gargantuan fish named Kun manifests the principle of fertility and life in the primordial ocean.

Paradoxically, the term "Kun" means fish roe, and thus connotes something small and incipient. With this name-play, Zhuangzi at once foreshadows two principal ideas of his philosophy: the identity of opposites and the identity of multiplicity. These are exemplified, for example, in the doctrines of the identity of all the phases of life, and the identity of birth and death: to be born is to die, to be an embryo is to be fully grown.[10]

"[The fish Kun] changes into a bird whose name is Peng." Kun is born of the yin-pole, but bears incipient yang-*qi*; Peng rising from Kun manifests the rise of incipient yang out of yin. Notably, whereas the yin fish lies hidden and mysterious in the dark northern sea, the yang bird is out in the open—it covers the sky and flies as a companion of the prevailing winds. Peng at once churns the air and flies south toward the yang-pole, centered in the Lake of Heaven—a crystalline yang body of water. But, as "return" and "reversal" are "the movement of *dao*," Peng eventually changes back into Kun and returns to the mysterious northern darkness.[11]

In sum, Zhuangzi portrays sky and sea as two primal realms of fluid *qi* complements, yin and yang. These complements in their complex of interactive relationships express the full operation of *dao*. Yet, in its primary originative and closure functions, it is the dark, mysterious primordial depths of the northern waters that are closest to *dao* that the *Laozi* and the *Zhuangzi* seek to accentuate. Accordingly:

> To be aware of the positive, yet to abide in the negative is to be the
>   abyss of the universe.
> To be the abyss of the universe is not to deviate from real attainment
>   and to remain like an innocent child.
> To be aware of the white, yet to abide in the black is to be the chasm
>   of the universe.
> To be the chasm of the universe is to have sufficient real attainment,
>   and to remain in the state of original non-differentiation.
>
> (*Laozi*, ch. 28)

All bodies of water—streams, rivers, lakes, seas—embody to some extent the depths and mysteries of the northern darkness, and bear primal *dao* properties of purity, transparency, reflectivity, passivity, formlessness, humility, fluidity, receptivity, and fertility. Thus, contemplative fishermen in long contact with such waters will spontaneously awaken to *dao*.

This recognition of water as a source of realization and insight is a seemingly universal human phenomenon. We find philosophers and poets across cultures and across the ages enchanted by and celebrating water. To mention just a few examples: Thales, the first Greek philosopher, declared water the first principle of all things.[12] The Greek poet Pindar called water "the best of all things."[13] An Indian *Purana* praises water as "the source of all things and existence."[14] Sounding somewhat like a Daoist, St. Francis celebrated water as the mirror of nature and the model of his conduct.[15] And Zhu Xi poeticized:

The wide pond expands like a mirror,
The heavenly light and cloud shadows play upon it.
How does such clarity occur? It is because it contains the living stream
from the Fountain.[16]

Mankind experiences flowing water as a living natural force. Springs and rivers display power and perpetual renewal; thus, they are deemed alive. Moreover, they vividly embody two basic features of existence: constancy and change. Between the relatively stable banks of a river, we observe waters in constant flux. As Heraclitus intoned, "We step and do not step into the same river twice, we are and we are not."[17]

A river's journey from source to mouth suggests the passage from innocence to experience, the sojourn from birth to death. The unity of the river thus implies the unity of the life process and the identity of life and death. When viewing a river from a position along its course, we experience its source and mouth as mysterious "beyonds." We imagine the source to be a pristine spring feeding the river from deep within the earth and the mouth as opening into a boundless sea, which absorbs the waters surging down from the river, effortlessly. Consequently, the sight of a river rouses our imaginations to deeper and wider conceptions of our worlds, our souls, our selves.[18]

Fish, too, are part of the fisherman's element. Fish display spontaneous, contented life. Zhuangzi tells of Confucius seeing sages who transcend society and "wander beyond the realm,"[19] such as the three friends who said to each other, " 'Who can join with others without doing with others? Who can do with others without joining with others? Who can climb up to Heaven and wander in the mists, roam the infinite, and forget life forever and forever?' The three men looked at each other and smiled." [20]

In attempting to characterize such men to his students, Confucius remarks, "Fish forget each other in the rivers and lakes, and men [such as these] forget each other in the Way."[21] Zhuangzi himself appreciated and vouched for the happiness of the fish.[22] He also affirmed that the True Man, the Spiritual Man "takes his cue from the fishes."[23]

From another perspective, Zhuangzi tells of Prince Ren fishing in the eastern sea for one year hoping to land a gigantic fish—a fish so big that it could feed all the people "from Zhihe east, from Cangwu north."[24] Through Ren's prolonged contemplation of the sea in angling for this avatar of Kun, he gains insight into *dao* and a grasp of the practical benefits of this insight, signified in his landing the colossal fish.

In sum, water, like *dao*, manifests formlessness and potential. Water spawns incipient life; fish, the fruit of their fecund element, flourish at one with their realm and manifest a free, spontaneous, contented life. Moreover, in the processes of dissolving forms and thus providing for the appearance of new forms, new life, water awakens the contemplative mind back to its original state, at one with *dao*:

> *Dao* is indistinct and ineffable.
> Ineffable and indistinct, yet therein are forms.
> Indistinct and ineffable, yet therein are objects.
> Unfathomable and invisible, yet therein are essences.
> . . . .
> Through [*dao*] we see *the beginnings of all things.*
> (*Laozi*, ch. 21, italics added)

> All things are together in action,
> But I look to their non-action.
> Things are unceasingly moving and restless,
> Yet each one is proceeding *back to the origin.*
> Proceeding back to the origin is quiescence.
> To be in quiescence is to *return* to the destiny of being.
> (*Laozi*, ch. 16, italics added)

The power and attraction of the fisherman figure in the *Zhuangzi* arises through our intimation of the enlightenment associated with the fisherman's reflective life on the water.

LEVELS OF REALIZATION AND INSIGHT OF FISHERMEN IN THE *ZHUANGZI*

Chapter 15, "Constrained in Will," sets forth a classification of scholars that distinguishes and profiles six different levels. The levels form an ascending scale of realization and conduct.[25] This apparently *ad hoc* yet meaningful assortment of levels consists of:

1. The scholar in the mountain valley who is a sullen social critic
2. The scholar in society who devotes himself to teaching and learning
3. The scholar in court and councils who serves his sovereign and state
4. The scholar of the rivers and seas who withdraws from the world, and *idles and fishes*
5. The scholar who devotes himself to practicing yoga and breathing exercises
6. The sage who transcends yet subsumes the other levels.[26]

In a sense the sage is beyond the scale, because he is independent and free in mind and spirit. Yet, under the sage, who acts by nonaction, the beneficial goals, actively though ineffectively pursued by scholars at other levels, are carried out and realized.

Our fisherman scholar is situated at the center, at the pivot, of this ascending scale of realization: he is engaged in withdrawing from society in spirit as well as in body. He is in the process of turning inward and dwelling in tranquillity in order to let his mind become detached and empty:

> To repair to the thickets and ponds, living idly in the wilderness, angling for fish in solitary places, inaction his only concern—such is the life favored by the scholar of the rivers and seas, the man who withdraws from the world, the unhurried idler.[27]

Initially, our fisherman scholar needs this wild, natural setting, this tonic of wildness (to borrow an expression from Thoreau) so as to cultivate and maintain his inner tranquillity, his sense of oneness with heaven, earth, and all things. The sage, by contrast, is already free; he will possess and maintain his enlightened state of mind, fed by the tonic of wildness, no matter what setting or situation he happens to be in. "The man who is not divorced from the great source is the natural man. The man who is not divorced from the essence is the spiritual man."[28] As Tao Yuanming poeticized:

> To build a house in the world of man
> And not to hear the noise of horse and carriage:
> How can this be done?
> When the mind is detached, the place is quiet.[29]

These six levels of scholars represent an ascending scale of realization, and the higher levels comprehend and subsume the five other levels; thus, the scholars who would cultivate *dao* at the higher levels should be conversant with the lower truths associated with lower levels. This accentuation on practical efficacy, even though it is rather light-handed, departs from the purely contemplative predilection exhibited in the first seven chapters of the *Zhuangzi*, and speaks to the later composition of this part of the text, perhaps early in the Han dynasty. In this light, it is assumed that the fisherman scholar, the yoga adept and the sage will grasp and have acquired insight into the structure and function of the government and society before withdrawing themselves and turning inward. *Laozi*, chapter 48, reads:

> To learn,
> One accumulates day by day.
> To study *dao*,
> One reduces day by day.

The process of reducing is a process of unlearning—it consists, in part, in releasing mental attachments to the social, political "knowledge" one has acquired, and then placing it into larger and larger perspectives, finally the perspective of *dao*. As Carl Jung affirms, "This Daoist view is typical of Chinese thinking. It is, when-

ever possible, *a thinking in terms of the whole.*"[30] Thus, the student of *dao* comes
to realize that the "knowledge" that had been transmitted to him through venerable texts by authority figures as sacrosanct, definite truths governing patterns of
interpersonal relationship and conduct are artificial stipulations and codifications,
true only for a certain time and place—even if they have a glorious history and are
shrouded in tradition.[31]

The sage thus conceived will be cognizant of the rituals and proprieties of
his society but he will respond to situations spontaneously according to his enlightened discernment. Even so, there is nothing to prevent his responses from
according with common practice.

Now let us consider examples of fisherman in the *Zhuangzi* to see if and how
they fit into this scale of realization.

First, we encounter Zhuangzi himself fishing and rejecting a generous offer
to administer the state of Chu in chapter 17, "Autumn Floods." In light of the
ascending scale of realization implied in the classification of scholars above, we
find Zhuangzi placing himself slightly past the midpoint, the pivot on the scale,
as a person who has turned inward, withdrawn himself from society to dwell in
nature, and who has begun to experience some enlightenment, some insight into
dao. Moreover, his disdainful rejection of the offer to take over the administration of the state shows that he still *depends on* being withdrawn and dwelling in a
secluded, tranquil setting to angle for contentment and deeper realization. Presumably, if he had acquired the spiritual autonomy of the sage, it would be all the
same to him whether he governed or wagged his tail in the mud.

Since Zhuangzi intends to communicate insights into human life, *dao* and
the condition of enlightenment to his readers through his writings, he would
naturally avoid official service and intentionally position himself at the halfway
point between sagehood and nonsagehood and thus truly "walk . . . two roads."[32]

Next, the account of Confucius heeding the advice of Taigong Ren in
chapter 20, "The Mountain Tree," places him poised to enter the midpoint of the
ascending scale of realization.

Confucius learns from Taigong Ren that his teachings about government and
society are not only a form of showing off and selling himself, but give rise to
dissatisfaction and strife. Confucius then bids his friends and associates adieu,
sends his disciples away, and retires to the great swamp, wearing animal skins and
coarsely woven cloth and feeding only on acorns and chestnuts. He grows so
"wild" (again, in Thoreau's positive sense of the term) there, so at one with the
swamp and wildlife, that he can "walk among the animals without alarming their
herds, walk among the birds without alarming their flocks."[33]

Stressing his sudden turn to hermitism, the anecdote doesn't mention Confucius angling, yet the author expects the reader to recall Confucius's enjoyment
of waters, his meditation on a stream and his preference for angling with a hook
rather than with a net as recorded in the *Analects*.[34]

Next, in chapter 21, "Tian Zifang," King Wen encounters a venerable old man fishing and at once recognizes him to be a sage. That his sagehood is authentic is underscored in the description:

> His fishing was not really fishing; he was not holding the fishing pole in hand in order to catch a fish. He was undertaking eternal fishing.[35]

King Wen has the discernment to see that this old man can manage the state administration perfectly and conceives of a way to persuade his high officials and relatives to accept him as the prime minister. A veritable Daoist sage, the old man goes on to rule by nonaction. During his three-year tenure, "the regular precedents and laws remained unchanged, and not a single new order was issued."[36] The established hierarchies and distinctions that had characterized government and society for generations fall away and people start to interrelate and conduct their lives in a simple, direct, sincere fashion. Pleased, King Wen seeks to extend the old man's dominion to the whole world. Hearing of King Wen's plan, the old man "looked blank and gave no answers, ... and when orders went out to make the attempt, the old man ran away ... and was never heard from again."[37]

As discussed above, in chapter 26, "External Things," Prince Ren makes an enormous fishhook and devotes himself to angling for the gigantic fish of the eastern sea for a full year. With its emphasis on Prince Ren's landing the fish, this story is not so much about the fisherman figure per se as it is intended to illustrate the benefits of cultivating broad-mindedness. Contemplating the wide sea for one year, Prince Ren's mind becomes so open and vast that he can comprehend and catch the giant fish: Daoist Great Understanding identifies with the cosmos and is sensitive and responsive to the pulse and rhythms of nature. Thus, the actions of the man of Great Understanding are, ultimately, more in harmony with the situation and fruitful than those of the more practical, goal-directed person.

Lastly, chapter 31, "The Old Fisherman," presents a sustained narrative of an encounter between Confucius and a nameless old fisherman sage. Confucius has brought several disciples to the Apricot Altar to study while he strums his lute and sings. The scene recalls *Analects* 11/26 where Confucius, in a relaxed mood, asks his disciples their respective ambitions. While acknowledging the younger disciples' grand ambitions to administer a state, he shares Zengxi's wish "to go bathing in the River Yi and enjoy the breeze in the Rain Altar, and then go home chanting poetry" with several adults and youths.[38]

Confucius settles down at the Apricot Altar; but, before he has completed playing his first song, an uncanny old fisherman pulls up in a boat, sizes him up, then lectures him on government and society, on eight faults and four evils, and finally on his need to be "diligent in improving [him]self, careful to hold fast to the Truth," Truth in the sense of inner genuineness.

The old fisherman's credentials as a sage are established at the outset of the narrative with his physical description:

His beard and eyebrows were pure white, his hair hung down over his shoulders, and his sleeves flapped at his sides.[39]

Moreover, toward the end of the narrative Confucius identifies the old man as a Perfect Man and then as a sage.[40]

Despite the disclaimer that he "will put aside his own ways for the moment and try applying [him]self to the things that [Confucius is] concerned with,"[41] the old fisherman's didactic lectures to Confucius on government and society mark him as a sage savvy about administration and society and place him squarely in our scale of scholars and realization. A genuine sage by that standard, he has transcended yet still comprehends, and perchance has impact upon, government and society in his "realm" of tacit influence. The old fisherman's savvy incorporates the "wisdom" of a laissez-faire nonaction approach, provided that people focus on the affairs within the purview of their concern; he strongly deprecates Confucian interventionism in other people's affairs.

The old fisherman then proceeds to espouse his own notion of Truth: Bearing Truth means being pure and sincere within so that one's manifest feelings and responses are genuine. "When a man has the Truth within himself, his spirit may move among external things."[42] To stand on tradition and custom is to dissipate the purity of one's emotions and complicate one's intentions. By responding directly, guided by one's spontaneous impulses, one will act appropriately and sincerely, and thus will "move" others and be appreciated by them.

Having said his piece, the old fisherman "poled away in his boat, threading a path through the weeds." Confucius watches transfixed, "until the ripples on the water were stilled and he could no longer hear the sound of the pole," before he ventures to mount the carriage back.[43] The old fisherman returns to the hidden Source whence pure waters emerge to purify himself, whereas Confucius rides a chariot back to artificial human society.

When the disciple Zilu dismisses the old fisherman in rather offhand fashion as a mere fisherman, not worthy of the profound respect Confucius has paid him, Confucius replies that to fail to treat an elder with respect is a breach of propriety, and to fail to treat a worthy with veneration is a violation of benevolence. He continues:

> If the fisherman were not a Perfect Man, he would not be able to make people humble themselves before him. And if men, in humbling themselves before him, lack purity of intention, then they will never attain the Truth. As a result they will go on forever bringing injury upon themselves.[44]

In concluding, Confucius identifies *dao* as the path along which the myriad things and human undertakings alike should proceed; things and undertakings that are in accord with the Way survive and flourish, those that do not, die and fail. Hence, the sage will pay homage wherever *dao* is to be found:

This old fisherman may certainly be said to possess [the Way]. How, then, would I dare fail to show respect to him!⁴⁵

A. C. Graham finds in the old fisherman's call to "hold fast to the Truth," to one's inner genuineness, an echo of Yang Zhu's egoistic hermitism.⁴⁶ Yang Zhu's position involves, however, an austere detachment from society and material things as well as a devotion to yogic practice. Yang Zhu would likely fall under the category of adepts devoted to breathing exercises and yoga in our scale of scholars and realization. The *Huainanzi*, chapter 13, for instance, attributes to Yang Zhu the principles of:

> keeping the body intact, protecting one's genuineness, and not tying the body by involvements with other things.⁴⁷

Many pre-Qin texts go on to attribute to Yang Zhu the extreme position of refusing to give anything of the self over to the world and of despising things and treasuring one's own life.⁴⁸

The old fisherman displays none of this excessive austerity. Whereas Yang Zhu simply has no thought about society, except perhaps to eschew it, the old fisherman has a positive view of society as possibly flourishing, on condition that people stay focused on their own duties at their respective social position. He also has a positive, almost Mencian view of human affairs, on condition that people maintain pure, sincere hearts and express their feelings truly and spontaneously. His views imply a detached attitude toward material things, but that is a far cry from the outright renunciation of them espoused by Yang Zhu.

Although similar in letter to Yang Zhu's saying, the old fisherman's call to "hold fast to the Truth," to inner genuineness, is much closer in spirit to views propounded throughout the *Laozi* and the *Zhuangzi*. The *Laozi* tells us to "manifest simplicity and embrace original non-differentiation" in chapter 19. Similarly, the *Zhanguoce* (Intrigues of the Warring States) suggests that we "return to inner genuineness and revert to original non-differentiation" ("Qice"). Moreover, the *Zhuangzi*, chapter 12, "Heaven and Earth," reads:

> The man of noble attainment moves in simplicity.... He takes his stand in the original source and his understanding reaches to the spirits. Therefore his attainment is far-reaching. His mind goes forth only when stirred by outer phenomena.... To preserve the self and live out life, to experience attainment and enlightenment into *Dao*—is this not noble attainment?⁴⁹

> The man with attainment is free of thoughts when at rest, and free of calculations when in action. He doesn't bear predetermined ideas of right and wrong, beautiful and ugly.⁵⁰

Above and beyond the affinity between the old fisherman and the *Laozi* and the *Zhuangzi* at this point, the old fisherman ascribes, as noted by Graham,⁵¹ a positive value to the feelings that stands out in the *Zhuangzi*, and that is absent from the *Laozi*. As noted, the old fisherman also displays a Mencian trust that people who have cultivated the Truth of inner purity and sincerity will be set to spontaneously express themselves with appropriate emotions and sentiments in various situations.

FISHERMAN SAGES

At this point, we would do well to pause and inquire whether the appearance of fisherman scholars and sages in the *Zhuangzi* signals a shift in the Daoist conception of sagehood. As we have seen, the ascending scale of scholars and realization into which all the fishermen figures in the *Zhuangzi* can be mapped, involves the assumption that scholars, worthies and sages at the higher levels will continue to understand and have insight into the ways of government and society. Those at the higher levels, even sages who have transcended all the mundane restrictions and concerns of society, will have a firm grasp of human affairs and will perchance exert a positive, generally harmonizing influence on government and society.

By contrast, the *Zhuangzi* usually portrays contemplative sages, figures detached from and unconcerned about mundane matters of interpersonal and social life. Emphasis is placed on the character of their enlightenment, their personal style, and their bearing and conduct. These sages tend to be elderly, with long, flowing white hair and beards, but with skin as smooth and soft as a baby's and eyes that are blank and innocent. They are as gentle and light-hearted as young girls. Their conduct is smooth and effortless and their existence in the world is never threatened; for their identity with heaven, earth, and the ten thousand things keeps them attuned to their setting and synchronized with the things transpiring around them.

Accordingly, the fisherman motif suggests an indirect shift to a slightly more practical conception of sagehood. To review, the fishing Zhuangzi refuses government service, preferring to wag his tail in the mud; as we have noted, this attitude was consistent with his position on the scale of realization. We, too, saw Confucius withdrawing from society to live as a hermit in the great swamp; again, this was consistent with his position on the scale. We may also observe that, whereas Zhuangzi would be particularly inclined, by temperament, toward a free, contemplative sagehood, Confucius would ultimately be inclined toward a more practical form. The old man fishing discovered by King Wen at first appears to be a contemplative sage, but once placed in charge of state administration he—by nonaction—infuses harmony into the realm by spurring the people to become simple, pure, sincere, and cooperative. Prince Ren's landing the gargantuan fish underscores the practical benefits of realizing *dao*. Finally, whereas the old fisherman dwells at the Source of the flowing river, alone and nameless, he displays impressive insight into government and society as well as into the subtleties of interpersonal intercourse. The profound impression he makes on Confucius is meant to confirm the "soundness" of his insights overall to the traditional reader.

How does the fisherman motif foster this subtle shift in the conception of sagehood? We recall that meditation and other yogic practices are part of Daoist cultivation. Meditation always involves the two poles of (1) opening up and freeing the mind, and (2) focusing and concentrating the mind. Examples of meditation presented in the "Inner Chapters" of the *Zhuangzi* are relatively free-style and nondirective; they involve opening up much more than focusing the mind, which is consistent with the entirely free, unattached contemplative sages presented there.[52] The fishing motif, on the other hand, places a new emphasis on focusing and concentrating the mind, with the point at which the fishing line enters the water providing the focal point of attention, while the fluid formless waters still act to open up and free the mind.[53]

The act of fishing itself provides an example of Zhuangzi's "walking two roads": the reflective fisherman will undertake eternal fishing while angling for fish.[54] It also exemplifies action by nonaction, nonintentional action: the reflective fisherman remains passive and indifferent while fishing. He is not really concerned whether he lands a fish; sometimes he even neglects to use bait or even a hook.[55] Nonetheless, fishing can and does yield practical results, in realization and enlightenment as well as in fresh fish.

FISHERMEN IN CHINESE POETRY

Many traditional Chinese poets and painters adopted images of the fisherman introduced into Chinese philosophy and literature by Zhuangzi. Because Zhuangzi had already invested the fishermen figure with philosophic significance and a wealth of associations, later poets and painters had just to present the fisherman in his element, and informed readers and viewers would make the connections and perchance feel moved. Even people unaware of the implicit associations and significances could feel the vastness and openness of the horizons, the fluidity and formlessness of the waters—whether of a still lake or a flowing stream—and the boundless, unfettered, detached, free spirit of the fisherman.

The theme of fishermen in Chinese poetry and painting deserves an in-depth inquiry; for present purposes, however, it will suffice to survey a few fisherman poems by Tang masters sympathetic to Daoism. Although these poets all drew inspiration and insight from Zhuangzi's portrayals of fishermen, each one accentuated a different aspect of the fisherman figure and his element.

First, let us consider Zhang Zhihe (730–810), a well-known poet-fisherman who reputedly preferred to fish without bait. His works, in fact, inspired the Yuan painter and poet of fishermen, Wu Zhen (1280–1354).[56] Zhang was charmed by the image of the fisherman floating freely along with the current in his boat, at one with the boundless, bountiful setting. His poems thus intone a sense of approaching the realm of the Immortals; they are, however, also laden with an overrichness of delight and bounty that runs counter to Zhuangzi's movement toward purity, tranquillity, and detachment. Consequently, while Zhang's poems are fine literary compositions, they do not capture the true spirit and depth of Zhuangzi's philosophy.

Zhang's fishermen take evident joy in the forces of nature and the profusion of life therein. The following is a typical example:

> In Jingdao Lake the moon is full,
> The Baling fisherman rows and chants.
> With fishing gear and dugout canoe,
> Happiness resides in the wind and wave.
> No need to follow the Immortals.[57]

Zhang's most famous poem, "The Fisherman's Song," celebrates the power and bounty of nature in the first two lines, but it steps back to suggest the isolation and austerity of the fisherman's life in the concluding two lines. Nonetheless, Zhang's fisherman prefers to stay on the river, feeling the wind and rain, rather than to retreat to human society:

> Before Xisai mountain the white egrets fly,
> Among the peach blossoms and flowing waters the Mandarin fish are
>   well-nourished.
> Hat of bamboo,
> Coat of green reeds,
> The driving wind and light mist do not necessitate the old fisherman's
>   return.[58]

Liu Zongyuan (773–819) was a Tang poet and essayist of philosophic acumen. His fisherman poems are masterpieces of the genre. More cognizant than Zhang Zhihe was of the hardship and isolation of the fisherman's life, Liu sketches imposing though secluded settings bordered by mountains that, rather than delimit and enclose, reach up and bring the earth up to the sky. Thus, Liu's poems effectively accentuate the fisherman's simultaneous seclusion in nature and access to the boundlessness of *dao*:

> River Snow
> Among thousands of mountain peaks,
>   not a single bird flies.
> Among the myriad mountain pathways,
>   not a single person plies.
> In this world of snow and mountains,
>   there is just an old fisherman in reed coat and straw hat,
> Alone in the cold river fishing.[59]

The Old Fisherman

At night the old fisherman docks his boat along the
    western cliff.
Before sunrise he draws up clear river water and
    burns Chu bamboo to cook.
Anon the sun rises and the fog disperses,
    there is not a soul to be seen.
With the sound of the oar in the water,
    the mountains and river are verdant.
Shifting our gaze, we see the waters flow out
    from the horizon.
The white clouds atop the cliffs pursue each other
    without intention.[60]

Wang Wei (699–759) expressed the essential thought of Daoism and Chan Buddhism in his best poetry. His poetic art achieved perfection in that he conveyed the philosophy directly through the juxtaposition of images, events and feelings, without recourse to special terms or jargon. In the following poem, the image of the fisherman's song entering deep into the river highlights the poet's sense of detachment from worldly concerns and sense of oneness and attunement with *dao*, as reflected in his tranquil setting and quiescent mind:

Of late I concern myself with quiescence.
Nothing in the world concerns my mind.

The breeze from the pine woods blows my sash;
The mountain moon shines upon my harp.
You ask me the reason of failure and success;
The fisherman's song goes deep into the river.[61]

Finally, the poet Sikong Shu (d. c. 790) actually speaks as a fisherman in the following poem. His degree of realization is manifested in his perfect comprehension of, and attunement with, his river setting:

Ceasing fishing, I return back for the day, but
    don't bother to fasten the boat to shore.
Unconcerned, I fall asleep just as the moon sets over
    the village.
Even though the night wind blows,
The boat will stay in the reeds and blossoms
    in the shallow water.[62]

Why needn't the fisherman secure his boat to the shore? Why can he fall asleep easily, unconcerned whether the boat will slip away and float downstream? He is at one with the river, the Way, attuned to the subtle ebb and flow of its current. Thus, he knows just where to leave his boat, at just the place where, held in place both by the reeds and by an equal balance between current and counter-current, the boat will remain, even more securely than if he were to fasten it down.

This poem recalls Zhuangzi's story about attempting to hide a boat:

> You hide your boat in the ravine and your fish net in the swamp and tell yourself that they will be safe. But in the middle of the night a strong man shoulders them and carries them off, and in your stupidity you don't know why it happened. You think you do right to hide little things in big ones, and yet they get away from you. But if you were to hide the world in the world, so that nothing could get away, this would be the final reality of the constancy of things.[63]

What does it mean to hide a universe in the universe? A person who has realized *dao* is at one with heaven, earth, and the myriad things. Since he (his Great Self) is at one with the world, he and the world are mutually dependent and sustain each other. Consequently, nothing can happen to either him or the world: even if his empirical self were to die or vanish, his Great Self would continue to persist in and through the totality. Similarly, Sikong Shu's fisherman persona is at one with heaven, earth and the myriad things. He is at one with the totality and is sensitive to the ebb and flow of the river. Thus, he knows intuitively where to leave his boat, without a care, in the knowledge that it will remain in place and nothing will move it. This signifies the wisdom of the fisherman sage.

NOTES

1. The chapter title is from "Qou Zhang Shaofu," a poem by Wang Wei. Translation adapted from Chang Chung-yuan, *Creativity and Taoism: A Study of Chinese Philosophy, Art, and Poetry* (New York: Julian Press, 1963), p. 91.

2. There are questions concerning the authorship of the *Zhuangzi*. See A. C. Graham's discussions in *Chuang-tzu: The Seven Inner Chapters and Other Writings from the Book*, trans. A. C. Graham (London: George Allen & Unwin, 1981), pp. 3–5, 27–30. See also Ping Wong Chin, *A Study of Chuang-tzu: Text, Author and Philosophy* (Ph.D. dissertation, University of Wisconsin, 1978), pp. 29–93. For ease of presentation, the author(s) will be treated simply as "Zhuangzi" in this paper.

3. For example, fishermen appear in chapters 15, 17, 21, 26, and 31. Fish appear in chapters 1, 6, 17 and elsewhere. Chapter 20 includes the recommendation to drift out to sea to realize *dao* (quoted at the head of this paper) and reports Confucius fleeing society to the great swamp where he becomes a bona fide hermit.

4. For a general survey, see William W. Lew, *The Fisherman in Yuan Painting and Literature as Reflected in Wu Chen's "Yu-fu T'u" in the Shanghai Museum* (Ph.D. dissertation, Ohio University, 1976), pp. 38–75, 161–81.

5. Graham provides some discussion on ch. 31, "The Old Fisherman," pp. 221 and 248.

6. Translations from the *Laozi* and the *Zhuangzi* in this paper are adopted from Chang Chung-yuan, trans., *Tao: A New Way of Thinking: A Translation of the "Tao Te Ching" with an Introduction and Commentaries* (New York: Harper & Row, 1975), and Burton Watson, trans., *The Complete Works of Chuang Tzu* (New York: Columbia University Press, 1968).

7. *Zhuangzi* (hereafter Z), ch. 1, p. 29.

8. Z, ch. 2, p. 43; see also Z, ch. 6, p. 83, and Z, ch. 17. p. 187 for the term *xuanming* 玄冥 (literally "mysterious darkness"), which Watson renders as "Dark-Obscurity."

9. Kuang-ming Wu, *The Butterfly as Companion: Meditations on the First Three Chapters of the Chuang Tzu* (Albany: State University of New York Press, 1990), p. 70. Wu's glosses and meditations on the opening paragraph have benefitted this discussion.

10. See, for example, Z, ch. 2, pp. 39 & 40, ch. 6, pp. 84–88, and ch. 17, pp. 175–82. For discussion, see Chang, *Tao: A New Way*, pp. xvi–xviii.

11. *Laozi*, ch. 48: "Reversal is the movement of *Dao*. Yielding is the action of *Dao*." The term "return" (*gui* 歸) appears throughout the *Laozi*.

12. Jonathan Barnes, *Early Greek Philosophy* (London: Penguin Books, 1987), p. 63.

13. Pindar, *Olympian Odes*.

14. Quoted in Mircea Eliade, *Patterns in Comparative Religion*, trans. R. Sheed (New York: New American Library, 1958), p. 188.

15. "The Canticle of Brother Sun," in L. S. Cunningham, *Saint Francis of Assisi* (Boston: G. K. Hall, 1976), p. 58.

16. Quoted in Chang Chung-yuan, *Creativity and Taoism* (New York: Harper Colophon, 1963), p. 182.

17. Quoted in Barnes, p. 117.

18. This is implied in Z, ch. 17, pp. 175–183. F. S. Colwell notes Coleridge's intriguing view of rivers and their sources as "companionable forms," and characterizes them as "agents that establish ... our most profound discourse with ourselves, offering a measure of self-knowledge otherwise inaccessible." *Rivermen: A Romantic Iconography of the River and the Source* (Kingston, Ontario: McGill–Queen's University Press, 1989), p. 5.

19. Z, ch. 6, p. 86.

20. Ibid.

21. Z, ch. 6, p. 87.

22. Z, ch. 17, pp. 188–89.

23. Z, ch. 24, p. 277.
24. Z, ch. 24, p. 276.
25. An implied scale of levels of realization and categories which differentiate among them appear elsewhere in the *Zhuangzi*, for example, in ch. 1, pp. 31–33, where Song Rongzi and Liezi are profiled, then three categories are given: the Perfect Man—who has no self, the Spiritual Man—who has no merit, and the Sage—who has no fame. Song Rongzi and Liezi have not quite reached these categories. Xu Yu appears to exemplify the Perfect Man, Jie Yu the Spiritual Man, and the Holy Man of Gushe Mountain the Sage. This classification, which reflects the position of Zhuangzi himself, is further removed from the realm of practical affairs than the classification that appears in chapter 15, which reflects the position, perhaps, of early Han Daoists who were developing the political and social side of their thought.
26. Z, ch. 15, pp. 167–68.
27. Z, ch. 15, p. 167.
28. Z, ch. 33, p. 362, with modifications.
29. Given in Chang, *Tao: A New Way of Thinking*, p. xxi.
30. C. G. Jung, *Jung on the East*, ed. J. J. Clark (London: Routledge, 1995), p. 74. (Selected from "Synchronicity: An Acausal Connecting Principle," par. 924.)
31. See, for example, Z, ch. 2, p. 40: "A road is made by people walking on it, things are so because they are called so. What makes them so? Making them so makes them so ... There is nothing that is not so, there is nothing that is not acceptable."
32. Z, ch. 2, p. 41. See also Z, ch. 6, pp. 79–80: "Therefore his liking was one and his not liking was one. His being one was one and his not being one was one. In being one, he was acting as a companion of Heaven. In not being one, he was acting as a companion of man. When Heaven and man do not defeat each other, then we may be said to have the True Man."
33. Z, p. 214.
34. *Analects* 6.23: "The wise find joy in water"; 7.27: "The Master used a fishing line but not a cable (attached to a net)"; and 9.17: "While standing by a river, the Master said, "What passes away is, perhaps, like this. Day and night it never lets up." D.C. Lau, trans., *Confucius: The Analects (Lun yu)* (Hong Kong: The Chinese University Press, 1979, 1983), pp. 53, 63, and 81.
35. Cf. Z, p. 229. The author retranslated this passage. Thoreau suggests eternal fishing at several points in *Walden*. He writes, for example:

> Time is but a stream I go a-fishing in. I drink at it; but while I drink I see the sandy bottom and detect how shallow it is. Its thin current slides away, but eternity remains. I would drink deeper; fish in the sky, whose bottom is pebbly with stars. I cannot count

one. I know not the first letter of the alphabet. I have always been
regretting that I am not as wise as the day I was born. (p. 66)

On midnight fishing: At length you slowly raise ... some horned
pout squeaking and squirming to the upper air. It was very queer,
especially in dark nights, when your thoughts had wandered to vast
and cosmogonal themes in other spheres, to feel this faint jerk,
which came to interrupt your dreams and link you to Nature again.
It seemed as if I might next cast my line upward into the air, as well
as downward into this element which was scarcely more dense.
Thus I caught two fishes as it were with one hook. (p. 117)

Commonly [my fellow citizens] did not think that they were lucky,
or well paid for their time, unless they got a long string of fish,
though they had the opportunity of seeing the pond all the while.
They might go there a thousand times before the sediment of
fishing would sink to the bottom and leave their purpose pure; but
no doubt such a clarifying process would be going on all the while.
(p. 142)

Henry David Thoreau, *Walden and Civil Disobedience*, ed. Owen Thomas
(New York: W. W. Norton, 1966).

36. Z, ch. 21, p. 229.
37. Z, ch. 21, p. 230.
38. Lau, p. 105.
39. Z, ch. 31, p. 344. The description bears comparison with that of the Spiritual
    Man ("Holy Man" in Watson's translation) of Gushe Mountain (Z, ch. 1,
    p. 33), the True Man of ancient times (Z, ch. 6, p. 78), and the Sage (Z, ch.
    13, p. 142).
40. Z, ch. 31, p. 351.
41. Z, ch. 31, p. 346.
42. Z, ch. 31, p. 349.
43. Z, ch. 31, p. 351.
44. Ibid.
45. Z, ch. 31, p. 352.
46. Graham, p. 248.
47. Graham, p. 221.
48. For discussion, see Fung Yu-lan, *A History of Chinese Philosophy*, vol. 1, trans.
    Derk Bodde (Princeton, N.J.: Princeton University Press, 1952), pp. 133–43.
49. Z, ch. 12, p. 128. Translation modified.
50. Z, ch. 12, p. 137. Translation modified. The discussion that follows in
    chapter 12 goes on to parallel the old fisherman's trust in aptness of the
    spontaneous feelings of pure, sincere people:

In an age of Perfect Attainment the worthy are not honored, the talented are not employed. The rulers are like the high branches of a tree, the people are like the deer of the fields. They do what is right but they do not know that this is appropriateness. They love one another but they do not know that this is benevolence. They are truehearted but they do not know that this is loyalty. They are trustworthy but they do not know that this is fidelity. They wriggle around like insects, performing services for one another, but do not know they are being kind. Therefore they move without leaving any trail behind, act without leaving memory of their deeds. (Z, ch. 12, p. 138)

51. Graham, p. 248.
52. See, for example, the account of Ziji of South Wall at the beginning of Z, ch. 2, pp. 36–37. For an overview of Daoist self-cultivation practices, see Chang Chung-yuan, "Processes of Self-Realization," *Creativity and Taoism* pp. 123–68.
53. Yoga and meditation practices implied in the *Laozi*, a text addressed to the ruler, are intended to induce both poles of opening and freeing and focusing and concentrating the mind. See chapters 10, 12, 16, 28, 56, and so on.
54. See note 35 above.
55. As noted above, the old man fishing discovered by King Wen in ch. 21 is "fishing without really fishing." In the *Shiji*, Sima Qian tells of a scholar in seclusion, Jiang Ziya, who fished with a straight hook and no bait, intending to catch only the fish that wanted to be caught. Jiang may well have been a model for the old man character in the *Zhuangzi*; he, too, was recruited by King Wen. Jiang, however, served for over twenty years as advisor to the throne, whereas the old man only served for three years—before fleeing, never to be seen or heard from again. See Burton Watson, trans., *Records of the Grand Historian of China: Translated from the* Shih-chi *of Ssu-ma Ch'ien* (New York: Columbia University Press, 1961), vol. 2, p. 453.
56. See Lew, pp. 66–74.
57. Translation given in Lew, p. 68.
58. Adapted from translation given in Lew, pp. 21–22.
59. Translation by the author.
60. Translation by the author.
61. Chang, *Creativity and Taoism*, p. 91. See Chang's discussion of the poem.
62. Translation by the author.
63. Z, ch. 6, pp. 8–81.

2

Just Say No to "No Self" in *Zhuangzi*

CHRIS JOCHIM

> Master Lie could ride upon the wind wherever he pleased,
> drifting marvelously, and returning only after fifteen days.
> Although he was not embroiled in the pursuit of blessings and
> thus was able to dispense with walking, still there was something
> that he had to rely upon.
>
> Supposing there were someone who could ride upon the
> truth of heaven and earth, who could chariot upon the
> transformations of the six vital breaths and thereby go
> wandering in infinity, what would he have had to rely on?
>
> Therefore, it is said that *the ultimate man has no self* [*wu ji*
> 無己], *the spiritual person has no accomplishment* [*wu gong* 無功],
> *and the sage has no name* [*wu ming* 無名].
>
> —*Zhuangzi* 莊子, chapter 1

The above epigraph concludes the first portion of chapter 1 ("Carefree Wandering") of *Zhuangzi* (Master Zhuang),[1] wherein he introduces the ideal of "wandering" ("*you*" 游) by telling marvelous tales about fish, birds, and unusual men like Master Lie. For some, the italicized aphorism at the end of the epigraph is the key to the whole of chapter 1. A clear example of this is Wu Yi 吳怡, *Xiaoyao de Zhuangzi* 逍遙的莊子 (The Carefree Wandering Master Zhuang).[2] Wu Yi is also typical in interpreting the passage by reference to concepts of "self," "no self," "true self," and the like. For others, parallel passages alleged to express Master Zhuang's teachings on "self" are the key to the whole text, or at least to the "Inner Chapters." An example of this is Wu Kuang-ming's view on the famous line near the start of chapter 2 ("On the Equality of Things"), which in his translation reads: "For-the-moment now I have lost me-myself" (*jinzhe wu sang wo* 今者吾喪我). What is lost during this paradigmatic experience is the "objectifiable self," as opposed to the authentic self.[3]

Moreover, leading English translations of *Zhuangzi* interpret "*wu ji*" in this passage by reference to a concept of "no self." Victor Mair and Burton Watson have "no self," and A. C. Graham has "selfless."[4] While they do not specifically stress concepts of "self" and "no self" in their own explanations of Master Zhuang's thought, their translations attribute these concepts to him and, in my opinion, thereby lead others astray. As a result, certain contemporary American thinkers interested in Master Zhuang have interpreted him as having a doctrine of "no self."[5]

In other words, whether intentionally or not, interpreters of *Zhuangzi* frequently attribute to him concepts of "self" and "no self" in the way they translate or explain key Chinese phrases in the text, such as *wu ji* and *sang wo*. Yet when we seek to understand these phrases in terms of Master Zhuang's overall message, these attributions are not only unnecessary, they are extremely misleading.

Master Zhuang did not preach a particular gospel or push his own brand of metaphysics, but he did have a consistent message about the art of living. I will characterize his ideal in the art of living as "flowing," making reference to contemporary theory on the "flow experience." Zhuang describes this ideal through sayings like the one in my epigraph, by means of philosophical dialogues, and with metaphorical tales about wandering, swimming in water like fish, flying like birds, or reaching states beyond flying (with hints of mystical experience).[6]

I believe one very useful way of understanding Zhuang's message on the art of living is to consider his views on the mental and behavioral traits that obstruct flowing. I will argue that he uses terms like *ji* and *wo*, not to mean selfhood in the modern Western or Chinese senses (represented, respectively, by the terms "self" and "*ziwo*" 自我), but only to identify traits that obstruct one's carefree flowing with the world of living things. As for my own interpretation of the passage at the end of the epigraph, in which *wu ji* is used for the first time, it will be clarified in due course, as we proceed through the stages outlined below.

ESSAY OVERVIEW

The first section below will discuss the modern Western concept of self in order to show its cultural specificity. The reason for doing so will be to indicate that the concept, and thus the term "self," carries so much cultural baggage that its use in the interpretation of ancient Chinese texts will inevitably mislead us.

The second section will further problematize the use of "self" as well as "no self" in interpreting *Zhuangzi* by considering key works of modern Chinese and Western scholars. These are all scholars who lean heavily on the concept of "self," assuming it has enough universal relevance to aid us in understanding Master Zhuang's thought.

The third section will consist of a detailed effort to contextualize the use of Chinese terms in *Zhuangzi* (*ji, wo,* and others) by looking at their use in late Zhou period texts other than *Zhuangzi* as well as at many passages from the text itself. By investigating this set of terms, which may overlap in meaning with modern terms for self (that is, "self" in English, "*ziwo*" in Chinese), I aim to contribute to the comparative study of concepts of the person, with specific reference to ancient China and the modern world. This will be necessary because, despite the many works that talk about Confucian and Daoist "selfhood," few begin with a linguistic survey of the relevant Chinese words.

The final section will aim to show what Master Zhuang probably *did* mean when he used those Chinese words that we normally render in English as "self." In doing so I will present, as the context for understanding what he meant, his essential message about the art of living. As already indicated, the key modern concept that I *will* use for this purpose is "the flow experience."

THE MODERN CONCEPT OF SELF

From Marcel Mauss through Charles Taylor, many thinkers have insisted that "self" is a modern Western (post-Cartesian) cultural construction.[7] Studies on concepts of the person in various non-Western societies have reinforced this view.[8] Moreover, the concept of self is actually a whole constellation of concepts. As Brian Morris points out: "The 'self' structure of Western culture has thus been widely described as individuated, detached, separate and self-sufficient, and involving a dualistic metaphysic."[9]

This cultural construction even intrudes on our way of thinking when we do not use the term, or think the concept, "self." In his seminal work, *Sources of the Self,* Charles Taylor begins by suggesting how wide is the range of the intrusion of this concept and its corollary, "the modern identity." In his words: "[In writing this book] I wanted to show how the ideals and interdicts of this identity—what it casts in relief and what it casts in shadow—shape our philosophical thought, our epistemology and our philosophy of language, largely without our awareness." The unconscious way in which we impose our concept of "self" on worlds of thought far removed from our own in time and place is of particular concern to me in this essay. In order that I can phenomenologically bracket it out of my effort to understand the concept of the person and the art of living in *Zhuangzi,* let us now survey key aspects of this cultural construction.

Among the aspects of our concept "self" that make it unique and differentiate it from the universally human "sense of me," and the ubiquitous terms of self-reference in human languages, Taylor points to the strong degree to which we have nominalized "self." He states:

> It is probable that in every language there are resources for self-reference
> and descriptions of reflexive thought, action, attitude.... But this is not
> at all the same as making "self" into a noun, preceded by a definite or
> indefinite article, speaking of "the" self, or "a" self. This reflects some-
> thing important which is peculiar to our modern sense of agency.[10]

This is part and parcel of our stress on inwardness, on a subjectivity that lives
within us, built on the dichotomy of inner and outer, which, thanks originally to
Augustine, is linked to a whole series of dichotomies. Augustine set us on this
path, building on Platonic oppositions he had inherited. According to Taylor,
"this same opposition of spirit/matter, higher/lower, eternal/temporal, immutable/
changing *is* described by Augustine, not just occasionally and peripherally, but
centrally and essentially in terms of inner/outer."[11]

After modern thinkers, from Descartes through Locke, had made their contributions, the "self" became, paradoxically, an inner object to be shaped by dis-
ciplined action as well as an inner subject seen as a privileged observer of objects
in the outer world. Radical objectivity and radical subjectivity thus became part of
the modern mind set. This is not so paradoxical if one accepts Taylor's argument
that Cartesian rational disengagement made possible the modern objectification
of both self and world. Speaking of a whole constellation of post-Cartesian,
Enlightenment era developments in European society, he offers this explanation:

> What one finds running through all the aspects of this constellation—
> the new philosophy, methods of administration and military organiza-
> tion, spirit of government and methods of discipline—is the growing
> ideal of a human agent who is able to remake himself by methodical
> and disciplined action. What this calls for is the ability to take an in-
> strumental stance to one's given properties, desires, inclinations, ten-
> dencies, habits of thought and feeling, so that they can be *worked on*,
> doing away with some and strengthening others, until one meets the
> desired specifications. My suggestion is that Descartes' picture of the
> disengaged subject articulates the understanding of agency which is
> most congenial to this whole movement, and that is part of the grounds
> for its great impact in his century and beyond.[12]

Thus, Taylor's search for the historical sources of the modern sense of
agency not only reiterates what many have said—that Cartesian subjectivity is a
uniquely modern concept of human agency—but he links this to the equally
"modern" proclivity to make one's "self" the object of methodical development.

In addition to Taylor's opus, I have also found Frank Johnson's briefer
treatment of the subject in "The Western Concept of Self" very useful. While
Johnson gives a short summary of historical developments, his main emphasis is

on the qualities that are imparted to "self," when the term is used in contemporary Western discourse in the humanities and social sciences. Johnson lists four such qualities: analytical, monotheistic, individualistic, and materialistic/rationalistic.[13] As this implies, a whole constellation of ways of thinking, or habits of thought, forms itself around the modern concept of self.

By "analytic" Johnson means, above all, "the tendency to see reality as an aggregation of parts." He adds: "This endorsement of a particulate universe of material objects is important given the western tendency toward an emphasis on 'taking things apart'—i.e., analysis—and on the consequent process—*deduction*." Thinking in the analytic-deductive mode leads to a view of "self" as an observer separate from external objects as well as to what Johnson calls static, structural models of "self as subject."[14]

Johnson is among a number of scholars who use the term "monotheism" to mean more than a theological position, that is, to mean a whole way of thinking. Naturally, he cites Nietzsche, who called monotheism "the rigid consequence of the doctrine of one normal being," as the initiator of this trend. One corollary of monotheism, so viewed, is a series of dualisms that begins with the true God/false gods opposition. Johnson lists various pairs of opposites, dividing them into two groups: "*qualities of existence* (for example, good/bad, beautiful/ugly, sacred/profane, and so on) and *categories of identity* (for example, God/Satan, mind/matter, love/lust, and so on)." Johnson identifies a second corollary of the monotheistic way of thinking—a closed-system cosmology—and explains its connection to modern concepts of self, as follows:

> Another corollary of monotheism is the tendency to support a closed-system cosmology whose limits are coterminous with a singular, all-encompassing deity. Such encapsulation of reality, modeled after a unitary, omnipotent power, has tended to reinforce the description of a closed-system *personology* as well as a closed-system theology.[15]

"Monotheism" thus involves the tendency toward unitary explanations of phenomena in general and, also, toward a closed-system view of self.

Of course, "individualism," as a quality of Western thinking and subjectivity, is closely related to the kind of "personology" that Johnson mentions. The "self" experienced as closed off from what is not self, in part, is a consequence of the personal anxiety connected with our cultural belief in ontological separation and estrangement from God. In tandem with this, the stress on individual freedom and rights, regardless of its merits in the political realm, produces feelings of loneliness and alienation. Self-expression and self-actualization become important ways of establishing who one is and how one will find satisfaction in the world. This affects, for example, the way children are raised. In Johnson's words: "Children are socialized simultaneously to be obedient, to submit to rules which protect the rights of others, *and* to develop a progressive independence."[16]

Finally, as for materialistic-rationalistic tendencies of thought, Johnson asks us to see these as a "belief system," rather than a privileged "rational, scientific approach to reality." This is a belief system defined by "acceptance of the mechanical and logical characteristics of a world of objects."[17] While general acceptance of this belief system does not preclude explanations of phenomena (such as a person's death) in terms of other, coexisting belief systems, it does lead to (1) the tendency for rationalistic and materialistic explanations to predominate, (2) the tendency to apply modes of understanding the material world to realms that are not easily "materialized," and (3) the tendency to discredit explanations not using the analytic-deductive mode of thinking.[18]

As Johnson indicates earlier in his essay, when this mode of thinking is applied to selfhood by contemporary authors in the humanities and social sciences, certain common trends emerge. "Self" is normally seen as a unitary phenomenon, although it is common to contrast this (inner) self with a social self. Another typical way of analyzing a person's (single) self is in terms of so-called "levels" (or "layers") of selfhood. Finally, as Taylor also stressed, "self" is presented as something to be "worked on," for example, through stages of development.[19]

"SELF" AND "NO SELF" IN *ZHUANGZI* STUDIES

In this section I give examples of approaches to Master Zhuang's thought that feature the concept of self (or no self). These include examples from the pens of both American scholars and Chinese scholars. The Chinese scholars, some of whose works are in English, are all part of the Chinese *Zhuangzi* studies milieu. Yet we should not expect them to be less under the influence of the modern concept of self than their "Western" counterparts, despite the fact that Taylor and Johnson, for example, stress the Western origins of this concept. Indeed, there are reasons for us to expect the opposite.

In his excellent survey of Chinese conceptions of the self through the centuries, Mark Elvin indicates that, since the late nineteenth century, modern Chinese thinkers have given "self" a central role in their philosophies, whether they advocate its liberation or propose its absorption into a collective consciousness.[20] Lin Tongqi, Henry Rosemont, and Roger Ames, covering contemporary developments in a recent essay on the state of the field in Chinese philosophy, explain that in recent years "self" has been, along with "culture," one of the two central concepts in Chinese thought. They not only underscore the continuing importance on debates over the status of "self" (*ziwo*) but also the new obsession with the concept of "subjectivity" (*zhutixing* 主體性). They quote a Chinese scholar (Wang Pengling) as saying, in 1987, that one can hardly open a journal without confronting a discussion of subjectivity.[21] These developments are, of course, in response to China's confrontation with Western philosophy, literature, social science, and so on, throughout which the modern concept of self is a taken-for-granted notion.

Indeed, my own reading of works by certain Chinese *Zhuangzi* scholars reveals a surprising degree of unconscious acceptance of Western dualistic, developmental, and other assumptions related to selfhood. I will begin here with these examples.

Lao Siguang 勞思光 is the author of a leading survey of Chinese thought, which gives considerable attention to Master Zhuang. "Self" (*ziwo*) is the central concept in his analysis of Zhuang's thought. Moreover, this analysis is built around a series of familiar dualisms: body/spirit, inner/outer, true/false, and cognitive/aesthetic. His analysis has three parts: Zhuang's rejection of the physical self (*xingqu wo* 形軀我), Zhuang's rejection of the "cognitive self" (*renzhi wo* 認知我), and a comparison with Confucian thought focused on the difference between the Confucian "moral self" (*daode wo* 道德我) and Zhuang's "aesthetic self" (*qingyi wo* 情意我).

He begins with Zhuang's alleged rejection of the physical self, because he feels that the aesthetic self, which is the true self for Zhuang, is easily confused with the physical self. Quoting numerous passages that link the body with the myriad living things (*wanwu* 萬物), he takes them as evidence that the true self is not bodily, because it exists beyond materiality. It is not merely one of the myriad things; it is beyond them. For Lao operates out of a body/spirit dualism that leads him to believe that because "the self is within present consciousness . . . thus the self does not take the physical form as its 'own body' (*zishen* 自身). . . . The self is a subject transcending the [material] series of events; thus, life and death of the physical form 'cannot change the self' (*buneng bianhua ziwo* 不能變化自我)."[22] Thus, for Zhuang, the true self is not only inner and spiritual, it is also immutable rather than subject to change.

It is impossible to imagine that, without being steeped in Western ideas about selfhood, a Chinese scholar would come to these conclusions. These conclusions are especially unfortunate in that they detract from what is, for me, an otherwise agreeable interpretation of Zhuang's thought. Lao's key point is that Zhuang prefers a nonevaluative, aesthetic appreciation of the world over a "cognitive" approach to reality, which creates mental obstructions to the enjoyment of life. Ironically, then, he criticizes "later Daoists," who grasped Zhuang's point about needing to break down cognitive obstructions, for failing to grasp Zhuang's theory on breaking through one's "physical self" (*xingqu wo*). He says this is why they made the mistake of trying methods to extend their life spans.[23]

Another Chinese scholar who sees Master Zhuang's concept of true self as central to his thought is Wu Yi, whose *Xiaoyao de Zhuangzi* was mentioned at the start of this essay. Thus, the title of the concluding chapter of Wu's work translates "The spirit of Master Zhuang's thought: manifesting true self." Having established that the phrase, "the ultimate man has 'no self,'" actually refers to a step on the way to realization of true self—"after reaching 'no self' one then sees 'true self' (*zhenji* 真己)"—he concludes that others have been wrong in stressing "forgetting oneself" (*wang wo* 忘我) as Zhuang's goal. Forgetting oneself, he says, is not the goal but only a kind of *via negativa.* Zhuang's positive path, or *gongfu* 功夫, is that of "realizing the true self" (*shizheng zhenwo* 實證真我).[24]

Another example, Liu Guangyi's 劉光義 *Zhuangxuezhong de chanqu* 莊學中 的禪趣 (The Zen Flavor within Zhuang Learning), shows how the imposition of concepts of true/false self on Zhuang's thought can become a complex triad of Western, Chinese, and Indian ways of thinking.[25] Liu sees *Zhuangzi* through the lens of Chan (Zen) Buddhism, having already colored this lens with modern notions of the search for a "true self" (*zhenwo* 真我) beneath the layers of "false self" (*jiawo* 假我). This shows, on the one hand, how one can use the Buddhist idea of a preexistent Buddha nature (*tatathagarbha* in its Chinese transformation) to interpret Zhuang's view of "true self" and, on the other hand, how one can further "clarify" this view by introducing the typically modern notion of a "false self" that conceals a truer self within. I believe this is what Liu is doing, even if not explicitly.

Moreover, Liu shares with Wu Yi the view that the "self" one "forgets" is not the true self. It is only one's false self. And he shares with Lao Siguang the notion that the false self to be "forgotten" is one characterized by physical and emotional qualities as opposed to truly spiritual ones. After quoting passages from *Zhuangzi* and Chan sources, such as the recorded sayings of Master Lin Ji 臨濟, he concludes that they convey a common message when portraying sages or Buddhas as impervious to material conditions, such as fire and flood. It is this: "When you have discovered true self, one's own nature, you are then liberated from all the troubles and fears formed by the ignorance and greed of the small self (the false self), allowing one to live in happiness, die in happiness, work in happiness, and wander in happiness."[26]

My final example of a Chinese *Zhuangzi* scholar is Wu Kuang-ming, who has published extensively, but not exclusively, in English. I already mentioned his *Butterfly as Companion* at the start of this essay for its strong emphasis on a passage where Zhuang allegedly presents a version of the false self versus true self contrast. To reiterate, the passage, in Wu's translation, is this: "For-the-moment now I [*wu*] have lost me-myself [*wo*]." Although Wu knows that *wu* and *wo* have their respective places in this passage because *wu* is typically in the subject position, *wo* in the object position, in sentences of this kind, he insists that Zhuang is intentionally establishing a contrast between *wu*, as the authentic transcendental *cogito*, and *wo*, as the identifiable, objectifiable self. Then, as one would expect, he argues that loss of the false self is the doorway into true self realization:

> If this obtrusive [*wo*] self is let go of, then the authentic self, the self that has been doing the losing, the self-shed self will appear as the self-that-has-lost-itself, as empty as dry wood and dead ashes [*ganmu sihui*; cf. *xu*]. Such *wu*-self is a catharted self, whose authenticity is certified precisely in its activity of self-catharsis (*sang-wo, sang-ou*).[27]

Looking at this situation, particularly in light of Wu's otherwise brilliant efforts to see Zhuang in his own terms, I cannot help but feel that Wu has come under the spell of modern "self" theory.

Paul Kjellberg, in an important review article on Wu's *Butterfly as Companion*, reaches the same conclusion. He does so in the context of criticizing Wu for presenting his own views (such as that of levels of self) under Zhuang's inspiration, rather than sticking to his intended work of exegesis. Here is what Kjellberg has to say:

> One wonders at times if the project of *understanding* Zhuang Zi is not being sacrificed in favor of being *inspired* by him. One particularly disturbing example of this is the very distinction he draws between *wu* and *wo*.... [Zhuang Zi's] use of these two terms here, both of which are first-person pronouns, is readily explained by the fact that, unlike *wo*, the word *wu* cannot function as the object of a verb unless pre-posed after a negation.... Thus, while it is certainly an interesting and useful distinction to draw, the implication that Zhuang Zi has a developed theory of two levels of the self for which *wu* and *wo* are technical terms is at the very least a bit precipitous, if not misleading.[28]

As we turn to several other key contributors to American *Zhuangzi* studies, we will see that their interpretations, while insightful in other respects, also suffer from being under the spell of modern "self" theory.

Judith Berling's essay, "Self and Whole in Chuang Tzu," exemplifies the best and the worst in this regard.[29] On the one hand, it is an insightful piece that articulates how, through teaching an art of living, Master Zhuang offers freedom from societal limitations without preaching the ascetic way of life that is so commonly advocated for this purpose. On the other hand, it reads into Zhuang's thought almost every imaginable feature of modern "self" theory, including a model of outer (social) self versus true inner self, a notion of layers of self, the goal of an autonomous perfected self, and a process whereby the spiritual quality of the inner self can shine through the layers of outer selfhood.

Interestingly, Berling stresses the importance of the passage on which this essay focuses, interpreting *zhiren* ("ultimate man" in Mair's translation) to mean "perfected self." She considers the passage to be one among several images and anecdotes used by Zhuang "which portray the transcendence of the perfected self." She interprets many other passages, in which various obstructions to freedom are the subject of humorous critiques, as Zhuang's presentation of two "extrinsic layers." The first layer consists of labels attached to persons. Of them, she states: "These labels represent judgments which in no way touch or reflect the true self." To complete this model, she adds: "A second layer of the socialized self consists of the various roles and functions designated by society."[30] Moreover, in common with some Chinese interpreters discussed above, she sees physical existence as another layer covering the real self, as if she were dealing with a tradition that posits a spirit/matter dualism (even though she knows she is not). Thus, she states: "Spirit [*shen* 神] is a quality of the inner self that lies beneath the layers of mind and things; it is the spirit which one tries to release or recover by moving toward the ideal of the perfected self."[31]

Ultimately, after setting socialized and physical existence into opposition with authentic selfhood, Berling shows how Master Zhuang is able to reconcile the two while avoiding ascetic withdrawal from ordinary life. Instead of ascetic withdrawal, Zhuang advocates joining the flow of life without sacrificing individual freedom. However, this reconciliation—"a balance between uncovering the inner core of the self and being open to the whole of life"—was only required, in the first place, because a foreign dichotomy had been imposed on Zhuang's thought.[32] As I will argue below, this imposition is not needed for one to understand Zhuang's message about joining the flow of life.

While Berling's work exemplifies the "layers" feature and dualistic tendency of modern "self" theory, Robert Allinson's *Chuang-Tzu for Spiritual Transformation* exemplifies the developmental tendency.[33] He argues that the Inner Chapters of *Zhuangzi* involve the reader in a project of self-transformation, taking him/her step by step away from conventional ways of thinking, through mental "forgetting," to an ideal state of mind. The strong point of this analysis is the emphasis, not on what Zhuang says, but on how he says it. The emphasis is on the language and literary devices (fantastic tales, uses of logic against logic, shocking humor, and so on) that allegedly lead us through the stages of self-transformation. Here I am not concerned with whether or not Allinson succeeds in proving that Zhuang's language is intended to transform readers step by step.[34] I am concerned mainly with his claim that the process of transformation taught by Zhuang was a step-by-step transformation of the "self." Allinson says *Zhuangzi* is "a chart of spiritual progress." He explains: "The literary conceits and linguistic techniques which make up the text of the *Zhuangzi* seem systematically and artfully arranged both to indicate the different levels of spiritual development which lie before us and to show which linguistic devices are appropriately applied to these differing and ascending levels."[35]

What is self-transformation? According to Allinson: "The project of self-transformation appears in the *Zhuangzi* under various labels, most frequently as entering into Heaven or obtaining the Tao or the Way. The master key to the attainment of the Tao or the entrance into Heaven is the employment of the strategy of forgetting the mind." Unable to find a suitable example of the phrase "forgetting the mind" (*wang xin* 忘心) in *Zhuangzi*, Allinson has to settle for a passage (outside the Inner Chapters) about forgetting the self, in which we read: "The man who has forgotten self may be said to have entered Heaven."[36] He takes this as a key passage on transformation of the self, for in his view: "Forgetting the self and transforming the self are more or less the same thing."[37] He comments on the passage in question, as follows:

> If we can take as the mark of attaining heavenliness the success that one has had in forgetting one's self, I think it is fair to say that mental forgetting is the master key to attaining the Tao. If we keep in mind that mental forgetting is the same as learning how not to operate through one's conscious mental functions, I believe that we will have found an explicit textual reference which identifies the project of self-transformation as the central project of the *Zhuang Zi*.[38]

Here *Zhuangzi* is taken to teach a project of self-transformation and, moreover, to present the human individual as having a "self" that s/he can forget. In other words, we have the developmental tendency of modern "self" theory built upon the idea, quite foreign to Master Zhuang, of "the self" as something that a person "has."

The same assumption—of "the self" as something to have or lose, to possess or forget, and so forth—underlies the interpretations of those who stress, not Zhuang's views on "self," but his views on "no self." One example of this is David Loy's attempt to compare Zhuang's views to Buddhist theories of "no self" (*anatman*) in "Zhuangzi and Nāgārjuna on the Truth of No Truth."[39] Loy reads Zhuang as taking the Buddhist position that "self" is an illusion that we possess and must eradicate to reach the realization of "no self." Buddhist interpretations of Zhuangzi, of course, are not new. They are not covered here because my interest is in the influence of Western, not Indian, views of selfhood.[40]

Our second example looks for parallels, not in Buddhism, but in postmodern thought. It is David Hall, "To Be or Not to Be: The Postmodern Self and the *Wu*-forms of Taoism."[41] After tracing the history of the Western concept of self, culminating in the modern notion that one "has" a self, Hall presents the postmodern rejection of the analytical-monotheistic-rationalistic model of "modern" thought about human agency. Thereafter, he discusses what postmodern thinkers have in common with Master Zhuang and, moreover, what they can learn from him.

There are many strengths in Hall's approach. First, he is fully aware of the cultural peculiarity of the modern concept of self. Second, he knows that the postmodern stance is a reaction to modernity, stating "I have claimed that the postmodern interpretation of self is a legitimate response to a serious impasse in the project of modernity."[42] Third, he sees key elements of what Zhuang and postmodern thinkers have in common. He states: "The postmodern, plural, aesthetic self has an awareness of its plurality and the insistent particularity of the elements that variously focus that plurality. This aesthetic self-consciousness rehearses the Taoist vision of no-soul, no-self (*wu-wo, wu-ji*)."[43] Finally, he insists that it would be a mistake to read "the Taoist no-soul doctrine" as a dialectical rejection of the Western concept of self. For not only was there no sense of a whole, unitary self to which Daoists could react, there was also no dialectical way of thinking that would require the rejection of one concept of self in favor of its alternative.[44]

Hall is perhaps right to believe Zhuang can help postmodern thinkers to see more clearly "that 'self' cannot be one, whole, or finally inclusive."[45] However, neither they nor other contemporary thinkers are helped by being told that Zhuang ever had a doctrine of "no-soul," or "no-self." Postmodernism has a concept of "self," even if it is that of a pluralistic "no-self" self. As far as I can tell, Zhuang had no such concept.

Hall's parallels could be valid, including his attribution to Zhuang of a no-self doctrine. This depends on whether or not, in using terms like *wu ji* [*wu-chi*] or *wu wo*, Zhuang was reacting to a concept of self or, in Hall's words, to the presumption of "the unity of rational self-consciousness."[46] This possibility should not be dismissed out of hand. Mark Elvin, in his survey of the history of conceptions of self in China, presents much evidence to show that those who wrote ancient Chinese texts, or were described in them, had a strong sense of identity and were even capable of radical individualism.[47] Surely Zhuang had something in mind when he intentionally placed terms of negation before the reflexive pronoun *ji* (-self) or the first-person pronoun *wo* (I, me), terms such as *wu* 無 (not be/not have), *shi* 失 (lose), *sang* 喪 (lose), *xu* 虛 (empty), or *qu* 去 (discard). But what did he have in mind?

I aim to answer this question on the basis of a careful investigation of the contextual meanings of terms that are usually rendered as "self" in translations of *Zhuangzi*, with particular attention to contexts in which there is some form of negation, either by a negative particle or by a verb that suggests loss or eradication. It has been necessary to undertake this investigation because so little attention has been paid to classical Chinese terms for "self" in the many existing discussions of selfhood in the Confucian as well as Daoist traditions. A notable exception to this is found in the debate between Herbert Fingarette and Roger Ames over Confucian conceptions of self. Interestingly, that debate ended with a question posed by Fingarette, which I take here as a starting point. This is the question: "Why should we reify 'self' by giving it the independent noun form in English, and thus to impute to Confucius [or Zhuangzi] the notion of some inner entity, some core of one's being—whether egoistic or ideal"?[48]

MASTER ZHUANG'S CONCEPT OF PERSONHOOD: A SURVEY OF KEY TERMS

This section will look at instances of *wo* and *ji*, the terms most frequently encountered above in others' discussions of Master Zhuang's concepts "self" and "no-self." It will also look at instances of two other terms whose use, in my view, sheds more light on Zhuang's concept of the person: *shen* 身 (body, person, "self") and *xin* 心 (heart, mind, heart-mind). All four terms are "negated" in the sense that they are preceded by words meaning losing, forgetting, and so on.

W. A. C. H. Dobson, in *A Dictionary of the Chinese Particles*, covers a full range of personal pronouns used in Late Archaic Chinese (Dobson's designation for Chinese of the late Zhou period). These include first person pronouns, such as *wo* (I, we, my, our, me), and pronouns used in a reflexive or emphatic sense, such as *ji* (reflexively as myself, himself, and emphatically as "[I] myself" and so forth) and *shen* (myself or himself, and, more emphatically, "in person"). His examples reveal that standard usage of *wo* and *ji* did not include nominalized forms that indicate a substantive entity, whether a "self" or something else.[49] Master Zhuang was unusual in frequently nominalizing these terms for special effect, although there are occasional examples in other Zhou period texts. For example, in *Lunyu* (Analects) 9.4, we are told that Master Kong 孔子 was free of *wo*, usually interpreted to mean "egoism."

Shen is of course another story. It was originally a noun meaning "body," which came to have the derivative meanings of "person" and the reflexive "self," often in combination with *ji* or other reflexive particles. In *Lunyu* 1.4, *shen* is what Zengzi "reflects on three times" in his daily regimen of character development. And it is that which one should "cultivate" (*xiu*), according to the famous opening chapter of *Daxue* 大學 (Great Learning). In *Zhuangzi* it is also the term that is consistently used when cultivation of personhood is discussed.

In my view, frequent use of *shen* in the sense of personhood as well as the innovative nominalizing of *wo* and *ji* has led translators of *Zhuangzi* to use the English word "self" and, therefore, consciously or unconsciously, to attribute the modern concept of self to him. In what follows, I begin with uses of *shen* in *Zhuangzi* because this is the best term to stress in presenting Zhuang's concept of personhood: the context for understanding his special nominalized uses of *ji* and *wo*.

Two things stand out when one surveys occurrences of *shen* in the sense of one's person (or "self") in *Zhuangzi*: (1) it designates something that one should "cultivate" (*xiu* 修), "preserve" (*bao* 保), and "nourish" (*yang* 養); and (2) it is almost always a bad idea to lose or to forget one's *shen*, and the same goes for putting it in danger or taking it lightly. The first occurrence of *shen* in the sense of "person" is at the beginning of chapter 3 ("Essentials for Nurturing Life"), where *baoshen* ("preserve one's person") occurs in a verse passage on ways to nourish life.[50] It is immediately followed by the famous story of Cook Ding, from whose skilled use of a meat cleaver Lord Wenhui learns how to nourish life. *Xiushen* ("to cultivate one's person") also occurs once in the Inner Chapters and half a dozen times in other parts of *Zhuangzi*.[51] *Yangshen* ("to nourish one's person") is an especially interesting phrase to consider because, at first sight, it would seem to have only the sense of nourishing oneself physically. Yet from the context in which it occurs in chapter 4 ("The Human World") of the Inner Chapters, we see that *shen* means one's person as something more than one's body. The context is a story about Scattered Apart, a man who had serious congenital defects that kept him from being conscripted by state authorities to be either a soldier or a laborer. As a result: "Though his body was scattered, it was sufficient to enable him to support himself [*yang qi shen* 養其身] and to live out the years allotted to him by heaven."[52]

Assuming that authors of the parts of *Zhuangzi* beyond the Inner Chapters were the first interpreters of his thought, their uses of *shen* and other key terms will help us to understand what the terms meant in their day, generally, and in the usage of Master Zhuang, in particular. Uses of *shen* outside the Inner Chapters strengthen the case for reading *shen*, in its philosophically most important uses, to mean the entire person—body, actions, attitudes, habits, and so forth—rather than as either one's inner self or one's body. These uses tell us not only that one should cultivate one's person but also that one should "preserve the existence" (*cun* 存) of it, "highly value" (*gui* 貴) it, and so forth. In chapter 21 (Sir Square Field), for example, Master Kong (Confucius) asks Lao Dan 老聃 (Old Longears) about his method of letting his mind wander in the origin of things. He is told about how the various living things accept their myriad transformations without concern for loss or gain, fortune or misfortune, and, finally, about the need to abandon concern for status, as follows:

> Abandoning subject status is like abandoning a clump of mud, because one knows that one's person is more valued than the subject status [*zhi shen gui yu li ye* 知身貴於隸也]. Value lies in oneself and is not lost by a change of status. Since there are myriad transformations that never begin to reach a limit, which of them is sufficient to trouble the mind? He who is already a doer of the Way comprehends this.[53]

Here *shen* refers to who one really is (not one's social status). One is tempted to say it refers to one's "true self," but to do so would take away from the meaning of *shen* as the entire person—including the body—and draw us into the semantic realm of spirit over body, inner over outer, and so forth. And this is best avoided.

Having established that *shen* is a key term to investigate in seeking to understand Master Zhuang's concept of the person, it will be instructive to look at those instances where he speaks of forgetting *shen*, taking it lightly, or otherwise harming it. In looking at such instances, one is struck by the extreme rarity of instances in which it is a good idea to forget one's "self," where *shen* defines selfhood. I have found only one clear instance of this, which comes from the mouth of "Master Kong" in chapter 4, a chapter that ends with the madman of Chu 楚 castigating Master Kong for his ignorant moralistic stance. Indeed, it would be quite appropriate to take Kong's advice in this context as the opposite of Master Zhuang's.

Kong gives his advice to the Duke of She as he leaves on a diplomatic mission to the state of Qi 齊. It is advice for "one who is a subject or a son," as follows: "he must carry out his affairs according to circumstances and forget about his own person [*wang qi shen* 忘其身]. What leisure has he for loving life and despising death? Thus, sir, you may proceed on your mission."[54] Since forgetting one's person is presented along with an admonition *against* "loving life and despising death," it is likely that these words do *not* represent Master Zhuang's position.

Moreover, all similar instances present forgetting, taking lightly, or losing *shen* as a bad idea. One passage that obviously expresses Zhuang's own viewpoint comes in his critique of Master Hui 惠子 at the end of chapter 5 ("Symbols of Integrity Fulfilled"), as follows:

> "What I mean by having emotions is to say that a man should not inwardly harm his person [*nei shang qi shen* 內傷其身] with 'good' and 'bad,' but rather should accord with the spontaneous and not add to life."
>
> "If he does not add to life," said Master Hui, "how can this person exist?"
>
> "The Way gives him an appearance," said Master Zhuang, "and heaven gives him a form. He does not inwardly harm his person with preferences and aversions. Now you, sir, dissipate your spirit and expend your essence by leaning against a tree while you mutter or by dozing over your study table. Heaven granted you a form, sir, but you go on babbling about 'hard' and 'white.' "[55]

This passage tells us at least two things: first, "the person," which is harmed, is not simply the physical person, the body; and, second, it is something that can be "hurt" by the kind of sophistry for which Master Hui was famous. Obviously, *shen* is taken to include mental as well as physical aspects of a person.

Of course, there are many uses of *shen* in the Inner Chapters where it un-ambiguously means "body" or where it is unclear whether it means the body or the entire person. However, it is clear in all these uses that preserving *shen* is good and losing it is bad. For example, the phrases "endanger my person/body" (*wei wu shen* 危吾身), "take his person/body lightly" (*qing yong qi shen* 輕用其身), and "take my person/body lightly" (*qing yong wu shen* 輕用吾身) all describe ex-tremely undesirable situations.[56]

Numerous examples from outside the Inner Chapters reiterate that forgetting one's *shen* is a bad idea. The most interesting of these examples is found in a story from chapter 20 ("The Mountain Tree") sometimes said to describe Master Zhuang's conversion experience.[57] It is a story in which Zhuang, out walking in a place called Eagle Mound, realizes that he is no different from other creatures ignorantly pursuing advantage in the world, while "forgetting" what is really im-portant: their "persons." Zhuang was so deeply affected by the experience that he sat depressed for three days and, then, explained why he was so unhappy, as follows:

> Zhuang Zhou said, "I have been guarding my physical form but for-
> gotten about my person [*wu shou xing er wang shen* 吾守形而忘身]; I
> have been observing the turbid water but am oblivious to the clear
> depths. Furthermore, I have heard my master say, 'When in a place
> where certain customs prevail, follow the rules of that place.' Now, as I
> was wandering at Eagle Mound, I forgot about my person [*wang wu
> shen* 忘吾身]. A strange magpie brushed against my forehead; and,
> wandering in the chestnut grove, [I] forgot about [my] true being [*wang
> zhen* 忘真]. The watchman of the chestnut grove considered me a
> poacher. That's why I am unhappy."[58]

Several things about this passage as a context for understanding the meaning of *shen* stand out: (1) Zhuang forgot about his *shen*, while guarding his physical form; (2) this happened while he was "wandering" (*you* 游), which normally indicates for Zhuang an ideal state of living; and (3) forgetting about one's "true being" (*zhen*) is made synonymous with forgetting about one's "person" (*shen*). Thus, even in a state of "wandering," one must *not* forget oneself in the most important sense: one's *shen*.

Moreover, the parallel use of *shen* and *zhen*, linking them conceptually, occurs again in chapter 31 ("An Old Fisherman"), where Master Kong receives rather than gives advice about life. In the course of responding to Kong's request for "the ultimate teaching," the old fisherman says:

> "Diligently cultivate your person; attentively guard your true nature
> [*zhen*]; let things return to the keeping of others—then there will be
> nothing in which you will be implicated. But now, instead of cultivat-
> ing your own person, you seek to cultivate others. Is this not paying
> attention to externals?"[59]

Thus, the term for the person, the so-called "self," that is linked to one's true being in *Zhuangzi* is one that refers to the entire person, pluralistically conceived, rather than to some inner or spiritual or transcendental entity.

Next to *shen*, *xin* (heart-mind) is the most important term for understanding Master Zhuang's concept of the person. Moreover, it is like *shen* in two important ways: (1) it's earliest reference was to something physical, namely, the human heart; (2) over time it came to cover an ever widening range of emotional and mental functions, not a distinct entity with a strictly mental or spiritual nature. In other words, it lacks the same qualities of the "self" and "soul," in the Western sense, that *shen* lacks. Both are pluralistic rather than unitary entities. Just as *shen* is the locus of various living habits that concern Master Zhuang, *xin* is the locus of habits of mind that concern him. It is an organ of various thoughts and feelings produced in a continuous stream. Finally, measured by frequency of usage, it is among the most important terms in the Inner Chapters, where it occurs forty-five times.

However, there is a major key difference between *shen* and *xin*. In contrast to Zhuang's consistently positive appraisals of *shen*, he is ambiguous about *xin*. As the locus of one's various thoughts and feelings, one's *xin* may either facilitate or obstruct one's quest to join the flow of life. An empty *xin* is good, a *xin* full of knowledge is not; a wandering *xin* is good, a sophistic *xin* is not; a peaceful *xin* is good, an agitated *xin* is not.

Some scholars suspect that the experience of mystical states or meditative practices led Master Zhuang to praise those who "can make the mind still like dead ashes" (*xin ke shi ru sihui* 心可使如死灰) or who can engage in "mind-fasting" (*xinzhai* 心齋). I will return to this issue in the final section of this essay. The relevant contexts tell us that the ideal is when *xin* is in a calm yet fluid state. It is best "to let [one's] heart-mind wander" (*you xin* 游心). This phrase, in which "to wander" is used as a transitive verb with *xin* as its object, occurs thrice in the Inner Chapters and twice outside them.[60] The first instance, in chapter 4, connects it with the ultimate course, as follows: "Just ride along with things as you let your [heart-]mind wander. Entrust yourself to inevitability and thereby nourish what is central. That's the ultimate course."[61]

This is "Master Kong" speaking, but presumably the one into whose mouth Zhuang has put his own message. The same is true at the start of chapter 5, where Master Kong is asked about another man of Lu 魯, called Princely Nag, who has just as many disciples as Master Kong, despite having been mutilated by having a foot cut off. With great humility, Kong explains what is special about the way Princely Nag uses his *xin*, as follows:

> "Life and death are of great moment," said Confucius, "but he is able to avoid their transformations...." If one sees things from the viewpoint of the differences ... the liver and the gall bladder are as distant as Chu is from Viet. If one sees things from the viewpoint of their similarities, the myriad things are all one. He who realizes this is unaware of the attractions of the senses but lets his [heart-]mind wander instead in the harmony of integrity. He sees what bespeaks the identity of things instead of what bespeaks their loss. He sees the loss of his foot as the sloughing off of a clump of earth."[62]

Letting the mind wander is here linked with the realization of relativity that is so important to Master Zhuang. Moreover, it is related to the ability to take oneself and the events which befall oneself as just part of the transformation of things, not as something special in which to invest ego concerns. In chapter 7 ("Responses for Emperors and Kings"), the "wandering" *xin* is linked to the ideal way of ruling, as follows:

"Let your mind wander in vapidity," said Anonymous, "blend your vital breath with immensity. Follow along with the nature of things and admit no personal preference. Then all under heaven will be well governed."[63]

What strikes one about this passage is that it also focuses on joining the flow of all things.

Even better known to readers of *Zhuangzi* than the concept of "letting the *xin* wander" is that of *xinzhai* (mind-fasting), although it occurs in only one story, where Master Kong instructs his favorite disciple, Yan Hui. This disciple asks what "mind-fasting" is, and his master responds:

"Listen not with your ears but with your [heart-]mind. Listen not with your [heart-]mind but with your primal breath. The ears are limited to listening, the [heart-]mind is limited to tallying. The primal breath, however, awaits things emptily. It is only through the Way that one can gather emptiness, and emptiness is the fasting of the mind."[64]

Here the mental stillness called "mind-fasting" is not so much an ideal state as a method to put one in touch with one's "primal breath" (*qi* 氣), the *dao* 道, and "emptiness" (*xu* 虛).

This passage, along with others from outside the Inner Chapters, praise the *xin* that is empty, forgotten, or just plain absent: "mindless" (*wu xin* 無心). The most interesting case of this is again from a story that hints of meditation. In this story, Wearcoat sings a happy song about his apparently sleeping compatriot, Gnaw Gap, as follows:

> His form is like a withered carcass,
> His [heart-]mind is like dead ashes;
> He verifies his real knowledge,
> But doesn't insist on his own reasoning.
> Obscure and dim,
> In his mindlessness [*wu xin*], you can't consult with him.
> What kind of man is he?[65]

The first two lines of the song contain wording found several places in *Zhuangzi* where we seem to meet a description of meditation. All of them may be based on the opening passage of chapter 2, in which Sir Motley of Southurb says "I lost me-myself" in explaining how his *xin* could be like dead ashes. In any case, the phrase "*xin* like dead ashes" became a key refrain for followers of Master Zhuang.

This and other phrases that seemingly negate the value of one's *xin* have contributed to theories that Master Zhuang advocated transcendence of an emotional or mental self in favor of something more essential, more spiritual. But this conclusion involves a misinterpretation of the phrases. Zhuang's point is not that one's *xin* is itself bad. Indeed, he can speak positively of it, as he does in contexts where he uses such phrases as "constant heart-mind' (*chang xin* 常心) and "heart-mind without knowledge" (*xin wusuozhi* 心無所知).

At the beginning of chapter 5, where Princely Nag's method of "cultivation of the person" is being praised, we are told that it goes from "knowledge" to "(ordinary) heart-mind," and, finally, to "constant heart-mind." The reference to the heart-mind that is without knowledge also occurs in a story on cultivation of the person (in chapter 11: "Preserving and Accepting"), one in which the Yellow Emperor gets advice from Master Broadly Complete about the ideal state that ensues when "the eyes see nothing, the ears hear nothing, and the mind knows nothing [*xin wusuozhi*]".[66] Thus, through cultivation of the person, the emotional and mental faculties covered by the term *xin* attain a proper state. They come to facilitate, rather than to obstruct, one's joining the flow of things.

Finally, now, we may use what we learned about Master Zhuang's concept of the person to understand what he probably meant in negating the so-called "self" in such phrases as *wu ji, xu ji, shi ji, qu ji,* and *wang ji;* or *wu wo, sang wo,* and *wang wo.* We learned that the concepts of *shen* and *xin* reflect a pluralistic conception of the person, not a unitary one built concentrically around an inner, spiritual core. We also learned that there is no place within this conception for a mind-body dualism. With this in hand, it is hard to imagine how modern interpreters found distaste for the physical dimensions of existence in *Zhuangzi.* In sum, to the extent that these two concepts define Zhuang's conception of the person, it is highly improbable that modern concepts of the self could serve any role, except perhaps as negative examples, in helping us to grasp what was going on with his experimental nominalizing of *ji* and *wo.*

Whether used in the ordinary way as a reflexive pronoun or in a special way as a noun, or whether used in *Zhuangzi* or in other texts of the same period, *ji* does imply a self/other contrast; it is often juxtaposed with *ren* 人 (other persons). The philosophical potential of this contrast was not lost on Zhuang. However, he did not develop it as we would, with our overriding sense of "self" versus "other." Instead, I believe, he was concerned with one's having an excessive sense of being different from others, a feeling of being better than others, and an *inability* to "go along with others" (*shun ren* 順人). Conversely, his ideal was that of "being free of *ji*" (*wu ji*) in the sense of blending in with other persons, not to mention "all living things" (*wan wu*). "The ultimate person" (*zhiren* 至人) was his key term for this ideal.

In my epigraph, the ultimate person, being free of *ji,* is akin to one who is free of "accomplishments" (*wu gong*) and free of "name" (*wu ming*). A reasonable explanation is that the passage is condemning three negative qualities of thought and behavior. *Ji* is on a par with the other two as a kind of bad habit, an obstruction to living in an ideal way. There is no need to hypostatize it as "self."

The two uses of *wu ji* outside the Inner Chapters support this interpretation. Both occur in what A. C. Graham has called "Great Man" passages, which he says

were probably written by disciples of Master Zhuang who tended to rationalize his
message.[67] One passage occurs in a section of chapter 11 on the Great Man's
teaching, as follows:

> The teaching of the great man is like the shadow from a form, like the
> echo from a sound. When questioned, he replies, sharing his thoughts
> fully and serving as the companion of all under heaven. He dwells in
> Neverland and travels to Utopia. He leads all of you teeming masses
> back to where you belong, to wander in limitlessness. He passes in and
> out of nonattachment, beginningless as the sun. His discourse and cor-
> poreal form join in the great commonality. Having joined in the great
> commonality, he has no self [*wu ji*]. Having no self, how could he have
> being? If you look at those who had being, they were the superior men
> of old. If you look at those who had nonbeing, they were the friends of
> heaven and earth.[68]

Here a remarkable set of elements of Zhuang's ultimate person are listed: he is a
companion of all under heaven; he "wanders"; he joins in the great commonality;
and, being free of *ji*, he is a friend of heaven and earth as opposed to a "superior
man."

In chapter 17 ("Autumn Floods"), a verse passage almost identical to the one
quoted at the outset of this essay occurs in a description of the Great Man's
conduct, as follows:

> Therefore, the conduct of the Great Man never takes a course harmful
> to others.... In conduct he differs from the vulgar, yet he does not
> make much of being eccentric and extraordinary; he lives as one of the
> common people, yet he does not despise the flatterers at court. The
> titles and salaries of the age are insufficient to induce him, its punish-
> ments and disgrace are insufficient to humiliate him.... I have heard
> said:
>
> > The man of the Way is not heard of,
> > The utmost man wins no gains,
> > The Great Man "has no self" [*wu ji*].[69]

Not only is the Great Man free of *ji* as well as of concern for reputation and gain,
he blends in with the common people, rather than seeking to stand out, to be well
known, to make gains, and so forth. This is why he is a model for others, not
because they "have selves," while he "has no self."

Similarly, I find no reason to take any of the other ways of negating *ji* in
Zhuangzi—by "losing" (*shi*), "emptying," (*xu*), "discarding" (*qu*), or "forgetting"
(*wang*) it—as implying that one "has a self" and must get rid of it. To begin with,
both instances of *shi ji* are in contexts where losing *ji* is a *bad* idea. In chapter 6

("Great Ancestral Teacher"), we read "if in pursuit of a name you lose your own self [*xing ming shi ji* 行名失己] you are not a knight."[70] The other instance is in a description of the ultimate person in chapter 26 ("External Things"), where we read: "Only the ultimate man can wander through the world [*you yu shi* 游於世] without deviation, accommodating others without losing himself [*shun ren er bu shi ji* 順人而不失己]."[71] This passage is interesting because, if *ji* meant "self" as opposed to "others," we would expect that losing oneself (rather than *not* losing oneself) would fit with accommodating others. My conclusion is that getting along with others, as part of "wandering through the world," is the important thing, not eradicating one's "self."

Significantly, in this regard, a key instance of *xu ji* 虛己 occurs in a section of chapter 20 that also features "wandering through the world." When Yiliao of Southmarket instructs the Marquis of Lu on how to avoid calamity, he states: "If a person can empty himself and go wandering in the world, who can harm him?"[72]

The one instance of *qu ji* comes from chapter 33 ("All Under Heaven"), which treats various thinkers of the time. The passage in question is in a section on the philosopher Shen Dao 慎到: "Shen Dao abandoned knowledge and rejected self [*qi zhi qu ji* 棄知去己], acquiescing in inevitability." Here *zhi* and *ji* are parallel terms indicating qualities that can keep one from following the flow of things. *Ji* suggests something like "egoism"; it does not mean "the self."

Finally, this brings us to the instance of *wang ji* that was so important for Robert Allinson. It is in a passage where, for the benefit of his friend Master Kong, Old Longears (Lao Dan) castigates "sophists" (*bianzhe* 辯者), concluding his critique with this: "To forget things and to forget heaven is called forgetting the self [*wang ji*]. The man who forgets himself may be said to have entered heaven."[73] There is no implication in this passage that *ji* (properly rendered "oneself," not "the self") is being negatively evaluated. On the contrary, it is parallel to "(all living) things" (*wu*) and "heaven" (*tian* 天). The total "forgetting" that is praised here affirms the central theme of *Zhuangzi*—letting go and wandering in the world—and once again hints of a meditative or mystical state. There is no need to read it as being about "the self."

Turning now to Master Zhuang's "no-self" doctrine in its final guise, related to uses of *wo*, we must begin by stating that there is no genuine case of "*wu wo*" anywhere in *Zhuangzi*. Although the phrase occurs in one of the most famous passages in the text, wherein *wo* is juxtaposed with *bi* 彼, meaning "other," the passage is about relativity of perspective, not about the negation of "self." It reads as follows: "If there were no 'other,' there would be no 'I' [*fei bi wu wo* 非彼無我]. If there were no 'I,' there would be nothing to apprehend the 'other.'"[74]

This passage is from the same chapter (chapter 2) that begins with an even more famous passage in this regard, the *wu sang wo* passage that is so crucial for Wu Kuang-ming's understanding of Master Zhuang's two levels of self: the "*wu*-self" (authentic transcendental *cogito*) and the "*wo*-self" (identifiable, objectifiable self). In looking at the context, we must remember that Sir Motley of Southurb uses the phrase in explaining what was happening when his body was "like a withered tree," and his mind "like dead ashes." These descriptions are used at several points in the text to indicate, most likely, a meditative or mystical state. If we free ourselves from the spell of modern "self" theory, we can interpret his words, "I have lost me-myself," to indicate the ultimate of unattached mental "wandering." In this state, there was no Cartesian residue, no authentic transcendental *cogito*, there was simply a "person" unaware of anything that distinguished him from the flow of all living things.

Moreover, if we broaden the context to look at seemingly parallel passages, in which the phrases *wang* (forget) *wo* and *shi* (lose) *wo* occur, there is no hint that *wo* means anything like "objectifiable self." *Wang wo* only occurs in a passage where *wo* indicates the reflexive "-self" in the second or third person, meaning "forget you" or "forget themselves," but surely not "forget the self."[75] The lone instance of *shi wo* also provides no evidence that *wo* can mean "self." It is from a story where a golden carp stuck in a rut says, "I have lost my normal environment (*wu shi wo changyu* 吾失我常與) and have no place to stay."[76] Moreover, this passage is among much evidence in *Zhuangzi* that *wu* occurs as the subject of a sentence, with *wo* in the predicate, with no hint of a philosophical distinction between a "*wu*-self" and a "*wo*-self." Thus, apart from the idiosyncratic phrase, "I lost me-myself," at the start of chapter 2, there is no evidence in the text that its author(s) used *wo* (I, me) to mean anything like "the self."

To summarize, although Master Zhuang occasionally nominalized *ji* and *wo* to designate certain undesirable habits of thought or behavior, he did not hypostatize these habits as a false "self"; nor did he hypostatize other ideal habits or inner qualities of the person as a true "self." He simply did not think in these terms. He was interested in the various habits and qualities of one's "person" (*shen*) and one's "heart-mind" (*xin*); and he taught of personal cultivation whereby one could let go of habits and qualities that obstructed one's innate tendencies to get along with others (*shun ren*), wander in the world (*you yu shi*), and join in the flow of all living things (*wan wu*). He had, at most, a pluralistic conception of "the person." Therefore, it does far more harm than good to interpret and to translate *Zhuangzi* by reference to concepts of "the self."

PERSONHOOD, MYSTICISM, AND THE FLOW EXPERIENCE

How should we interpret the references in *Zhuangzi* that praise the loss of habits and qualities designated by "*ji*" or "*wo*"? How can we step outside of our modern frame of interpretation, dispense with the concept of self, and determine what the text probably meant? I would suggest that a starting point lies in the earliest complete interpretation we have, the commentary included in the *textus receptus.*

the edition of *Zhuangzi* edited and interpreted by Guo Xiang 郭象 (died 312), whose commentary was free of Western conceptions of selfhood.

The Ideal Person

Guo assigns great importance to the ideal described in my epigraph in both its forms: the "ultimate man" described in the aphorism as well as the hypothetical "someone who could ride upon the truth of Heaven and Earth" and "chariot upon the transformations of the six vital breaths and thereby go wandering in infinity." He interprets the passage as helping us to understand the message of Master Zhuang's stories, all the way back to the tales of the Peng bird and the long-lived cedrella tree at the start of chapter 1. For Guo, this message is that each living thing has its own unique way of being, which is *natural* to it, and each is not better or worse than any other. And the human ideal lies in being in accord with all living things. As Paul Kjellberg has shown, the key concept that Guo adds in thus interpreting Master Zhuang is that of the "nature" (*xing* 性) of each thing, a concept foreign to the Inner Chapters of *Zhuangzi*.

Guo comments on the ideal of one who can chariot upon the transformations of the six vital breaths, as follows:

> Heaven and Earth is a cumulative name for all living things. Heaven and Earth take all living things as their body, and all living things must take Nature's course as their true being (*zheng* 正). Nature's course is that which is natural through non-purposeful action (*bu wei* 不為). Thus, the Peng's ability to fly high, the dovelet's to fly low, the cedrella tree's ability to grow (tall), and the morning mushroom's to stay short—all these are abilities from naturalness, not abilities from purposeful action. Naturally able without purposeful action, they act in true being. Therefore, [Zhuang's phrase] "to ride upon the truth of Heaven and Earth" means to accord with the natures of all living things; and "to ride upon the transformations of the six vital breaths" means to wander along the course of [Nature's] transformations.[77]

This passage sets the stage for Guo's perspective on the aphorism about the ultimate person.

In his commentary on the phrase "the ultimate person has no *ji*," he says: "Without *ji* and thus in accord with living things (*wu ji gu shun wu* 無己故順物); in accord with living things and thus being (true) king (*shun wu er wang yi* 順物 而王矣)." Obviously, Guo has his own bias, or frame of interpretation, which leads him to read the passage more politically than others may. But he has no concept of "self" to read into the text and, therefore, simply interprets *ji* to be that which stands in the way of one's accord with (other) living things.[78]

His comments on the other two occurrences of *wu ji* in *Zhuangzi* are perfectly in line with this. Commenting on the passage in chapter 11, where *wu ji* helps describe what it means to join the great commonality, he simply says: "If one has *ji*, then one cannot join the great commonality" (*you ji ze buneng datong ye* 有己則不能大同也). In commenting on the passage in chapter 17, where we are told the Great Man has no *ji*, he says: "It's just a matter of letting things be" (*ren wu eryi* 任物而已).[79] Whatever qualities are represented by the term *ji*, Guo does not hypostatize them into a single entity. His interest is only with their potential to keep one from harmonizing with other living things, joining the great commonality, and letting things be. In line with Guo's commentary, then, one should simply call them "ego concerns," as in the following retranslation of the passage from my epigraph.

> The ultimate person has no ego concerns,
> The spiritual person has no merit concerns,
> And the sage has no name concerns.

In this translation, all three kinds of obstructions to joining the flow of life are taken as plural in nature, and all three are assumed to be qualities of a person conceived pluralistically, not of a unitary self.

Less sympathetic interpretations of Master Zhuang's thought, by Confucians, for example, also endorse this interpretation. In an appendix to his three-volume compendium of commentary on *Zhuangzi*, Wang Shumin 王叔岷 takes pains to show how Confucian scholars from Yang Xiong 楊雄 through Zhu Xi 朱熹 to Qian Mu 錢穆 have slandered Master Zhuang by pairing him with Yang Zhu as another proponent of egoism (*wei wo zhi xue* 為我之學). While Wang easily marshals evidence showing these Confucians were grossly mistaken, the very fact that they conceived the problem in terms of egoistic tendencies—and whether one encourages or discourages them—shows they were in line with a sympathetic commentator like Guo Xiang in their basic assumptions.[80] Because these assumptions are so different from those behind the modern concept of "the self," we must abandon it in favor of a concept of "the person" that is more hospitable to Master Zhuang's thought.

However, even those who accept this view may feel that, as long as I say Zhuang has a concept of the person, then he has a concept of self, even if not the typical modern one. Among students of Chinese conceptions of "self" whose works I have consulted, Mark Elvin would most likely feel this way. As indicated previously, he offers a strong defense of the position that texts from Zhou period China can reveal a strong sense of identity, and even radical individualism, although he sees significant differences between Chinese and Western assumptions about selfhood. Nonetheless, I still reject the term "self" because of all the cultural baggage it carries. I acknowledge that "person" is not completely free of cultural baggage, but I insist that it is by far the lesser of two evils.

In the second section of this essay, we saw how easy it is for the cultural baggage carried by "self" to lead us to read all manner of modern theories of selfhood into *Zhuangzi*. Simply by using the term "self," regardless of one's efforts to shun its cultural baggage, one endorses the unification ("monotheistically") of a variety of thoughts, feelings, and attitudes into a single entity. Moreover, as we saw in the third section, there are alternatives to the use of "self" and "no self" that are more in line with the general cultural milieu as well as the specific message of Master Zhuang.

In this section, I will shift my attention from Zhuang's critique of various obstructions to joining the flow of life to his advice on cultivating this ideal. In doing so, I will look at three literary genres found in *Zhuangzi*: knack stories, fantastic tales, and accounts of ecstatic experience. In starting out, let me praise A. C. Graham's excellent commentary on this matter, which he expresses by reference to what he calls "cultivating the spontaneous energies." As Graham notes, Zhuang conceives these energies in terms of physiological ideas *current in his own time*, as follows:

> He assumes that the organ of thought is not the brain but the heart [*xin*], and also that everything in motion in the universe is activated by *ch'i* [*qi*], "breath, energy," conceived as a fluid which in its purest state is the breath which vitalizes us.... Thinking in terms of the traditional physiology, he recommends us to educate the spontaneous energies rather than use the heart to think, name, categorize and conceive ends and principles of action.[81]

Graham notes that Zhuang has some advice on a specific method of cultivation (i.e., controlled breathing) and occasionally describes ecstatic experience. However, in Graham's view, the "knack stories" of *Zhuangzi* offer the best sources of advice on how to cultivate the spontaneous energies.

Knack Stories

Graham is especially fond of one knack story in the Inner Chapters, the episode of Cook Ding in chapter 3, but also provides for us a large collection of knack stories from elsewhere in *Zhuangzi* under the chapter heading "The Advantages of Spontaneity."[82] Because the story of Cook Ding is so well known, now let me use another of Graham's favorites as my key example: the story of a swimmer who could navigate waters so turbulent that even fish, turtles, and crocodiles avoided them. Master Kong was so amazed by this fellow that he asked him about his "Way to stay afloat in water." His reply was this: "No, I have no Way. I began in what is native to me, grew up in what is natural to me, matured in what is destined for me. I enter with the inflow, and emerge with the outflow, follow the Way of the water and do not impose my selfishness upon it. This is how I stay afloat in it."[83] In my view, this passage is important not only because it is about a "knack" to perform something effortlessly, but also because it is about *water*.

Water was a key symbol for Master Zhuang because its fluid nature so well represents the flow of life. Thus, he presents Master Kong as comparing a person "forgetting" himself in the Way to how a fish "forgets" itself in water. He does so in a truly fascinating story in chapter 6. Master Kong sends his disciple Zigong to the funeral of one among three friends who, we are told, "can ascend to heaven and wander in the mists ... forgetting themselves in life forever and ever without end." When Zigong arrives for the funeral he finds two of the men singing a song about their deceased friend, Sir Mulberry Door. Zigong returns to Master Kong to ask: "What kind of people are they?" "[And what is] their secret?" Here is the response he gets from Master Kong:

> "Fish delight in water," said Confucius [Master Kong], "and man de-lights in the Way. Delighting in water, fish find adequate nourishment just by passing through their ponds. Delighting in the Way, man's life is stabilized without ado. Therefore, it is said, 'Fish forget themselves in the rivers and lakes; men forget themselves in the arts of the Way.'"[84]

Of course, the arts of the Way are elsewhere symbolized by the arts of craftsman in "knack stories." Whether it is Cook Ding carving up an ox, Engraver Qing making a bell stand, or Hunchback catching cicadas, their "knack" is that of effortless involvement in the flow of their work. According to Graham, all these figures are heroes for Master Zhuang for this reason: "They spread their attention over the whole situation, let its focus roam freely, forget themselves in their total absorption in the object, and then the trained hand reacts spontaneously with a confidence and precision impossible to anyone who is applying rules and thinking out moves."[85] The figures in the knack stories, thus, resonate with us, suggesting how we can transcend our limitations even while performing everyday tasks. In this way they aid Master Zhuang in "teaching" us to see the value of joining the flow of life.

Fantastic Tales

Though quite different as a literary genre, fantastic tales may function like knack stories. Judith Berling, who considers participation in the flow of life to be the aim of Master Zhuang's teaching, links fantastic tales to this aim because they help one's imagination to wander. In other words, the flight of the imagination is en-hanced by stories of "flight," both literal and figurative. She gives special attention to the story in my epigraph about the flying ability of Master Lie and, then, someone else's talent for a kind of "flight" beyond flying. According to the tale, "Master Lie could ride upon the wind wherever he pleased"; but this was nothing compared to one "who could ride upon the truth of heaven and earth," without

even having to rely upon the wind. Berling feels that in this passage Master
Zhuang "questions whether flying is an adequate image of freedom" on the
grounds that flying is but an extension of walking and only hints at true freedom
from the limitations of human mobility.[86] Of course, flying without relying on
anything, even air, seems incredible. Yet it is precisely because of the "fantastic"
quality of the experiences Zhuang describes, the figures he creates, and the situations he portrays that they push us beyond limited perspectives in the same way
that knack stories suggest how we can transcend our behavioral limitations.

Ecstatic Experiences

While contemplating fantastic tales may lead to flights of the imagination, it does
not induce actual ecstatic states, of which Master Zhuang gave accounts. Some
feel confident in asserting that Master Zhuang was quite aware of ecstatic states,
even to the point of being able to differentiate between different types of states.
For example, Jordan Paper interprets the tale of Master Lie's flying as Zhuang's
effort to indicate the superiority of a mystical state over that of shamanic flight.
After establishing to his own satisfaction that shamanic activity was present in
Zhuang's China, Paper claims that Zhuang was familiar not only with shamanic
flight but also with true mystical states. He differentiates the two states by reference to Agehananda Bharati's "zero experience." Thus, Paper explains that "all
ecstatic experiences are not mystical experiences (this point is of the essence in
comparison to shamanism); only the ecstatic experience of complete loss of self-
identity—union with the ultimate in some sense (Bharati) ... is properly the
mystic (or zero) experience."[87] In the tale of Master Lie, Zhuang wants to explain
that the "ultimate person," who has "no self," is one who has gone beyond the
experience of shamanic flight. Thus, he slights "flying" in favor of what is beyond
flight: wandering in infinity with nothing to rely on. It is necessary for Zhuang to
make this comparison with shamanic experience because he has no other frame of
reference in trying to talk about mystical states. Since Zhuang was at the beginning of the Daoist mystical tradition, he had no established frame of reference or
vocabulary to use, whether native or foreign (for example, Buddhist).

Ultimately, Paper's claim depends on cross-cultural comparisons that I am
not competent to judge. He suggests that, in making a comparison between shamanic flight and (true) mystical experience, Zhuang is like others who, knowing
ecstatic states, have made the same comparison. In any case, for me, Paper helps to
open the door to accepting that certain fantastic tales as well as more straightforward accounts of ecstatic states in *Zhuangzi* mark the beginnings of a mystical
tradition in Daoism. After all, if Master Zhuang had mystical experiences in a
cultural milieu that lacked any frame of reference or vocabulary with which to
describe them, it would be unrealistic to expect his descriptions to be any more
explicit than they are. Moreover, given his penchant toward the fantastic, we

would hardly expect him to give the kind of technical descriptions that we find, for example, in Buddhist sources.

Apparently, it is the lack of explicit descriptions of mystical experience that led Livia Kohn to downplay the role of mysticism, as opposed to philosophical speculation, in *Zhuangzi,* and to claim that it had a different and larger role in later Daoism, as represented, for example, by Guo Xiang. This is noted in Harold Roth's excellent review of her *Early Chinese Mysticism.*[88] Roth himself is a proponent of the view that Zhuang's "mind fasting" and "sitting and forgetting" (*zuo wang* 坐忘), for example, do refer to practices that lead to a mystical state: "consciousness devoid of egoistic bias" and "full participation in the world free from the biased strategies and perspectives of one's limited ego."[89] Most important for our present purpose, Roth joins other interpreters of *Zhuangzi* who stress that it advocates a mystical goal of participation in the world, not that of merging with a transcendental Absolute. This is the goal of an intraworldly mysticism: joining the flow of life.

The Flow Experience

At the same time, joining the flow of life is more than a goal of mystical practice. It is an art of living and, thus, something that Master Zhuang saw in a variety of experiences, including what we now call "mystical experience." In other words, he saw the same quality in certain experiences people can have during work, play, imaginative creativity, and, perhaps consummately, mystical practice. In my view, he saw something that Mihaly Csikszentmihalyi recently "discovered" as a result of his psychological research on happiness. In *Flow: The Psychology of Optimal Experience,* he describes how he made this discovery in these words:

> My first studies involved a few hundred "experts"—artists, athletes, musicians, chess masters, surgeons—in other words, people who seemed to spend their time in precisely those activities they preferred. From their accounts of what it felt like to do what they were doing, I developed a theory of optimal experience based on the concept of flow—the state in which people are so involved in an activity that nothing seems to matter; the experience itself is so enjoyable that people will do it even at great cost, for the sheer sake of doing it.[90]

For Csikszentmihalyi, this experience defines "happiness" for all kinds of individuals in human societies, not only for the kinds of individuals who were the subjects of his early studies. With the help of colleagues all around the world, he came to see that people could have "the flow experience" during a wide variety of activities from assembly line work to meditation. Like Master Zhuang, he began to see "flow" almost everywhere he looked, engendering a multiplication of striking examples.

The key element of the experience of flow is that it is "autotelic," which means it is intrinsically rewarding rather than tied to any future goal or benefit. As the optimally "enjoyable" experience, it has eight major components, as described in these words:

> When people reflect on how it feels when their experience is most positive, they mention at least one, if not all, of the following. First, the experience usually occurs when we confront tasks we have a chance of completing. Second, we must be able to concentrate on what we are doing. Third and fourth, the concentration is usually possible because the task undertaken has clear goals and provides immediate feedback. Fifth, one acts with a deep but effortless involvement that removes from awareness the troubles and frustrations of everyday life. Sixth, enjoyable experiences allow people to exercise a sense of control over their actions. Seventh, concern for the self disappears, yet paradoxically the sense of self emerges stronger after the flow experience is over. Finally, the sense of the duration of time is altered; hours pass by in minutes, and minutes can seem to stretch out like hours.[91]

In these components we see both the similarities and the differences between how Csikszentmihalyi and Master Zhuang described the flow experience after each "discovered" it.

The first two components indicate "flow" is something that happens when one works with a certain kind of concentration. Not surprisingly, in his chapter on "Work as Flow," Csikszentmihalyi discusses examples from *Zhuangzi*, such as the story of Cook Ding. Moreover, although he stresses that clear goals are important, he acknowledges that goal-consciousness disappears *during flow*. In relation to this, the "joy" of flow results from the effortless involvement that lays one's troubles aside as well as from the fact that, during flow, "concern for the self" is gone. Finally, there is reported to be a change in one's experience of time. Zhuang, of course, reports changes in both dimensions of experience—spatial and temporal—in connection with "wandering" (*you*). This is not lost on Csikszentmihalyi, who considers *you* a key cross-cultural example of "total autotelic experience."[92]

What are the differences? And, if "flow" is a universal phenomenon, how do we explain the differences? For Csikszentmihalyi, the differences are insignificant and do not need a special explanation. The elements of seeking challenges and attaining mastery, he says, may seem to be absent in *Zhuangzi*. Yet, on the basis of his understanding of the story of Cook Ding, he sees these features in what I have called the intraworldly mysticism behind various stories in the text. He states:

> the mystical heights of the *You* [wandering] are not attained by some superhuman quantum jump, but simply by the gradual focusing of

attention on the opportunities for action in one's environment, which results in a perfection of skills that with time becomes so thoroughly automatic as to seem spontaneous and otherworldy.... Lord Wen-hui's cook is an excellent example of how one can find flow in the most unlikely places, in the most humble jobs of daily life.[93]

Although other genres of stories that I covered above—fantastic tales and accounts of mystical states—do not fit his model as well as do the knack stories of *Zhuangzi*, I accept that Master Zhuang "discovered" the flow experience just as surely as did Csikszentmihalyi. At the same time, I accept that each presents a culturally different understanding of flow.

Views of Personhood

As to how we can account for the differences, perhaps looking at each thinker's different view of personhood will help, especially since Csikszentmihalyi's view owes so much to modern conceptions of "the self." Indeed, "the self" is a central concept in Csikszentmihalyi's "anatomy of consciousness." He tells us that it is part of the contents of consciousness, but no ordinary part. In his words:

> The self is no ordinary piece of information ... it contains everything else that has passed through consciousness: all the memories, actions, desires, pleasures, and pains are included in it.... [T]he self is in many ways the most important element of consciousness, for it represents symbolically all of consciousness's other contents, as well as the pattern of their interrelations.[94]

The self plays a powerful role in life. Even during the flow experience, it is still a guiding influence. And in order for someone to turn all life into a unified flow experience, the role of a goal-oriented sense of self is absolutely crucial.

In discussing loss of self-consciousness as a component of flow, Csikszentmihalyi says it would be wrong to think that "the self" gives up its role, "that the person in flow has given up the control of his psychic energy." "[I]n fact the optimal experience involves a very active role for the self ... loss of self-consciousness does not involve a loss of self, and certainly not a loss of consciousness, but rather, only a loss of consciousness *of* the self." We forget temporarily who we are, but the self makes sure the activity continues. If it is a violin performance, for example, the self is active in one's awareness of the finger's movements, of the sounds the ears hear, and even of the form of the musical piece.[95]

Csikszentmihalyi's stress on control is even more striking when he discusses the final ideal: "turning all life into a unified flow experience." Although "flow" is something one just lets happen, a unified lifetime of flow requires a strong sense of self, careful planning, and setting of goals. Indeed, it is best if one has one ultimate goal, no matter what it is. In his words: "it does not matter what the ultimate goal is—provided it is compelling enough to order a lifetime's worth of psychic energy." This is the best way to stave off the enemy: the "chaos" of a life that lacks purpose or over which one has no control.[96]

Predictably, Csikszentmihalyi's discussion of flow conforms to its cultural context: just as a teleologically conceived God brought order out of chaos, a "self" focused on an ultimate goal can bring order into one's life. This "cosmogonic" fear of chaos and the "monotheistic" need for unitary order manifest themselves in his description of the ideal life, despite the claim that un-self-conscious flow experiences make it a "happy" life.[97] This puts the very nature of flow itself in tension with a self-conscious, goal-oriented lifestyle. There is also a conflict, or at least a paradox, inherent in the claim that a strong sense of self lies behind, and in some way facilitates, the periodic "joy" of the loss of self-consciousness.

In my view, Master Zhuang's chaos-friendly cosmology and pluralistic conception of the person provide a much better context for presenting the joy of flow as the source of human happiness. This essay focuses on Zhuang's view of the person, rather than on his cosmological views. Nonetheless, here I must stress that Zhuang's cosmology parallels his view of personhood in that it lacks the concept of "God" as a macrocosmic "self" directing the behavior of all living things. Indeed, Zhuang stands out among thinkers, Chinese and Western, for his positive appreciation of "chaos."[98] He maintains a consistent emphasis on letting things happen, rather than making them happen, at both levels: person and cosmos. Regarding persons, like Csikszentmihalyi, he appreciates effortless concentration on certain tasks; yet he also appreciates flights of the imagination and ecstatic states that feature loss of control. Finally, when it comes to leading a whole lifetime of flow, Zhuang de-emphasizes control as well as the pursuit of success (merit, name, etc.). He does not advocate a well-planned life punctuated by enjoyable moments of flow. Seeing a universe in flow, he invites us to participate in the flow, like fish swimming in water.

CONCLUSION: ETHICS WITHOUT THE MORAL SELF

Csikszentmihalyi appreciates the joys brought into life by the periodic unleashing of one's "spontaneous energies," to use A. C. Graham's term, but he is unwilling to give these energies a role in determining the broader course and aims of life. He assumes that only a goal-focused self can play this role; that is, without the guidance of "the self" making moral choices, flow activities would be nothing more than momentary joys. There would be no way to connect these activities into a meaningful "life" or to determine what value a particular activity would have beyond its addictive joy as a flow experience.

In other words, we seem to be left with only two alternatives. On the one hand, we can take the position that flow activities are valuable in themselves as sources of cognitive, aesthetic, or sensual joy, regardless of their moral status (good or bad, benign or harmful). On the other hand, we can take the position that flow activities have value only as parts of an ethically meaningful course of life, which depends on the role of "the self" making rational choices about life's aims. If these were indeed the only alternatives, we could distinguish our two thinkers by saying that Zhuang takes the former position, while Csikszentmihalyi takes the latter. This would probably make a great deal of sense to those who consider Zhuang a radical moral relativist.

In fact, some interpreters who consider Zhuang to be a radical relativist, or skeptic, claim that he would indeed not distinguish between good or bad, harmful or benign, flow activities (defined as the kind of activities described in his "knack" passages).[99] One such interpreter, Robert Eno, goes as far as to argue that Zhuang values spontaneity for its own sake and, thus, idealizes those activities that produce unique feelings of freedom and joy just because of the spontaneity involved. The moral status of those activities is irrelevant. In an apparent reference to the skill of Cook Ding, Eno states "the dao of butchering people might provide the same spiritual spontaneity as the dao of butchering oxen."[100] Eno himself, however, does not identify with the position he attributes to Zhuang. By contrast, he takes a position close to that of Csikszentmihalyi. He prefers the Confucian appreciation of spontaneous activities over that of Zhuang precisely because Confucians locate them in a life unified by specific goals within a social world.[101] My own view is that Eno is not so much in the sway of Confucianism as he is, like Csikszentmihalyi, under the spell of modern "self" theory, according to which the ethical life must be built around the rational ordering principle of moral selfhood.

Other interpreters of Master Zhuang have criticized Eno and like-minded scholars for characterizing Zhuang as a radical moral relativist, pointing out that he never uses an example of harmful behavior to exemplify the joys of spontaneity. These interpreters include Ivanhoe and Kjellberg, both of whom owe a debt to A. C. Graham's discussion of spontaneity in *Zhuangzi*, as referred to above.[102] In his efforts to establish a role for spontaneous energies in guiding life, Graham characterizes Zhuang's view of persons as opposite that of Western views that dichotomize persons, separating these energies from rational faculties and denying them a role in moral life. Graham's exposure to Zhuang has made him question the modern Western assumption that a person deprived of the guidance of a reasoning self will have no moral compass. Accordingly, Graham avoids the bias involved in taking Zhuang to be a moral relativist because he stresses spontaneous energies, rather than a reasoning self, in his examples of ideal behavior.

Interestingly, Bernard Williams has found a similar bias at work in interpretations of early Greek literature. In *Shame and Necessity*, he shows how a certain modern Western bias has colored the study of early Greek literature, and Homer's works in particular. In his view, most students of this literature find in it an undeveloped sense of selfhood and, linked to this, "an ethical experience that is primitive, unreflective, defective in morality, and, at the limit, incoherent."[103] Because Homeric man lacked key features of our modern conception of personhood, built upon notions of body-soul dualism, moral agency, and "the self," Homeric man has been seen as something less than a true and full person. In Williams's words: "One of the reasons for thinking that Homeric man could not decide for himself was that he supposedly had no self to decide for: he was, in his own conception, not what we could consider as a whole person at all."[104] From Williams's discussion I have come to believe that Homer had a pluralistic conception of the person parallel to Zhuang's conception of personhood as something without a unitary self behind the thoughts, habits, actions, feelings, and so forth of which we are made. Of course, their views of personhood may be otherwise quite different. For example, Zhuang's optimistic assessment of the results of humans following their spontaneous energies contrasts with Homer's sense of human tragedy.

Williams feels we can learn something from pre-Socratic Greeks precisely because their way of thinking about persons was not conditioned by modern assumptions concerning reason and moral selfhood, including the key notion of a "criticizing self" that lies beyond one's social habits, bodily functions, and other elements of the process by which one is contingently formed. Originally Platonic, says Williams, this is the idea that "the criticizing self can be separated from everything that a person contingently is—in itself, the criticizing self is simply the perspective of reason or morality."[105] It is in terms of this idea that the modern West defined the role of reason in conceiving the person and the cosmos. To wit:

> Plato, Aristotle, Kant, Hegel are all on the same side, all believing in one way or another that the universe or history or the structure of human reason can, when properly understood, yield a pattern that makes sense of human life and aspirations. Sophocles and Thucydides, by contrast, are alike in leaving us with no such sense. Each of them represents human beings as dealing sensibly, foolishly, sometimes catastrophically, sometimes nobly, with a world that is only partially intelligible to human agency and in itself not necessarily well adjusted to ethical aspirations.[106]

Needless to say, Master Zhuang fits on the latter of these two sides.

Williams is not concerned only that we appreciate Greeks before Plato for having coherent views of personhood—albeit without "the self"—but also that we learn from them. Indeed, we must entertain the idea that, by having a pluralistic conception of the person, their views are more nuanced and in tune with the experienced world than those of many modern thinkers.

Having benefited from Williams's analysis, on the one hand, I want to assert that Master Zhuang was not hampered by an undeveloped understanding of personhood. This would certainly not be what I intend in arguing that *Zhuangzi* contains no modern concept of self. On the other hand, I do not want to praise Zhuang for precociously adopting, ahead of his time, a postmodern or Buddhistic rejection of "the self." I simply want to credit him with having a pluralistic conception of the person, based upon such concepts as *shen* (body-person) and *xin* (heart-mind). According to this view, in its simplest form, cultivation of the person involves letting go of certain bad habits that make life unsatisfactory: ego concerns that obstruct one's cooperation with other beings, merit concerns that leave one worrying about the score instead of enjoying the game, and name concerns that make one frustrated when failing to gain others' attention. It does not involve believing in but abandoning the (false) self in order that one can discover a deeper and truer no-self "self."

NOTES

1. Victor Mair, trans., *Wandering on the Way: Early Taoist Tales and Parables of Chuang Tzu* (New York: Bantam Books, 1994), pp. 5–6. HY 2.1.21–22. Here and throughout this essay, I change Chinese names and terms from Wade-Giles to Pinyin Romanization (e.g., from "Lieh" to "Lie"), whenever the original has Wade-Giles forms. In citing *Zhuangzi*, in addition to an English translation, I give the page, chapter, and line number(s) for each passage from *Concordance to Chuang Tzu*, Harvard Yenching Sinological Index Series, Supplement No. 20, 1947, abbreviated as HY.

2. See Wu Yi, *Xiaoyao de Zhuangzi* (The Carefree Wandering Master Zhuang) Taipei: Dong Da Tushu, 1984), p. 47. He later (p. 56) discusses the passage in connection with Master Zhuang's views about the (mere) "self" and the (no-self) "true self" (*zhen ji* 真己). Another work that reaches the same conclusion about this passage is Jiang Xichang 蔣錫昌, *Zhuangzi Zhexue* 莊子哲學 (Master Zhuang's Philosophy) (Taipei: Huanyu Publishing, 1970). See p. 83.

3. The translation is in Kuang-ming Wu, *The Butterfly as Companion: Meditations on the First Three Chapters of the Chuang Tzu* (Albany: State University of New York Press, 1990), p. 135. The term "objectifiable self" is his "gloss" on the passage in question (his line 10), p. 155, and in the many places where he discusses the difference between this "self" and authentic self, p. 16 *et passim*.

4. Mair, *Wandering*, p. 5; Burton Watson, *The Complete Works of Chuang Tzu* (New York: Columbia University Press, 1968), p. 32; A. C. Graham, *Chuang-tzu: The Seven Inner Chapters and Other Writings from the Book Chuang-tzu* (London: George Allen and Unwin, 1981), p. 45. In what follows, I will normally quote Mair's translation. In addition to being the most recent translation by a well-trained scholar of classical Chinese, it is the most readable. I especially like the way Mair has translated most names of

persons and places, rather than avoiding translation by using romanization of Chinese. Mair's translations allow readers to see the humor of these made-up names in the same way that readers of the Chinese text would see this.

5. See, for example, David L. Hall, "To Be or Not to Be: The Postmodern Self and the *Wu*-Forms of Taoism," in *Self as Person in Asian Theory and Practice*, ed. Roger T. Ames et al. (Albany: State University of New York Press, 1994), pp. 213–34; and David Loy, "Zhuangzi and Nāgārjuna on the Truth of No Truth," in *Essays on Skepticism, Relativism, and Ethics in the "Zhuangzi,"* ed. Paul Kjellberg and Philip J. Ivanhoe (Albany: State University of New York Press, 1996), pp. 50–67.

6. I am aware of the dangers in attributing anything at all to a single thinker named Zhuang, since in the text bearing his name only the first 7 out of 33 chapters, the "Inner Chapters," are widely acknowledged to have the imprint of his original mind. Obviously, the quest for "the historical Master Zhuang" is just as problematic as the quest for "the historical Jesus," which has occupied (perhaps wasted) the time of countless scholars. Nonetheless, I will adopt the convention of using his name to identify the source of the message we find in the work, looking for evidence of it above all in the Inner Chapters. For an excellent overview and creative treatment of authorship issues, see Graham, *Chuang-tzu* and A. C. Graham, "How Much of *Chuang-tzu* Did Chuang-tzu Write?" *Journal of the American Academy of Religion Thematic Issue* 47.3 (1979), ed. H. Rosemont Jr. and B. Schwartz, pp. 459–502.

7. See Marcel Mauss, "A Category of the Human Mind: The Notion of the Person, the Notion of the Self," in *The Category of the Person: Anthropology, Philosophy, History*, ed. M. Carrithers et al. (Cambridge: Cambridge University Press, 1985); and Charles Taylor, *Sources of the Self: The Making of Modern Identity* (Cambridge, Mass.: Harvard University Press, 1989).

8. See Ames et al., *Self as Person*; Anthony J. Marsella, George DeVos, and Francis L. K. Hsu, eds., *Culture and Self: Asian and Western Perspectives* (New York and London: Tavistock Publications, 1985); and Brian Morris, *Anthropology of the Self: The Individual in Cultural Perspective* (London and Boulder: Pluto Press, 1994).

9. Morris, p. 16.

10. Taylor, p. 113.

11. Taylor, pp. 128–29.

12. Taylor, pp. 159–60.

13. Frank Johnson, "The Western Concept of Self," in Marsella, DeVos, and Hsu (cited above), pp. 91–138. The four qualities are explained on pp. 113–28.

14. Johnson, 114–15. In Roger T. Ames and David Hall, *Anticipating China: Thinking Through the Narratives of Chinese and Western Culture* (Albany:

State University of New York Press, 1995), this analytic-deductive mode of thinking, described by reference to the idea of "rational order," is contrasted with early Chinese ways of thinking that were built around a conception of order which is called "analogical" or "aesthetic."

15. Johnson, pp. 118–19. He cites Nietzsche on p. 116; and he follows David Miller, *The New Polytheism* (New York: Harper & Row, 1981) in listing two groups of oppositions on p. 117.

16. Johnson, p. 123.

17. Johnson, p. 124.

18. Johnson, p. 125.

19. Johnson, pp. 92–98.

20. Mark Elvin, "Between Heaven and Earth: Conceptions of the Self in China," in M. Carrithers et al. (cited above), covers "the self in modern Chinese thought" on pp. 174–86.

21. Lin Tongqi, Henry Rosemont Jr., and Roger T. Ames, "Chinese Philosophy: A Philosophical Essay on the 'State of the Art,'" *Journal of Asian Studies* 54.3 (August 1995): 733; the statement on self and culture is on p. 730.

22. Lao Siguang, *Xinbian Zhongguo zhexueshi* 新編中國哲學史 (Sanmin Shuju, 1981), pp. 258–59.

23. Lao, p. 284.

24. Wu, p. 118. The interpretation of the phrase "the ultimate man has 'no self'" is on p. 56.

25. Liu Guangyi, *Zhuangxue zhong de chanqu* (Taipei: Taiwan Shangwu Yinshuguan, 1989).

26. Liu Guangyi, p. 103.

27. Kuang-ming Wu, p. 184. On pp. 416–17, n. 28, he discusses the grammatical and etymological issues related to his *wu* versus *wo* theory. Rather than take the facts concerning *wu-wo* word order in the passage as evidence against his theory, which they seem to be, he argues that knowledge of grammar supports his view that Zhuang consistently uses *wu* and *wo* to indicate levels of selfhood.

28. Paul Kjellberg, "Feature Review"of *Butterfly as Companion, Philosophy East and West* 43.1 (January 1993): 113.

29. Judith Berling, "Self and Whole in Chuang Tzu," in *Individualism and Holism: Studies in Confucian and Taoist Values*, ed. D. Munro (Ann Arbor: University of Michigan, Center for Chinese Studies, 1985), pp. 101–20.

30. Berling, p. 105; the statement about the perfected self is from p. 109.

31. Berling, p. 112.

32. Berling, p. 117.

33. Robert E. Allinson, *Chuang-Tzu for Spiritual Transformation: An Analysis of the Inner Chapters* (Albany: State University of New York Press, 1989).

34. See Randall Nadeau's review of *Chuang-Tzu for Spiritual Transformation, Journal of Chinese Religions* 18 (Fall 1990): 187–88, for a critique of the extent to which Allinson adequately deals with the linguistic issues on which his argument depends.
35. Allinson, p. 9.
36. Cited in Allinson, p. 144. The preceding material is from p. 143. The phrase *wang-xin* occurs once in *Zhuangzi*, in chapter 28, which is not known for having much in common with the Inner Chapters.
37. Allinson, p. 195, n. 1.
38. Allinson, p. 144.
39. David Loy (cited above).
40. Paul Kjellberg, "Zhuangzi and Skepticism" (Ph.D. diss.; Stanford University, 1993), has a chapter on Buddhist readings of *Zhuangzi*; see pp. 30–40. He indicates that Chinese Buddhists started reading the text at the time of Guo Xiang (d. 312 C.E.), author of the earliest extant Daoist commentary and editor of the *textus recensus*. Moreover, they interpreted the text differently from Guo. The Buddhist concept of *Kong* (Sanskrit, *sunyata*; English, emptiness)—indicating that all things are devoid of permanent and independent existence—conditioned Buddhist readings of *Zhuangzi* from the start.
41. David L. Hall, cited above.
42. Hall, p. 231.
43. Hall, p. 232.
44. Hall, pp. 229–30.
45. Hall, p. 230.
46. Hall, p. 232.
47. Elvin, cited above.
48. See Herbert Fingarette, "The Problem of the Self in the *Analects,*" *Philosophy East and West* 29.2 (April 1979): 129–40; and Roger T. Ames, "Reflections on the Confucian Self: A Response to Fingarette," in *Rules, Rituals, and Responsibility: Essays Dedicated to Herbert Fingarette,* ed. Mary I. Bockover (La Salle, Ill.: Open Court, 1991), pp. 104–14, with Fingarette's response to Ames on pp. 194–200. The question is posed on p. 199. Incidentally, the position implied in Fingarette's rhetorical question was later endorsed in Roger T. Ames, "The Focus-Field Self in Classical Confucianism," in Ames et al., *Self as Person,* p. 198.
49. W. A. C. H. Dobson, *A Dictionary of the Chinese Particles* (Toronto: University of Toronto Press, 1974), pp. 87–88 (reflexive pronouns covered), and under each word in alphabetical listing.
50. HY 7/3/2.
51. HY 9/4/12, 27/11/39, 34/13/36, 35/13/58, 51/19/67, 52/20/32, and 87/31/31.

52. Mair, p. 40. HY 12/4/86.
53. Mair, pp. 202–3. HY 55/20/34.
54. Mair, p. 34. HY 10/4/44.
55. Mair, 49–50. HY 15/5/57–59.
56. Cf. Mair, p. 36, p. 45, p. 48. HY 10/4/55, 13/5/25, and 14/5/49.
57. According to P. J. Ivanhoe, "Zhuangzi's Conversion Experience," *Journal of Chinese Religions* 19 (Fall 1991): 13, Henri Maspero was first to so characterize the story. I am also indebted to Ivanhoe for alerting me to the need to alter Mair's translation of the story, as cited below, by inserting "I" (meaning Zhuang) as the subject of the phrase in which there is a reference to forgetting one's "true being."
58. Mair, p. 197. HY 54/20/66–68. Mair's translation has "body" for *shen* in the two places where I have "person." Also, Mair takes magpie to be the subject of the phrase that I have altered to read: "[I] forgot about [my] true being." I have done so because (1) Zhuang is the one who is "wandering," and (2) the magpie is the cause of Zhuang's regretful lack of awareness. Also, as Ivanhoe points out, there is little reason to depict Zhuang as a "poacher," rather than just a trespasser. See Ivanhoe, "Zhuangzi's Conversion," pp. 21–24.
59. Mair, p. 321. HY 87/31/32–33.
60. In addition to the examples from the Inner Chapters given immediately below, see HY 55.21.26, where Lao Dan says "I was letting my mind wander in the origin of things" (Mair, p. 202). Also see HY 70/25/29, where the phrase "let your mind wander in infinity" occurs (Mair, p. 258).
61. Mair, p. 35. HY 9/4/52–53.
62. Mair, p. 43. HY 12/5/5–8.
63. Mair, p. 68. HY 20/7/11.
64. Mair, p. 32. HY 9/4/26–28.
65. Mair, p. 214. HY 58/22/24–25.
66. See, respectively, HY 13/5/9 (Mair, p. 43) and HY 27/11/37 (Mair, p. 96).
67. Graham, *Chuang-tzu*, pp. 143–44.
68. Mair, p. 101. HY 28/11/63–66.
69. Graham, *Chuang-tzu*, p. 150; quotation marks added in the final line. Mair does not translate this passage, following Chen Guying 陳鼓應, *Zhuangzi jinzhu jinshi* 莊子今註今釋 (Master Zhuang: modern new notes and modern interpretations) (Taipei: Taiwan Shangwu publishing, 1975), p. 461, n. 6. Mair uses Chen's edition of *Zhuangzi* as the basis for his translation. In this case, because the Great Man passage interrupts a dialogue between Earl of Yellow River and Northern Sea, Chen considers it an improper insertion. Graham translates it along with other Great Man passages, not as part of this dialogue.

70. Graham, *Chuang-tzu*, p. 91. HY 15/6/12. Mair does not translate this passage, following Chen Guying's judgment. Graham also treats it as probably being a late insertion into the text.

71. Mair, p. 275. HY 74/26/37.

72. Mair, p. 190. HY 52/20/24.

73. Mair, p. 109. HY 30/12/45.

74. Mair, p. 13. HY 4/2/14–15.

75. HY 37/14/10–11. Mair, p. 132, translates "forget themselves." Watson, p. 155, translates "forget you."

76. Mair, p. 269. HY 73/26/10.

77. Sibubeiyao 四部備要 edition of *Zhuangzi* with Guo Xiang's commentary, 8th printing (Taipei: Zhonghua Book Co., 1983), first *juan*, p. 5a.

78. *Zhuangzi*, first *juan*, p. 5a.

79. *Zhuangzi*, fourth *juan*, p. 22a; and sixth *juan*, p. 8b.

80. Wang Shumin, *Zhuangzi jiao quan* 莊子校詮 (Master Zhuang: collated interpretations), vol. 3 (Taipei: Academia Sinica, Institute of History and Philology, 1994), pp. 1426–28. In his rebuttal of Confucian views, Wang quotes many of the same passages used in this essay's treatment of Master Zhuang's so-called "no self" doctrine.

81. Graham, *Chuang-tzu*, p. 7.

82. Ibid., pp. 135–142. The episode of Cook Ding is translated on pp. 63–64.

83. Ibid., p. 136. HY 50.19.52–53. Cf. Mair, p. 182.

84. Mair, p. 61. HY 18.6.72–73. The entire story is on pp. 59–61.

85. Graham, *Chuang-tzu*, p. 6. See pp. 135 and 138 for his treatment of the stories of the bell stand maker and the cicada catcher, respectively.

86. Berling, p. 110. Also see Michael Crandell, "On Walking without Touching the Ground: 'Play' in the *Inner Chapters* of the *Chuang-tzu*," in *Experimental Essays on Chuang-tzu*, ed. V. Mair (Honolulu: University of Hawaii Press, 1983), pp. 101–24.

87. Jordan Paper, *The Spirits are Drunk: Comparative Approaches to Chinese Religion* (Albany: State University of New York Press, 1995), p. 127.

88. Livia Kohn, *Early Chinese Mysticism: Philosophy and Soteriology in the Taoist Tradition* (Princeton, N.J.: Princeton University Press, 1992).

89. Harold D. Roth, "Some Issues in the Study of Chinese Mysticism: A Review Essay," *China Review International* 2.1 (Spring 1995): 160–61. This "review" runs twenty pages and is a marvelous introduction to the issues and sources relevant to the study of Chinese mysticism. I also like it because it avoids using modern "self" theory in approaching these issues and sources.

90. Mihaly Csikszentmihalyi, *Flow: The Psychology of Optimal Experience* (New York, 1990), p. 4.

91. Csikszentmihalyi, p. 49.

92. Csikszentmihalyi, p. 150. "Work as Flow" is covered on pp. 143–63.
93. Csikszentmihalyi, p. 151.
94. Csikszentmihalyi, p. 34.
95. Csikszentmihalyi, p. 64.
96. Csikszentmihalyi, pp. 214–15. Also see the chapter preceding these comments, chapter 9, "Cheating Chaos," pp. 192–213.
97. Earlier in this essay, I explained the use of "monotheistic" as a cultural characteristic. On such a use of "cosmogonic," see Ames and Hall, *Anticipating China*, pp. 3–11.
98. See Norman J. Girardot, *Myth and Meaning in Early Taoism: The Theme of Chaos* (hun-tun) (Berkeley: University of California Press, 1983).
99. The most straightforward exposition of this position is found in Robert Eno, "Cook Ding's Dao and the Limits of Philosophy," in Kjellberg and Ivanhoe, pp. 127–51. This essay reiterates a position taken in Robert Eno, "Creating Nature: Ruist and Taoist Approaches," in *Chuang Tzu: Rationality; Interpretation*, ed. Kidder Smith (Brunswick: Breckinridge Public Affairs Center, 1991), pp. 3–28. Kjellberg, "Feature Review," discusses others who portray Zhuangzi as uninterested in the moral status (evil or benign) of flow ("knack") activities, including Antonio Cua and Chad Hansen. In particular, see pp. 78–86 (on Hansen) and pp. 108–111 (on Cua). Kjellberg also covers Eno's position, pp. 104–8.
100. Eno, "Cook Ding's Dao and the Limits of Philosophy," p. 142.
101. See ibid., p. 143.
102. See Kjellberg, "Feature Review," pp. 113–25; and Philip J. Ivanhoe, "Was Zhuangzi a Relativist?" in Kjellberg and Ivanhoe, pp. 196–214.
103. Bernard Williams, *Shame and Necessity* (Berkeley: University of California Press, 1993), p. 21.
104. Ibid., p. 23.
105. Ibid., p. 159.
106. Ibid., pp. 163–64.

3

Between Chen and Cai:
Zhuangzi and the *Analects*

JOHN MAKEHAM

Curious though it may seem to us now, there was a tradition, shared by a number of Chinese commentators, which considered Zhuangzi 莊子 (fourth century B.C.E.) to have been an heir to the teachings of Confucius (trad. 551–479).[1] A. C. Graham also notes that the "*Inner chapters*, permeated by an obsession with the life and legend of Confucius, invite the suspicion that the author must have been brought up a Confucian. . . . It is almost as if Confucius were a father-figure whose blessing the rebellious son likes to imagine would have been granted in the end."[2] In the outer and mixed *pian*, however, especially in the dialogues with Laozi 老子, and the Yangist compilations, "Dao Zhi" 盜跖 (Robber Zhi) and "Yu fu" 漁夫 (The Old Fisherman), Confucius is portrayed far less sympathetically. Yet, sympathetically portrayed or otherwise, Confucius is the most cited character in the whole of *Zhuangzi*, and the frequency with which he is cited allows the various contributors to this disparate collection plenty of scope to use him as a spokesman for a host of opinions.

Now just as these various appropriations of the image of Confucius contributed to the collection of essays that constitutes *Zhuangzi*, in keeping with this spirit, it is my intention to reappropriate one of these images to contribute to this particular collection of essays on *Zhuangzi*. The opinions for which I will enlist this reappropriated image of Confucius to act as spokesman are, naturally enough, my own. The challenge I have set myself is to show that they are also the views of a Confucius to be found in the *Analects*, and yet are strikingly at odds with the image of Confucius depicted in *Mencius* 孟子 and *Xunzi* 荀子. To this end, I have selected a story which appears both in the *Analects* and *Zhuangzi*—indeed seven times in *Zhuangzi*. This is the story of the trying plight faced by Confucius while travelling between the states of Chen 陳 and Cai 蔡.

I will, however, be focusing on the particular version of the story (and the image of Confucius) found in *pian* 28 of *Zhuangzi*, "Rang wang" 讓王 (Yielding the Throne).[3] I will begin by examining the range of significance the story took on during the formative phases of its transmission so as to be better able to identify the unique import of the "Rang wang" version of the story.

It has long been assumed that the *locus classicus* of the incident described in "Rang wang" is *Analects* 15.2:[4]

> In Chen they ran out of grain. Those accompanying him fell ill and none was able to get up. Zilu 子路 was angry and went to see Confucius: "Does even the gentlemen fall on hard times?"
>
> Confucius said, "The gentleman resolutely embraces hard times while when the petty man meets with hard times he is unable to keep himself in check."[5]

There is no reliable evidence to date this particular *zhang* ("section") or the *pian* ("book") in which it is included; therefore we have no solid grounds for assuming that it must predate, say, the related account in *Mencius* (7B.18). My own view is that given the rather simple form that events in the story take, it is more likely to be an earlier rather than a later version of the story. And given that it *might* be earlier than the *Mencius* passage, then in the absence of any compelling arguments to think otherwise, for ease of exposition and as an expeditious means of breaking into this particular hermeneutic circle, I will tentatively assume that it does.

The first problem to be confronted is whether this passage forms part of the opening *zhang* of "Wei Ling gong" 衛靈公, 15.1, or whether it is a separate *zhang*:

> When Duke Ling of Wei asked Confucius about military formations, he replied, "While I have heard something about the objects used in ceremonial, I have never learned anything about military matters." The next day Confucius left.

Certainly 15.2 seems to follow on from 15.1 naturally enough. Historically, however, the connection would be problematical, if, as some accounts have it, Confucius did not leave Wei until after Duke Ling had died.[6] Yet there were early commentators, such as Gao You 高誘 (*c.* 168–212), who did treat 15.1 and 15.2 as a single *zhang* or at least as related passages.[7] In doing so, they would appear to have been following the interpretative lead of Sima Qian 司馬遷 (145–*c.* 86), who, after describing the exchange in 15.1, goes on to say, "The next day, while the duke was speaking with Confucius, he saw a flying goose, and as he raised his head to look at it, his attention was no longer directed at Confucius. Thereupon, Confucius left, going back to Chen."[8]

By interpreting 15.1 and 15.2 as a single passage Sima Qian is able to portray Confucius as one who would rather move to another state than advise a ruler on matters that he found abhorrent. Yet it should also be noted that the story related in 15.1 is strikingly similar to another story about Confucius in Wei, that is recorded in *Zuozhuan* 左傳:

> As Kong Wenzi 孔文子 (a Wei minister) was about to attack Taishu Ji 大叔疾 (a Wei minister), he solicited Confucius' views.
>
> Confucius said, "While I learned something about the items used in ceremonial, I have never heard anything about military matters." He left the room, called someone to get his carriage ready and, as he departed, said, "While a bird may choose which tree it will settle on, who ever heard of a tree being able to choose the bird?!"
>
> Kong Wenzi immediately halted him, saying, "I would never dare to do this for my own benefit, but only to avoid calamity befalling the state of Wei." Confucius decided to stay but then people from Lu enticed him with gifts, so he returned to Lu.[9]

Like Cui Shu 崔述 (1740–1816),[10] I believe that this passage and 15.1 are two versions of what was once the same story. It will be noted that in the *Zuozhuan* version, Confucius's decision to leave Wei is prompted by the prospect of material rewards. Omitting this detail, Sima Qian may be seen to have adapted the general outline of the *Zuozhuan* version to the task of reading 15.1 and 15.2 as either one continuous passage or two intimately related passages. In doing so he is able to interpret Confucius's decision to leave Wei as one based on an unwillingness to serve under a ruler if this means compromising his moral principles (in this case, by being requested to advise on matters of warfare).

If we accept that 15.1 and the above passage from *Zuozhuan* are different versions of the same story, then we have some reason to suspect that originally 15.2 had nothing to do with 15.1. When, then, did they become associated? No other version of this story where Confucius runs into difficulties in the Chen-Cai region, which predates Sima Qian's account, assumes or draws a direct connection between his decision to leave Wei and go to Chen.[11] Where Wei is mentioned, such as at *Mencius* 5A.8, the connection is purely contingent. According to this passage, Confucius did encounter some unspecified trouble in Chen, but only after he left Lu to proceed to Wei, then moved from Wei to Song, after which he moved on to Chen. We know that Sima Qian did not take this passage as the authority for his association of 15.1 and 15.2 because in his biography of Confucius, "Kongzi shi jia" 孔子世家, he records the encounter with Huan Tui 桓魋 that is a feature of this *Mencius* passage, as occurring on a previous occasion (495?)

when Confucius had departed Wei.[12] This *Mencius* passage does, however, introduce a new dimension into the story of Confucius's difficulties in Chen: that it was but one in a series of unfortunate incidents, one that was to be further embellished in still later versions of the story. The immediate point I wish to establish, however, is that the association Sima Qian draws between 15.1 and 15.2—while natural enough given the juxtaposition of the two *zhang*—was a possibility that was opened up only when the *Analects* text was edited such that 15.1 and 15.2 were placed as consecutive passages. For reasons that will become plain later in this essay, it is possible that this editorial juxtapositioning may only have occurred shortly before Sima Qian wrote his "Kongzi shi jia."

Accordingly, if we set aside the historical background that Sima Qian brings to his reading of *Analects* 15.2, the only discernible problem confronting Confucius and his party is that they have run out of food. Given that there is no hint in *Analects* 15.2 of there being a further cause of their hardship, then one would have no difficulty in understanding the key word in this passage, *qiong*, simply to mean "poor, impoverished, to have fallen on hard times" and Confucius's concluding remark to mean that one should not buckle when impecunious.

When, however, we turn to examine a version of what is purported to be the same story in *Mencius* 7B.18, we are presented with a different perspective on the matter: "Mencius said, 'The gentleman's difficulties between Chen and Cai were brought about by not having any influence with those in positions of authority.'" Traditional commentators have had little difficulty in associating this passage with *Analects* 15.2 despite the fact that in this passage Confucius is not specifically mentioned and the geographical area is slightly different. Indeed, all subsequent versions of the story refer to "the area between Chen and Cai"; "Chen," by itself, is abandoned. According to this passage, whatever difficulties Confucius found himself in, were the result of his lack of political connections, thus even if this meant that he and his disciples went hungry, the root problem was not poverty but powerlessness, a lack of position. If according to one reading of *Mencius* 5A.8 it is accepted that Confucius's host in Chen, Sicheng Zhenzi 司城貞子, was an official in the employ of Zhou 周, the marquis of the Chen,[13] and that Sicheng was not a particularly high-ranking official,[14] this would further support this interpretation.

From this point on, until Sima Qian's reconstitution of the particular events that comprise the story, it becomes increasingly untenable to assign a diachronic framework for the story's transmission. Even where two texts, A and B, which record similar versions of the story and can be dated with some accuracy (which is the exception rather than the rule) such that text A may be said to predate text B, this is no guarantee that the version of the story in text B is later than or has been influenced by the version in text A. Given this situation, as a general principle, it is more realistic to proceed on the assumption that from about 250 B.C.E. until about 120 B.C.E. the story was widely circulated and that not long into this period, in a number of cases, alternative contemporaneous versions of the story became as, if not more, influential on a given version of the story as any version/s that preceded it. Having said this, however, once again for ease of exposition, I will tentatively assume that the next stage in the shuffling of events which constitute the story is found in *Xunzi*, "You zuo" 宥坐:[15]

> When Confucius was travelling south to Chu, he ran into difficulties in the region between Chen and Cai. For seven days he had nothing cooked to eat, and his soup of wild herbs had no grain to thicken it. All of his disciples had a hungry look about them. Zilu came forward and asked, "I have heard that 'heaven will repay those who do good with good fortune and those who do bad with misfortune.' Now, Master, for a long time you have been accumulating potency, building up a store of rightful acts and cherishing morally excellent behavior. Why, then, do you find yourself in such distressing circumstances as this?"
>
> Confucius replied, "You 由, you have not memorized what I have told you. Do you really believe that the wise are certain to be heeded? But did not Prince Bigan 比干[16] have his heart cut out?! Do you really believe that those who do their best on behalf of others are certain to be heeded? But was not Guan Longfeng 關龍逢 punished?![17] Do you really think that those who remonstrate with their superiors will be heeded? But was not Wu Zixu's 伍子胥 body hung up and displayed outside the city of Gusu 姑蘇?![18] Seen from this perspective, there are many gentleman of wide learning and profound strategies who do not encounter the right times. How am I unique?[19]
>
> "Further, although angelica and the orchid grow in the forest, they do not lose their fragrance because there are no people there to appreciate them. The gentleman engages in learning not so that he may become successful (*tong* 通) but rather so that when times are hard (*qiong* 窮) he will not be at a loss as to what to do; so that in times of anxiety he will remain steadfast of purpose; and so that by knowing that misfortune and good fortune follow one another just as do ends and beginnings his heart will not become confused. Being either a worthy or a good-for-nothing depends on ability; the decision to act or not to act depends on the man; meeting with success or not depends on timing; and life and death depend on circumstances beyond individual control. Now, if a person does not encounter the right times, then even if he were a worthy, would he be able to make any headway? If, however, he should encounter the right times, what difficulties would he have? Hence, the gentleman broadens his learning, deepens his strategies, cultivates his person, and makes his conduct proper while he waits for the right times."

Confucius said, "You, sit down and I'll tell you. In the past, Chonger 重耳 (i.e., the future Duke Wen 文 of Jin 晉; r. 636–628), the son of the Duke of Jin, conceived his ambition to become overlord when he was fleeing from Cao 曹; King Goujian 勾踐 (r. 496–465) of Yue conceived his ambition to become overlord when he was trying to hold off a siege at Guiji 會稽. Xiaobo 小白, the future Duke Huan 桓 (r. 685–643) of Qi 齊 conceived his ambition to become overlord when he was fleeing from Ju 莒.[20] Hence, one who has not been exposed to distressing circumstances will reflect only on matters close at hand; one who has not personally experienced being passed over will set himself a narrow ambition. How do you know that I will not benefit from being here in this situation in Sangluo 桑落?[21]

As with the version of the story at *Analects* 15.2 the plight that Confucius and his company face is a lack of food; Mencius's explicit introduction of matters relating to office and political connections does not constitute the "nucleus" of the story as it is related in the first paragraph. Instead a new element, "heaven" (*tian* 天) is introduced, thereby framing Confucius's predicament within a cosmological context: if there is a morally normative cosmic order, then how is it that a morally exemplary person, such as Confucius, seemingly finds himself out of favor with heaven? Variations on this question were of central concern to thinkers from the middle of the third century B.C.E. right through to the end of the Han and, in turn, generated a host of different responses. It will be noted that in this passage, two quite different accounts of Confucius's reply to Zilu are recorded. In the first account, Confucius cites the examples of three exemplary ministers who, despite doing what good ministers should do, all met with misfortune. Clearly for this Confucius, there was no anthropomorphic heaven that mechanistically rewards good deeds and punishes bad deeds. Instead, he invokes the concept of timeliness: encountering the right combination of circumstances at the appropriate time. If these good ministers had lived in different times, their fates may well have been different. In citing these examples, the issue of office, which is not assumed in the opening paragraph, is reintroduced into the story, thereby implying that Confucius's real concern was his failure to have secured substantive office. Confucius's remarks in the third paragraph reinforce the view that the opportunity to hold office is not a matter that an individual can determine. Through his understanding of the cycles of change the gentleman should bide his time, cultivating himself until the right opportunity comes once again into cycle. This is not so much resignation as strategic planning. The final paragraph, which does not appeal to timeliness, seems also to abandon the belief in a morally normative heaven, and identifies individual effort and ambition as the determinants of success and failure. Confucius's ambitions are greatly magnified in this alternative reply. No longer simply aspiring to office, we find Confucius citing the examples of celebrated overlords of the Spring and Autumn period as models of men who used adversity to fire their ambitions and thereby secure genuine political power. More than just an optimist in the face of adversity, Confucius is transformed into a figure harboring powerful political aspirations.

In contrast to this portrayal of an ambitious Confucius, the story takes on a different significance for the author/s of the essay, "Fei ru" 非儒, included in *Mozi* 墨子. Identified as a late Warring States writing,[22] this polemical essay belongs to a genre in which the principal aim is to expose the alleged hypocrisy of Confucius and, by implication, the tradition that looked back to him as a foundational sagely teacher:

> When that person named Kong fell on hard times between Chen and Cai, his soup of wild herbs had no grain to thicken it. On the tenth day[23] Zilu cooked a suckling pig.[24] Without inquiring where the meat had come from, Kong proceeded to eat it. Zilu stripped off[25] his lower garment and sold it for some wine. Kong drank the wine without enquiring where it had come from.[26]
>
> Later, when being entertained by Duke Ai of Lu, Confucius would not be seated because his mat was not correctly positioned[27] and he would not eat the meat because the carcass had not been correctly dismembered.[28] Zilu entered and politely inquired, "Why is your behavior contrary to how it was when you were between Chen and Cai?"
>
> Kong replied, "Come here, I will tell you. When I was with you at that time, I behaved as I did in order somehow to stay alive; when I was with you just now, I behaved as I did in order somehow to do what was right."
>
> When he was hungry and poor, he did not decline from indiscriminately taking what he could in order to stay alive, yet when he was sated, he put on a false show of upright behavior in order to make a display of himself. How could there be anything more low or hypocritical?![29]

Unfortunately, this passage has sustained some degree of corruption and abridgment. The references to "that person named Kong" and "Confucius" attest to editors using different source materials, while the lack of an explanation of how Zilu acquired the suckling pig (while it is explained how he acquired the wine) is anomalous. Nevertheless, the gist of this unsympathetic account is clear enough: what for Confucius is expediency, is for his critics hypocrisy. This hypocrisy is epitomized by Confucius's unwillingness to tell Duke Ai that he has already had enough to eat and instead make excuses by invoking the conventions of ritual etiquette, conventions that, in any case, he would appear to have contravened by having already eaten until sated.[30] This version of the story does evidence some formal features in common with the passage from *Xunzi* already discussed, in particular the role of Zilu as interlocutor and the line, "Come here, I will tell you." And while preserving the older theme that Confucius's troubles were due to impoverishment, rather than the issue of office, the attendant theme of steadfastness in the face of adversity is, of course, missing entirely.

A passage in the "Ren shu" 任數 (Relying upon Logistics) essay of the eclectic *Lüshi chunqiu*[31] might conceivably be read as a response to this anti-Confucius polemic. This essay is one of two versions of the Chen-Cai story preserved in this work:

> When Confucius fell on hard times between Chen and Cai, for seven days he had not eaten a single grain, and even his soup of wild herbs had no grain to thicken it. Day and night Yan Hui 顏回 searched for grain and when he finally got some he prepared a fire and started to cook. When the grain was nearly cooked, Confucius looked over at Yan Hui only to see him quickly grab some of the grain and eat it. Confucius pretended not to have noticed. Before long the food was ready to eat, and having called Confucius, Yan Hui served him the food.[32] At this point, Confucius got to his feet and said, "Today I dreamt about my father. As this food is clean I will make an offering of it to him."[33]
>
> Yan Hui replied, "You cannot do that. Just a moment ago some dust from the smoke got into the steamer. As it would have been inauspicious to have thrown the food away, I grabbed the soiled portion and ate it."
>
> Confucius sighed and said, "That which one believes is one's eyes, and yet there are times when one cannot even believe one's eyes. That which one relies upon is one's heart, and yet there are times when even it is unreliable. My disciple, remember this. Knowing people is certainly not easy, hence to know this is not difficult;[34] rather, it is how you come to know them that is difficult."[35]

Like the above passage from *Mozi*, the focal event of this version of the story is Confucius's attitude to food at a time of shortage. Although Confucius's interlocutor has changed from Zilu to Yan Hui, the acts of procurement and preparation are common to both versions despite the differences in detail. The possibility for reading this specifically as a response to the "Mohist" passage is suggested by the inclusion of these common events in the story. In the passage under discussion, Confucius is cast in an antithetical role to that of a self-centered glutton only too ready to put principle to one side. And what better way to portray this than to have him decline the food despite his hunger? Yet there is a further twist. As it transpires, although Confucius was prepared to forego the food on the pretext that he wanted to use it as an offering to his departed father, this was really a ploy to test whether Yan Hui would allow him to do so in the knowledge that he had defiled it for such a purpose. Confucius was testing his disciple. But as we subsequently learn, this defilement had occurred not because of Yan Hui's greed, but rather in order to keep the food clean for Confucius's consumption. Thus in the end, even Confucius is humbled into admitting that he had judged Yan Hui unfairly, thus leaving the reader to admire Yan Hui's honesty and selfless devotion to his master.

What examples such as this suggest is that the retrospective application of the label "Confucian "to late Warring States and early Han thinkers has its limitations and that we might be better served by adopting more specific locutions. Yet even this approach has its limitations to the extent that it is biased toward identifying thinkers and ideas with particular "schools" or "lineages" (Zi Si, Yan Hui, or whatever). This is clearly not always justified, as the passage under discussion well illustrates. Thus while this passage articulates the views of a thinker or thinkers who had come to see Yan Hui as a person who exemplified certain moral qualities that put even Confucius to shame, this may have been a view shared by a number of contemporaneous or near contemporaneous thinkers who were nevertheless each sympathetic to a range of ideologies not all of which were mutually compatible. In view of this, while lineages of thinkers should be identified where possible, equally, where particular ideas are privileged at a particular period, our focus should shift more to the extent of the diffusion of these ideas and to the range of individual expressions of these ideas.

One book that allows us some scope to do this with reference to the Chen-Cai story is *Zhuangzi*, where in the outer and mixed *pian* of the received text the story occurs no less than seven times in various formulations. It is impossible to be sure which version/s of the story is the earliest, so I will begin with a version found in the mixed *pian*, "Tian yun" 天運 (The Turning of Heaven), which, like the "Fei ru" passage from *Mozi*, is critical of Confucius, but from the perspective of thinkers who possibly lived several generations after Zhuangzi's death. The gist of the story is a criticism of Confucius's vain attempt in travelling to various states of China, including Lu, to convince their rulers to adopt the old institutions of Zhou. Confucius's quixotic misadventures are blamed on his ignorance of "the turning which has no fixed direction and which endlessly accommodates things."[36] This last comment is clearly reminiscent of Zhuangzi's description of the "way" in the inner *pian*. For our interests, one detail in this particular version of the story distinguishing it from any discussed so far, is that Confucius is described as having been besieged (*wei* 圍) between Chen and Cai and that this was why he and his party ran out of food. Also worthy of note is that like the account at *Mencius* 5A.8, the Chen-Cai incident is portrayed as the last in a series of misadventures that had befallen Confucius on his travels. The series of events, however, is somewhat different: "a tree was felled on him in Song, he had to wipe away his footprints in Wei, and he fell on hard times (*qiong*) in Shang and Zhou."[37]

The tradition that a tree was felled on Confucius is developed in a number of sources in the period spanning *circa* 250-120. Watanabe Takashi has developed an intriguing theory about how the origins of this incident can be traced to the pithy and cryptic account in *Analects* 7.23, "Heaven has given birth to the potency in me, what can Huan Tui do to me?" Huan Tui is also mentioned in *Mencius* (5A.8) as the Song minister of war who attempted to kill Confucius when he was in Song. Watanabe argues that this incident developed during the Warring States period such that, by a process of word association, the name Huan Tui came to mean "to fell a tree," which, if true, would explain how the mutated versions of the story found in the above and three other passages from *Zhuangzi*[38] came to mean that when Confucius was in Song a tree was felled on him.[39] As for the other two incidents—the wiping away of his footprints in Wei, and falling on hard times (*qiong*) in Shang and Zhou—there appear to be no earlier extant sources that shed further light on them.[40] In summary, then, this version of the story is used to make the point that Confucius's troubles are the product of his misguided ambitions in the public/political sphere.

As with this version of the story, the three versions clustered in close succession in the "Shan mu" 山木 (Mountain Tree) *pian* of *Zhuangzi*, have also been classed as "School of Zhuangzi."[41] I will refer to them as Mountain Tree A, B, and C.[42] A and B are critical of the Confucius committed to learning and to worldly success. Importantly, however, they go one step further: they both portray an alternative, positive image of Confucius as well. Mountain Tree B is similar to the version of the story just discussed in that again Confucius is described as having been besieged between Chen and Cai, and again this is the last in a series of misadventures. Here, however, it is not so much Confucius's political ambitions that are the subject of criticism, but rather his dependence on bookish learning. Having been convinced by his interlocutor that this was the cause of his troubles, Confucius makes the following resolution:

> "I respectfully submit to your instructions!" Thereupon, walking slowly and relaxed, he returned home. He put an end to his learning and abandoned his books. His disciples, no longer presenting themselves before him to take from him, developed an affection for him greater than it had ever been before.

What is important to note here is that while one particular image of Confucius is rejected, it is a Confucius cast in a different image who makes the decision to reject learning. In other words, it is not Confucius who is rejected, but only one particular image of him. The implication that is meant to be drawn is that the "real" Confucius, the Confucius who won the undisputed affection of his disciples, is the one who came to change his mind about the value of learning. Hence, by implication, those traditions that promote an image of the Confucius devoted to learning are, in fact, not fully informed about the full course of events in Confucius's life.

A similar strategy is employed in Mountain Tree A. The passage begins with Confucius starving, having been besieged between Chen and Cai. It turns out that

Confucius's predicament had been brought about by his vanity in pursuing success and fame. "Your aim has been to startle stupid people by showing off your knowledge, to cultivate your own person so as to show up the corruption of others, and to go around all radiant and shining as if you were holding up the sun and moon." Instead, he is advised to be like "the man of great integrity" who is "focused and constant, just like a madman; he wipes away his footprints,[43] forsakes political purchase, and does not pursue success and fame." Upon hearing this, Confucius was so impressed that he decided to leave his friends and disciples to become a hermit in the wilderness. The message is clear: the real Confucius saw the error of his ways and so he finally chose to abandon the pursuit of fame and success.

Mountain Tree C is of particular interest because of all the versions of the story discussed so far it bears the closest relationship to the version in "Rang wang" (Yielding the Throne). Version C may also be distinguished from A and B in that Confucius is nowhere portrayed critically; instead the story is adapted so as to present a thoroughly positive image of Confucius. The passage opens with Confucius besieged between Chen and Cai. Despite not having eaten any cooked food for seven days, he remains unperturbed as he taps a tree and sings. Concerned that Yan Hui might be feeling sorry for him, he sings the following lines to him:

> It is easy not be affected by the losses from heaven;
> It is hard not to be affected by the gains from man.
> There is no start which is not an end;
> Heaven and man are one.

The third line is reminiscent of the line from *Xunzi* quoted above, "misfortune and good fortune follow one another just as do ends and beginnings," but the attitude to heaven in the first and last lines is plainly different. Here there is a sense that heaven's order can be discerned, allowing one to identify with it and so accommodate one's behavior accordingly. As Confucius explains:

> Hunger and thirst, cold and heat stop advancing when they grow exhausted and become sealed off. This is the movement of heaven and earth, the cyclical flow of things. The point is to join this flow.

Confucius proceeds to explain that one should serve heaven, not an earthly ruler; that to enjoy titles and emoluments is tantamount to stealing; and that it is by making himself part of this flow that the sage manages to live out the fullness of his days. The image of Confucius presented here is that of a sage who has identified with the way of heaven and as such has come to disdain the holding of office, seeing it really to be an act of robbery. One should not, however, interpret this simply as "the Daoists" irreverently poking fun at "the Confucians" by perverting the true image of their sage. Rather, it should be seen as a serious attempt to mould a particular image of Confucius and in doing so appropriate his authority.

The version of the Chen-Cai story in the "Shen ren" 慎人 (Treating Others with Care) *pian* of *Lüshi chunqiu* bears an even closer relationship to the "Rang wang" (Yielding the Throne) version. The compilation of *Lüshi chunqiu* was completed around 239 B.C.E. while "Rang wang" was compiled some time between then and the end of the second century.[44] This might suggest that the "Rang wang" version of the story took the "Shen ren" version as its source, a position argued for by Graham,[45] although the possibility remains quite open that both were based on a third source. Graham makes a plausible case for his thesis that "Rang Wang" was a reference book for debaters of the "Yang school," and comments that it "would be useful for a debater of the Yang school to have a miscellany of such examples at his elbow, copied from a standard source such as *Lü-shih ch'un-ch'iu.* . . . Nor would it matter that a story is obviously Confucian; it would be up to the debater to use it for his own purposes."[46] This in turn prompts the question of what makes a story "obviously Confucian." As we will see, while the version of the Chen-Cai story in these two *pian* does specifically accord humaneness and rightness a high regard, the concluding sentence, which champions withdrawal from the world of men, is less readily identifiable as "Confucian."

Given that these two accounts are so similar to one another, I will only translate the version in "Rang wang" and address its key differences from the "Shen ren" version in subsequent discussion. The stories included in this *pian* fall into two series, our particular story being the last in the first series. Four of the fifteen stories in the first series are about Confucius or his disciples, and as with the other eleven, all illustrate that one can be happy in poverty.

> When Confucius was trapped (*qiong*) between Chen and Cai, for seven days he had nothing cooked to eat and his soup of wild herbs had no grain to thicken it. Despite having a very hungry look about him he strummed his zither and sang inside a room.
>
> While Yan Hui was picking vegetables, Zilu and Zigong 子貢 said to him, "The Master was chased out of Lu twice, he had to scrape away his footprints in Wei, he had a tree felled on him in Song, he fell on hard times in Shang and Zhou, and now he is besieged between Chen and Cai. It is not a crime to kill him, and there is nothing to stop people from stabbing[47] him. And yet there he is, playing his zither as he sings, and drumming as he dances,[48] without a pause in the sound—can a gentleman be so without shame?"
>
> Yan Hui was speechless. He went in and told Confucius. Pushing away his zither, Confucius sighed deeply, "You 由 and Si 賜 are petty men. Call them here I will speak with them."
>
> Zilu and Zigong came in and Zilu said, "Things being as they are is what I call being impeded (*qiong*)."
>
> Confucius said, "What are you talking about?! To have access to the way is what is meant by getting through (*tong*), and to have no

access to the way is what is meant by being impeded. Now, by embracing the way of humaneness and rightness I happen to come across the troubles of a world in chaos; what has this to do with being impeded? Hence by reflecting within myself I do not lose access to the way, and as I confront difficulties I do not lose my potency. When the coldest time of year has arrived and the frosts and snows have already descended, this is how I know that the pines and cypress will be thriving. Is this strait between Chen and Cai not a blessing to me?"

He returned to his zither and resumed his strumming and singing with a flourish,[49] while Zilu grabbed a shield and danced with all the ardour of a warrior.

Zigong said, "I must confess that until now I had no idea about how things really stood."

Those men in antiquity who had obtained the way were happy whether they were impeded or whether they got through. Yet that in which they delighted had nothing to do with being impeded or getting through. When one obtains[50] the way in this life then being impeded and getting through are the same as the cycles of cold and heat, wind and rain. Therefore Xu You 許由 was content on the northern bank of the Ying river[51] and Gongbo 共伯 attained his fulfilment on the summit of Mount Gong 共.[52]

In the first two paragraphs, although Confucius's troubles between Chen and Cai are first referred to by the more general term *qiong*, the subsequent use of *wei* specifies that the fundamental trouble was being besieged. This effectively brings both traditions together—starvation and physical danger—thus compounding the sense of adversity. Yet, in the face of this adversity, Confucius remains calm and optimistic, singing, dancing, and playing music. This image of calmness and optimism in the face of adversity has an obvious parallel in the *Xunzi* version of the story.

The reference to cypresses and pines thriving in the coldest part of winter also parallels a sentiment expressed in the *Xunzi* version of the story: "one who has not been exposed to distressing circumstances will reflect only on matters close at hand; one who has not personally experienced being passed over will set himself a narrow ambition." Where this parallelism ends, however, is of greater significance. In the "twin" version of this "Rang wang" (Yielding the Throne) passage in the "Shen ren" (Treating Others with Care) *pian* of *Lüshi chunqiu*, immediately after the line on pines and cypresses is a reference to the same three overlords and their inspired ambitions that feature in the *Xunzi* passage. In the "Rang wang" passage, however, these lines have been expunged. Now while one might speculate that this is the product of later editing,[53] it is more likely to reflect the editing of the "Yangist" compilers of this passage. It would, after all, be quite in keeping with their disdain of political ambition. Thus, rather than portray

Confucius as a figure who harbored political ambitions, the Yangist editors chose to expunge the reference to the three overlords.

Removal of the reference to the three overlords also removes what for the *Lüshi chunqiu* compilers was the very raison d'être for including this passage in the first place: to illustrate the importance of "timeliness." We can infer this because "Shen ren" is placed as the fourth in series of six essays[54] which share "timeliness" as their common theme. The real purport of this passage for the *Lüshi chunqiu* compilers is that success depends on meeting particular people and making particular decisions at the right time.

Removing the reference to the "three overlords" allows the Yangist compiler to juxtapose two other themes. The first of these themes (which also happens to be paralleled in the Mountain Tree C version of the story) is that the sage identifies with the cyclical flow of the cosmos.[55] The second is that of eremitic withdrawal. The juxtaposition of these two themes (no longer being separated by the theme of timeliness) clears the way for the Yangist's reading: since worldly success and failure "are the same as the cycles of cold and heat, wind and rain" then why not simply wash one's hands of them and retire from the world? The importance that the last line of the story has for the Yangist compiler (unlike the *Lüshi chunqiu* compilers whose purpose lay elsewhere, as we have already seen) is twofold. First, its endorsement of eremitic withdrawal would have been consistent with his own position of not risking harm to oneself for the sake of others; second it allows him to reject Confucius's way of humaneness and rightness, which is attainable in the world of men both in and out of office. Thus we should not understand the author to be advocating *both* Confucius's happy embrace of the way of humaneness and rightness in the world of men *and* eremitic withdrawal; rather it is the latter position only that the compilers of "Rang wang" privilege.

Almost immediately after the Yangists were writing, this image of Confucius is singled out for criticism from another quarter: the Syncretists.[56] Their objection, however, is not that Confucius and others like him refused to withdraw from the world of men, but rather that this itinerant-teacher-and-expounder-of-humaneness-and-rightness refused to further his career:

> To expound on humaneness and rightness, doing one's best on behalf of others and living up to one's word; to be respectful, temperate, modest, deferential, interested only in improving themselves—such are the tastes of the men who go putting the world to right, the teachers and instructors, the itinerant and the stay-at-home scholars.[57]

As Graham remarks, "[P]ublic life is even more important for the Syncretist than for a Confucian, who can at least withdraw from it on moral grounds."[58] Yet why should this particular image of Confucius—itinerant teacher and expounder of the way of humaneness and rightness, impoverished yet unattracted to public office; in short the Confucius depicted in the "Rang wang" versions of the Chen-Cai story—be highlighted (critically) by two quite different[59] groups of thinkers in the *Zhuangzi?* Could it be because at the time when these essays were compiled this image of Confucius had become authoritative enough to pose a challenge to both Yangist and Syncretist values?

By contrast, it is as a politically motivated figure that Confucius is portrayed in *Mencius* and *Xunzi.* In *Mencius,* this portrayal is by no means limited to the Chen-Cai story. For example, Mencius maintains that Confucius would grow anxious if three months had passed without securing some official position, and that whenever he went to a different state he always took a present for his first audience with the ruler of that state.[60] A key factor determining whether Confucius would take office or not also differs from the account in "Rang wang." As Mencius explains:

> When Confucius left Qi, he was in such a hurry that he departed as soon as his rice was dry, not even bothering to wash it. When he left Lu, however, he said, "I will proceed slowly, as is the way when departing the country of one's parents." Confucius was the sort of man who would hurry or take his time, would remain in a state or take office, all depending on what was appropriate.... *Confucius was the sage of timely action.*[61]

As we have already seen, whereas "timeliness" is also employed in the *Xunzi* and "Shen ren" interpretations of the Chen-Cai story, in the "Rang wang" interpretation, it is not addressed, being displaced by the cyclical flow of the way. For this Confucius it was not his assessment of the "timeliness" of a given situation that determined his actions, but, rather, whether or not he could engage the way in a given situation. Elsewhere Mencius maintains that Confucius never stayed at any one court for more than three years because of the difficulties he invariably confronted in having his ideas put into practice. As he proceeds to explain, Confucius's desire to take office was motivated not only by the possibility of putting the way into practice, but also, variously, because he was received courteously by some rulers, or because other rulers happened to support men of worth.[62] In short, the impression Mencius gives is that Confucius was regularly "job hunting" and regularly being frustrated.

Similarly, in *Xunzi,* it is a politically ambitious Confucius who not only informs the interpretation of the Chen-Cai story but also other passages. As already discussed, one of the characteristics of Confucius's alternative reply to Zilu in "You zuo" is that his high regard for the three overlords is used to present him as a figure harboring powerful political aspirations. Now while this is inconsistent with Xunzi's criticism of these overlords in "Zhongni" 仲尼—"even an adolescent disciple of Confucius would have been ashamed to praise the five overlords in his speech"[63]—in a later writing, "Wang ba" 王霸, Xunzi significantly recants on this view:

> Although their potency was still lacking and although rightness had not yet been achieved, yet by and large they had brought together the pat-

terns for ordering the world.... The unity of their own countries was extremely[64] evident and so their allies trusted them.... That these five overlords—all of whom lived in backward and lowly states—were able to inspire awe throughout the world and threaten the central states was because they practised trustworthiness.[65]

Xunzi is, however, careful to distinguish Confucius from these overlords, arguing that even though he lacked a scrap of land, he left a lasting reputation.[66] Yet Xunzi does not try to conceal his concern that the attainment of reputation, while of value, is not as desirable as the attainment of office:

Zaofu 造父 was the best charioteer in the world, but without a chariot and a team of horses there was no way to evidence his ability. Yi 羿 was the best archer in the world, but without a bow and arrows there was no way to evidence his skill. A great *ru* 儒 is the best at adjusting and unifying the world, but without a minimum of one hundred square *li* 里 of territory, there is no way to evidence his meritorious achievements.... When he is out of office (*qiong*) the vulgar *ru* deride him. When he attains office, outstanding men are transformed by him, crazed people flee from him, the heretical fear him and the mass of people are put to shame by him. When he attains office, then he unifies the whole world, but when he is out of office he establishes a noble reputation alone.[67]

And, as for the specific example of Confucius, the greatest of the great *ru*:

Bigan had his heart cut out;
Confucius was trapped at Kuang.
How resplendent was the clarity of their wisdom!
How depressing it is that the times which they encountered
(*yu shi* 遇時) were so unpropitious![68]

Contrary to the image of Confucius portrayed in *Mencius* and *Xunzi*, rarely in the entire *Zhuangzi* is Confucius explicitly portrayed as an ambitious office seeker, successful or otherwise.[69] Where he is criticized for fame seeking, it seems to be Confucius the teacher-cum-moraliser who is the object of this criticism.[70] Similarly, when we turn to the *Analects*, rather than a politically ambitious figure, we find that the attainment of office is not a motivating concern for Confucius. Rather, his goal is to act in accord with the way, and that frequently this end (*zhi* 志) is best served by not serving in office even though this means facing poverty and hardship. In short, we find a Confucius who closely resembles the Confucius of the "Rang wang" version of the Chen-Cai story.

The fundamental importance of the way for Confucius is most succinctly expressed in *Analects* 4.8: "Confucius said, 'If one morning you were to learn of the way, but die the same evening, it would be worth it.'" One should even be prepared to lay down one's life for it (8.13). If one lives in accord with the way, then one can find delight even in poverty, hardship (7.16; 6.11; 1.15; 9.28; 14.2) and obscurity (1.1). Accordingly, it is not essential to take office (2.21; 3.24); rather, the whole purpose of learning is to align oneself with the way (1.14). If wealth and title come one's way as a consequence of according with the way, well and good; if not, then they must be forsaken (4.4; 8.13) for they are goods external to the practice of the way (4.9).[71] How one speaks and acts, whether one takes office or withdraws from office, whether one shows one's knowledge or feigns stupidity, and whether one is poor and of lowly status or wealthy and of honourable status, should all depend on whether or not the country one is in possesses the way (14.3; 14.1; 15.7; 5.21; 8.13).

These interlinking themes are entirely compatible with Confucius's comment in the *Analects* version of the Chen-Cai story: "The gentleman resolutely embraces (*gu* 固) hard times, while when the petty man meets with hard times he is unable to keep himself in check." With his aim fixed on the way, the gentleman embraces hard times, even if this means leading a dangerous and insecure existence. This sense of resolutely pursuing the way also throws light on 14.32, which I believe has long been misinterpreted:

> Weisheng Mou 微生畝 asked Confucius, "Qiu 丘, what is your object in going around perching now here, now there? Is it not to show off your eloquence?"
>
> Confucius said, "It is not that I dare to show off my eloquence; rather it is because of my pressing resoluteness (*gu*)."

A similar motivation is also evident in 18.6, which relates Confucius and Zilu's encounter with two tillers. Upon learning that Zilu's companion is Confucius, one of the tillers says to Zilu, "The flood now spreads throughout the world, and yet who in the world is prepared to change to something better? Rather than following a man who is fleeing from some men, would you not be better off following men who are fleeing from the age?" When Confucius learnt of this he said to Zilu, "One cannot take the birds and beasts as one's companions. If I am not a man among men, then who am I? So long as there is the way in the world, I will not change it for anything else." Despite being pursued by some enemy, Confucius chooses to remain in the world of men, practicing the way of rightness and humanity, rather than opt for eremitic withdrawal. As confirmed in 8.13, only when the way is no longer to be found anywhere in the world is withdrawal an option for Confucius.[72] Or, as expressed in the metaphor of 9.28, "Only when the coldest time of the year is reached does one learn that it is the pine and cypress which are the last to shed their leaves."

If one were to accept that the *Analects* is "a rough consensus text, whose contents were more or less endorsed by all factions of the Ruist community over a period of time",[73] the incompatibility between the portrayal of Confucius in *Xunzi* and *Mencius*, on the one hand, and the above reading of the *Analects*, on the other hand, could only strike one as anomalous. Given this, then, would it not be more reasonable to suggest that the *Analects* (and particularly the image of Confucius in the *Analects*) drew substantially on traditions and records that were only partly shared and/or accepted by the authors of *Xunzi* and *Mencius*? This speculation is further supported by the fact that in *Xunzi*, the *Analects* is not cited once, and of those many passages that quote Confucius, not one is found in the received *Analects*. Similarly, of the twenty-eight passages in *Mencius* that begin with "*Kongzi yue* 孔子曰" or "*Zhongni yue* 仲尼曰", a mere eight are found in the received *Lunyu*. Of these eight only one is identical with the received text; of the other seven, one is slightly different while of the other six, the wording is substantially different. This hardly betokens a significant commonality of "collected sayings."[74]

Elsewhere I have argued that it is was not until around 150–140 B.C.E. that the *Analects* came into existence as a book and that this book was based on a number of earlier "collected sayings" of the Master.[75] The principal source for the book which subsequently became known as *Lunyu*, was the twenty-one *pian* of collected sayings purportedly discovered in the wall of Confucius's house during the reign of Emperor Wu 武 (r. 141–87). Originally these twenty-one *pian* were several collections of *pian* recording Confucius's and his disciples' speech and actions, and that only subsequent to their discovery were these collections regarded as a single book. Nor is there any reason to believe that these twenty-one *pian* represented the entire corpus of such early collections of the Master's sayings, or that in pre-Qin times they had been privileged as a single collection or as a group of collections over any other early collection or collections of the Master's sayings. The status afforded these *pian* as constituting an integral book was a product of being singled out for special attention in the Western Han precisely because they had been found in the wall of Confucius's house and the ascendancy of Confucianism at this time required that an orthodox and standard (although not yet standardized) version of Confucius's recorded sayings be established. And once these twenty-one *pian* were regarded as forming a book in their own right and conferred a name to signal this status and homogeneity, the process of textual closure was imminent. Subsequently, the assumption became that these twenty-one *pian* had existed as a book ever since they were first recorded, when actually it was a Western Han invention. We do not know when these *pian* were compiled in the Warring States period, nor the extent to which they were subsequently edited after their initial discovery. Yet despite the ample evidence we have for judging the composition of the received text to be disparate, the theme of Confucius's attitude to office, such as I have sketched above, displays a remarkable consistency throughout the book, including the last ten *pian*, which in many other respects evidence significant inconsistencies with the first ten *pian*.[77] How is it, then, that the *Analects* did include so many passages that portray a Confucius who is not intent on securing office?

That there were many records of the Master's sayings transmitted in the Warring States period is further evidenced by the many and varied images of Confucius current in that period. As we have seen, in the different versions of the Chen-Cai story alone, Confucius is variously cast as being out in the cold for want of political connections; as a man frustrated in his political ambitions; as a man harboring strong political ambitions; as a hypocrite and glutton; as a man lacking in character judgment; as a quixotic figure; as a man of misguided ambitions; as a teacher who came to realise the futility of learning; as one who came to see the folly of success and fame; and as one who had learnt to accommodate the movements of heaven and earth. In more detailed portrayals of Confucius's character, such as in *Xunzi,* the narrative genre in which his character is given definition is the tragedy. Confucius's tragedy stems not from a fault in his character but from the fact that "the times which he encountered were so unpropitious." In *Mencius,* it is again in a narrative with a tragic undertone that elements in Confucius's character are revealed. Echoing his comment that Confucius's plight between Chen and Cai was a consequence of having no political connections, Mencius explains that, despite the quality of his potency, Confucius never came to "possess the world" because he never received the recommendation of an emperor.[78] Not only this, Confucius is also sadly misunderstood by ordinary men.[79] Yet, as evidenced by the *Analects,* there were also other traditions in which the unity of Confucius's character was informed by a different narrative genre: the heroic quest. The collected sayings that were incorporated into the *Analects* were, in significant measure, heirs to this alternative narrative tradition (whether by dint of geography and/or particular lineages of transmission we cannot know), and hence the Chen-Cai story, as a narrative within this larger narrative of heroic quest, was made intelligible by being read in the context of this larger narrative. Now given that this particular image of Confucius's character was transmitted not only in those Warring States collections of the Master's sayings that were subsequently edited into the book, the *Analects,* but also in Yangist and Syncretist writings, it clearly was not an image known only to a few "Confucian" scholars. In short, probably already by the late Warring States period it had come to be accepted as an (although not necessarily the) authoritative tradition. The fact that in the *Analects* there is little evidence[80] of an attempt to reconcile this image with the alternative one promoted in *Mencius* and *Xunzi,*[81] testifies to the continued regard accorded the authority of this image by as late as 150–140 B.C.E.

Ironically, it is in a version of a story edited by Yangist editors, and included in a collection of writings historically labelled "Daoist," that preserves an image of Confucius consistent with his image in the *Analects* (yet at odds with his image in *Mencius* and *Xunzi*). The moral of this story is that "Confucian" sources are not always our only or necessarily our best guide for understanding the Confucius of the *Analects*, and that as invaluable as *Mencius* and *Xunzi* are as sources which develop and comment on the images of Confucius and on his thought, they are interpretations, not authorities. To treat them as somehow privileged because together with the *Analects* they were all eventually labelled Confucian/*ru* writings is unwarranted. If interpretations found in *Zhuangzi*, or indeed any other "non-Confucian" writing, produce more consistent readings of the *Analects*, then they should be followed. Finally, when it is appreciated that pre-Qin thinkers themselves regarded "*ru*" as a heterogeneous concept,[82] then perhaps it is not so surprising that "the *ru*" failed to share a consistent image of Confucius.

NOTES

1. Han Yu 韓愈 (762–828), for example, in his "Song Wang xiu cai xu" 送王秀才序, in *Zhu Wen Gong jiao Changli xiansheng wenji* 朱文公昌黎先生文集, 20.6a, Sibu congkan ed., asserts a direct line of transmission from Zixia 子夏 to Tian Zifang 田子方 to Zhuangzi. While not going as far as this, Wang Anshi 王安石 (1021–86), "Zhuang Zhou shang" 莊周上, *Linchuan wenji* 臨川文集, 68.10b–13a, *Siku quanshu*, vol. 1105, pp. 563–64, nevertheless advocates an apologist reading of *Zhuangzi* in which Zhuangzi is said to be sympathetic to the fundamental import of Confucius's teachings. Su Shi 蘇軾 (1037–1101), "Zhuangzi Si Tang ji" 莊子祠堂記, *Dongpo quanji* 東坡全集, 36.14b–16a, *Siku quanshu*, vol. 1103, pp. 510–11, on grounds similar to those cited by Wang, claims that Zhuangzi's real motive was to aid Confucius, not to criticize him.
2. A. C. Graham, *Chuang-tzu: The Inner Chapters* (London: Unwin Paperbacks, 1986), pp. 117, 18.
3. *Zhuangzi*, Harvard-Yenching Institute Sinological Series, Supplement 20, (Peking: Harvard-Yenching Institute, 1947), 79.28.59–68. Translated below.
4. References to the *Analects pian* and *zhang* divisions follow those used in the Harvard-Yenching Institute Sinological Series, Supplement 16 (Peking: Harvard-Yenching Institute, 1940).
5. Alternatively, "The gentleman remains steadfast in hard times while the petty man is swept away as if caught in a deluge."
6. See Qian Mu 錢穆 *Xian Qin zhuzi xinian* 先秦諸子繫年 (Taipei: Sanmin shuju 1981), 1:41–42. Qian's account may be supplemented by Zheng Xuan's 鄭玄 (127–200) commentary to *Lunyu*, 7.15, as preserved in the Pelliot #2510 Dunhuang manuscript (reproduced in Kanaya Osamu 金谷治, *Tō shohon Jō shi chū Rongo shūsei* 唐抄本鄭氏注論語集成 (Tokyo: Heibonsha, 1978, 312):

> *After Duke Ling died*, his grandson, Zhe, was enthroned. After this, Zhao Yang of Jin installed Kuai Kui in the city of Qi. Shi Wangu of Wei, leading an army, surrounded him. *At this time, Confucius*

was in Wei. Hence Zilu asked Confucius if he intended to assist Zhe or not.

7. See his commentary to *Lüshi chunqiu* 呂氏春秋, Sibu beiyao edition (Beijing: Zhonghua, 1927–35), 14.15b.

8. *Shiji* 史記 (Beijing: Zhonghua shuju, 1982), 47.1926.

9. Ai 11, *Shisanjing zhushu* edition (Taipei: Yiwen yinshuguan 1985), 58.27a–27b.

10. Cui Shu, "Zhu Si kao xin lu" 洙泗考信錄, 3.28–29, in his *Cui Dongbi yishu* 崔東壁遺書 (Shanghai: Yadong tushuguan, 1936).

11. His biography of Confucius does not make it clear in which year Confucius left Wei and arrived in Chen. (According to the *Suo yin* 索隱 commentary, 47.1927, it was in the second year of Duke Ai of Lu's reign, 493). Sima Qian records that in the summer of the third year of Duke Ai of Lu's rule, 492, Duke Ling of Wei died (47.1927). (In his chronological tables [14.672], however, he records that Duke Ling died in the second year of Duke Ai's reign, 493; see also *Shiji*, 14.672.) Next he states that in the following year, 491 (the date of the assassination of Duke Zhao 昭 of Cai 蔡 is consistent in both the biography, 47.1928, and the chronological tables, 14.673), Confucius moved from Chen to Cai and in the year after that, 490, he went from Cai to She, later returning to Cai (47.1928). While it is not recorded when he left She to return to Cai, it is recorded that in the third year after he had moved to Cai, 489, Wu sent a punitive expedition against Chen (47.1926–30; the year 489 concurs with the account in the chronological tables). It is against this general background that Sima Qian narrates his account of the troubles that befell Confucius:

> In the third year after Confucius had moved to Cai, Wu sent a punitive expedition against Chen. To assist Chen, Chu had dispatched troops, stationing them at Chengfu. Learning that Confucius was living in the area bordering Chen and Cai, Chu sent envoys to invite Confucius to take up a position in Chu. Just as Confucius was preparing to go and pay his respects, the senior ministers of Chen and Cai plotted amongst themselves, saying, "Confucius is a worthy man and the target of his criticisms is the faults of the feudal lords. He has been in our region for a long time now, and none of the activities of we senior ministers would be likely to have met with his approval. Now, although Chu is a large state, it has sent an envoy here to invite Confucius to take up a position there. If Confucius were called upon to assist in Chu's government, then we senior ministers in charge of matters here in Chen and Cai would be in danger." Thereupon they dispatched footsoldiers who surrounded Confucius and his followers in the countryside.

But, again, no account confirms that the immediate cause of Confucius's troubles was the fears harbored by powerful ministers about Confucius's imminent rise to substantive office. It is, however, consistent with the prominence Sima Qian gives to the theme of jealousy in his account of Confucius's life. Sima Qian's account of the historical context of the story, incorporating it within his larger portrayal of events in Confucius's life, has exerted a profound influence on how Confucius has been understood in subsequent history.

12. *Shiji*, 47.1921. Incidentally, the reference to passing through Song and encountering Huan Tui is dated as occurring in the twenty-fifth year of Duke Jing of Song's reign (492) at *Shiji*, 38.1630 and 14.673, which is several years later than Sima Qian's account at 47.1921. In any case, trying to get much consistent chronological sense out of Sima Qian's reconstruction of Confucius' life is frequently an exercise in futility.

13. Jiao Xun's 焦循 (1703–1760) interpretation, *Mengzi zhengyi* 孟子正義, (Beijing: Zhonghua shuju, 1991), 19.659–62.

14. As may be inferred from the comparison with Yong Ju 癰疽 and Ji Huan 瘠環 mentioned earlier in the passage. If the alternative interpretation is followed, that is, that not only was Confucius hosted by Sicheng Zhenzi, a Song official, but that he also gained employment with the marquis of Chen, then there is a clear inconsistency between this situation and the claim that Confucius had no political connections.

15. John Knoblock, *Xunzi*, vol. 3, (Stanford, Calif.: Stanford University Press, 1994), pp. 237–38, for example, maintains that the *pian* in which this story appears as one of a collection of "school sayings," is part of an oral tradition that predates Xunzi.

16. Bigan was an uncle (younger brother of the father) of the tyrant Zhou 紂. *Shiji*, 38.1607–10, records that after he had remonstrated with Zhou, Zhou cut out his heart to see if it had the seven openings of a sage's heart.

17. Little else is known about Guanlong Feng. From this and the brief account in *Xunzi*, "Jie bi" 解蔽, Harvard-Yenching Institute Sinological Series, Supplement 22 (Peking: Harvard-Yenching Institute, 1950), 78/21/8, we may deduce that despite being a loyal minister to Jie 桀, the tyrannical last ruler of the Xia dynasty, Guan was punished.

18. Loyal minister of King Fuchai 夫差 of Wu 吳 (r. 495–473). The king ignored Wu's warnings about the state of Yue, and instead believed slanders about him perpetrated by the traitorous minister Bo Pi 伯嚭, forcing him to commit suicide. Before Wu did so, he instructed his retainers to pluck out his eyes and hang them over the city gate of the capital of Wu so that he could witness Yue invade and destroy Wu. See *Zuozhuan*, 57.2b–5a; *Shiji, juan* 66.

19. Following the emendments to this passage proposed by Wang Shumin 王叔岷, *Zhuzi jiaozheng* 諸子斠證, (Taipei: Shijie shuju, 1964), p. 253.

20. For a concise introduction to these three overlords, see Knoblock, *Xunzi,* vol. 2 (Stanford, Calif.: Stanford University Press, 1990), pp. 140–42, 145–46, 196–97.

21. *Xunzi,* 103/20/32–43.

22. Watanabe Takashi 渡邊卓, *Chūgoku kodai shisō no kenkyū* 中國古代思想の研究 (Tokyo: Sōbunsha, 1973), p. 110.

23. The word *shi* 十 here is probably a copyist's mistake for *qi* 七.

24. Emending *xiang* 享 to *peng* 烹 and omitting *wei* 為; see Sun Yirang 孫詒讓 commentary, *Mozi jiangu* 墨子閒詁 (Beijing: Zhonghua shuju, 1986), 1:275.

25. Following Sun Yirang, *Mozi jiangu,* 1: 275, in reading *hao* 號 as *chi* 褫.

26. Cf. *Analects* 10.8: "One should not consume wine and meat that have been purchased."

27. Cf. *Analects* 10.12: "One should not sit on a mat if it has not been correctly positioned."

28. Cf. *Analects* 10.8: "Do not eat the meat from an animal that has not been dismembered properly."

29. *Mozi jiangu,* 1: 275–77.

30. Cf. *Analects* 1.14: "The Master said, 'A gentleman seeks neither satiation in food nor comfort in accommodation.'"

31. Compiled under the patronage of Lü Buwei 呂不韋 (d. 235 B.C.E.) and completed about 239 B.C.E.

32. Following Yu Yue 俞樾, *Zhuzi pingyi* 諸子平議 (Taipei: Shijie shuju, 1973), p. 281, in reversing the order of these two sentences.

33. Following the alternative reading, *shi jie gu kui* 食絜故饋 cited by Li Shan 李善 (d. 689) in his commentary to Lu Ji 陸機 (261–303), "Jun zi xing" 君子行, *Wenxuan* 文選, compiled by Xiao Tong 蕭統 (501–31) (Beijing: Zhonghua shuju, 1977), 28.3a.

34. Cf. *Analects* 2.1: "Knowledge is to recognize that when you know something you know it and when you do not know something that your do not know it."

35. Following Tao Hongqing 陶鴻慶, *Du zhuzi zhaji* 讀諸子札記 (Taipei: Yiwen yinshuguan, 1971), p. 123, in regarding the three words *Kongzi zhi* 孔子之 before *suo yi zhi ren nan ye* 所以知人難也 as excrescent.

36. 38/14/37–38.

37. *Zhuangzi,* 38/14/34.

38. 53/20/37; 73/28/61; 87/31/27.

39. Watanabe, *Chūgoku kodai shisō no kenkyū,* pp. 92–95.

40. Related criticisms are also a feature of two "Yangist" *pian,* "Dao Zhi" and "Yu fu," the dates of which, Graham says, "need not be more than a decade or so after 202 B.C.," but may be even later. See "How Much of *Chuang-tzu* did Chuang-tzu Write," *Studies in Chinese Philosophy & Philosophical Literature* (Singapore: National University of Singapore, 1986), p. 309. Both accounts of the Chen-Cai story recorded in these two *pian* rehearse a similar

litany of misadventures, with the "Dao Zhi" (Robber Zhi) version concluding that Confucius was in no position to look after others as he could not even look after himself and the "Yu fu" (The Old Fisherman) version concluding that he should stop being such a busybody and leave other things to other people. In both cases, the attacks on Confucius allow the Yangist to parade his own ideas about preserving one's own life at all cost.

41. Guan Feng, "Zhuangzi waiza pian chutan" 莊子外雜篇初探, in *Zhuangzi neipian yijie he pipan* 莊子內篇譯解和批判, (Beijing: Zhonghua shuju, 1961), pp. 340, 343; A. C. Graham, *Chuang-tzu, The Inner Chapters*, (London: Unwin Paperbacks, 1986), p. 115; *Disputers of the Tao: Philosophical Argument in Ancient China* (La Salle, Ill.: Open Court, 1989), p. 173.

42. Mountain Tree A (20.52.28–37); B (20.53.37–45); C (20.53.50–61).

43. Note the different use to which this phrase is put.

44. See Graham, "How Much of *Chuang-tzu* did Chuang-tzu Write?," pp. 307–13. In his more recent *Disputers of the Tao*, p. 173, however, as with the other Yangist writings, he dates it "from in or near the same period" as the Primitivist writings, that is, 209–202 B.C.E.

45. See ibid., p. 308.

46. See ibid., p. 311.

47. Following Wang Shumin, *Zhuangzi jiaoquan* 莊子校詮 (Taipei: Sanmin shuju, 1988), 3:1154, n. 10, in reading *ji* 藉 as a loan word for *ci* 刺.

48. Following *Lüshi chunqiu*, SBBY, 14.16a, in emending *qin* 琴 to *wu* 舞.

49. Following *Lüshi chunqiu*, 14.16a, in emending *xiao* 削 to *lie* 烈. I have also followed Graham's inspired rendering of *lie ran* as "with a flourish," See *Chuang-tzu: The Inner Chapters*, p. 230.

50. Following *Lüshi chunqiu*, 14.16a, in emending *de* 德 to *de* 得.

51. Xu You was a hermit who is said to have fled to Mount Ji 箕 (to the north of the Ying River) rather than accept the throne from Yao 堯.

52. After serving as a caretaker emperor, Gongbo abdicated the throne to King Xuan 宣 in 828.

53. Alternatively, it might even be seen as an interpolation in the "Shen ren" passage.

54. From "Shou shi" 首時 to "Bi ji" 必己.

55. One difference, however, is that whereas in the former it is the movement of heaven and earth that constitutes this flow, in the latter and the "Shen ren" versions it is the way. Thus the use of the "way" might be seen as an attempt by the original author of this passage to privilege the "way" of Confucius over the more naturalistic "movement of heaven and earth."

56. In his "How Much of *Chuang-Tzu* did Chuang-tzu Write," p. 317, Graham dates the Syncretist stratum as "not too long after 202 B.C."; in his later *Disputers of the Tao*, p. 173, he dates it more generally as second century B.C.E. Harold Roth, "Who Compiled the *Chuang Tzu*," in *Chinese Texts and*

Philosophical Contexts, ed. Henry Rosemont Jr., pp. 79–128, argues that it was Syncretists at the court of Liu An, king of Huainan, *circa* 130, who compiled *Zhuangzi*. In his reply to this essay, pp. 279–83, Graham criticizes this hypothesis on the grounds that the type of Syncretism evidenced in *Zhuangzi* is not specific to the Huainan circle and that Roth is too reductive in identifying early Han Daoism as Huang-Lao Daoism.

57. *Zhuangzi*, "Ke yi" 刻意, 40.15.2–3; Graham, *Chuang-tzu, The Inner Chapters*, p. 264, modified.

58. Graham, "How Much of *Chuang-Tzu*," p. 319. The Syncretists commitment to public life is particularly evident in the essay "Tian xia" 天下 (In the World). In their other writings as well, they developed a robust political dimension that integrated the political ideas of various thinkers into a comprehensive framework that was given its fullest expression in the *Huainanzi* essay, "Zhu shu" 主術 (The Art of Rulership). See Roger T. Ames, *The Art of Rulership*, (Honolulu: University of Hawaii Press, 1983). See also my review of the second edition of this work, in *Australian Asian Studies Review* 19.1 (1995): 136–38.

59. The Syncretist would have regarded the Yangist as he did anyone who advocated only the views of one philosophical tradition or school of thought. Certainly the Yangist's espousal of withdrawal from the world would have qualified him to be included in the following category criticized in the Syncretist essay, "Ke yi," 40.15.3–5; Graham, *Chuang-tzu, The Inner Chapters*, p. 264, modified:

> To live in the woods and marshes, settle in an untroubled wilderness, angle for fish and live untroubled, interested only in doing nothing—such are the tastes of the recluses of the riverbanks and seaside, the shunners of the age, the untroubled idlers.

60. 3B.3.

61. 5B.1.

62. 5B.4.

63. These five overlords, were: Duke Huan of Qi, Duke Wen of Jin, King Zhuang 莊 of Chu 楚 (r. 613–591), King Helü 闔閭 of Wu 吳 (r. 514–496), and King Goujian of Yue. On the dating of "Zhongni" and "Wang ba," see Knoblock, *Xunzi, vol. 1* (Stanford, Calif.: Stanford University Press, 1988), pp. 6, 11–13.

64. Following Liu Taigong 劉台拱 (1751–1805), as cited in Liang Qixiong 梁啟雄, *Xunzi jianshi* 荀子柬釋 (Taipei: Taiwan shangwu yinshuguan, 1978), p. 140, who glosses *qi* 綦 as *ji* 極.

65. *Xunzi* 38.11.13–18.

66. *Xunzi* 37.11.8–9.

67. *Xunzi* 23.8.80–81, 87–89.

68. *Xunzi* 95.26.31–32.

69. The few examples would include the Mountain Tree A passage, and the passage in the Yangist diatribe, "Dao Zhi," where Confucius is criticized for trying to get riches and honors from various rulers. See 81.29.33.

70. One passage, 71.23.33–38, which Graham, *Chuang-Tzu, The Inner Chapters*, p. 190, assigns to a group "related to the Inner Chapters," is ambiguous on the point of whether Confucius is being criticized simply as a "fawner on princes" or for seeking office.

71. For the concepts of "practice" and "internal and external goods," see Alasdair McIntyre's discussion in chapter 14 of his *After Virtue: A Study of Moral Theory*, 2nd ed. (London: Duckworth, 1993).

72. Similarly, Zilu's concluding remarks in 18.7 should be understood to mean that the hermit in this passage would not have withdrawn from the world if the way was still to be found there; the fact of his withdrawal is taken by Zilu as evidence that the way is no longer operative in the world.

73. Robert Eno, *The Confucian Creation of Heaven* (Albany: State University of New York Press, 1990), p. 80. The "period of time" he refers to is the Warring States period.

74. Further evidence of this is to be found in such examples as *Mencius* 1A.7, where Mencius claims that none of the followers of Confucius spoke about the matters of Dukes Huan and Wen, whereas in *Analects* 14.15 and 14.16 Confucius does precisely this, even praising Duke Huan in both passages. It would certainly be strange for Mencius to have made this claim if he had known of these passages in writings that he believed did reflect the views of Confucius. If he had not seen them, then the evidence is equally telling.

75. Rather than rehearse the details of my long argument, I refer the reader to the article: "On the Formation of *Lun yu* as a Book," *Monumenta Serica* 44 (1996).

76. *Lunheng* 論衡, Huang Hui 黃暉 ed., *Lunheng jiaoshi* 校釋 (Taipei: Taiwan shangwu yinshuguan, 1983), 28.1132.

77. See, for example, Cui Shu, *Cui Dongbi yishu*; Hu Zhikui 胡志奎, *Lunyu bianzheng* 論語辨證 (Taipei: Lianjing chuban shiye gongsi, 1978); and my discussion of their arguments in "The Formation of the *Lun yu* as a Book."

78. 5A.6.

79. 6B.6; 7B.19.

80. Which would include the juxtaposition of 15.1 and 15.2 discussed at the beginning of this essay.

81. And still being transmitted in early Western Han versions of the story such as *Hanshi waizhuan* 韓詩外傳 (*juan* 7, *zhang* 6), *Hanshi waizhuan jishi* 集釋, ed. Xu Weiyu 許維遹 (Beijing: Zhonghua shuju, 1980), pp. 242–46, which appears to take the *Xunzi* version of the story as its basis.

82. See, for example, *Xunzi*, "Fei ru" and "Ru xiao."

4

How to Interpret Chapter 16 of the *Zhuangzi*

"Repairers of Nature (Shan Xing 繕性)"

HENRY G. SKAJA

CONSIDERING THE PROBLEM IN CONTEXT

Chapter 16 of the *Zhuangzi*, "Repairers of Nature (*Shan Xing* 繕性)," continues to pose significant interpretive difficulties for translators and commentators. For example, as indicated by Burton Watson, perhaps the most significant of these difficulties is that the chapter (lines 2–5) "attempts to derive the Confucian virtues and concerns from the Way [*dao*]" as presented by the Daoists.[1] A related difficulty (line 17) is indicated by Watson as follows: "Why the writer quotes such an un-[D]aoist injunction as 'Rectify yourself,' or what he means by it, I do not know."[2] According to A. C. Graham, the chapter is "unrelated to anything elsewhere in the book."[3]

In this paper I wish to show how these and other interpretive difficulties associated with chapter 16 can be resolved by considering more closely the historical, political, intellectual, and textual context in which the chapter was written (the problem of textual corruption notwithstanding).[4] In light of these contextual considerations, we find that the chapter acknowledges and resonates clearly with the teachings of the Confucian philosopher Mencius, in regard to his conception of human nature (*renxing* 人性) and the Way (*dao* 道) as *fundamentally social and cooperative* in "virtue" or "character" (*de* 德).[5] On the other hand, we find that the chapter is highly critical of the teachings presented by the Confucian philosopher Xunzi, who, in direct opposition to Mencius, argued that people are by nature selfish and uncooperative (*xinge* 性惡), so that human nature needs to be "trans-

formed" or "repaired" through the "artifice" (*wei* 偽) of scholars versed in the
Way.[6] Thus, we can understand the title of chapter 16 and its primary subject of
criticism: "Repairers of Nature." As indicated by the author of the chapter, those
who attempt to repair our nature actually destroy our naturally social and harmonious virtue or character (*de*)—and, thus, depart from the Way (*dao*).

In order to better understand my argument in regard to resolving the interpretive difficulties associated with chapter 16 of the *Zhuangzi*, consider the following remarks by James Campbell in regard to his recent book, *Understanding
John Dewey: Nature and Cooperative Intelligence* (1995). Although Campbell's remarks are directed primarily to the contemporary situation in Western philosophy,
they are nevertheless relevant. Therefore, I quote Campbell at length:[8]

Accordingly, I shall argue that, in a manner reminiscent of the social philosophy presented by John Dewey,[7] both Mencius and the author of chapter 16
conceive human nature and the Way as fundamentally social and cooperative
in character. Consequently, both philosophers appeal to the natural cooperation
and "cooperative intelligence" of people as the only means or "Way" of attaining
lasting fulfillment in human life (*rensheng* 人生), and of addressing and resolving
adequately the social and political problems that divided classical China into
competing factions during the "Warring States period" (463–222 B.C.E.). If my
argument is correct, then we find that a number of the interpretive difficulties
associated with chapter 16 tend to dissipate, so that the genuine philosophical or
social issues which are addressed in the chapter can be brought to light for contemporary philosophical discussion. In what follows, I shall attempt to bring these
issues to light and, at the end of this paper, I shall provide a complete, annotated
translation of the chapter.

In order to better understand my argument in regard to resolving the interpretive difficulties associated with chapter 16 of the *Zhuangzi*, consider the following remarks by James Campbell in regard to his recent book, *Understanding
John Dewey: Nature and Cooperative Intelligence* (1995). Although Campbell's remarks are directed primarily to the contemporary situation in Western philosophy,
they are nevertheless relevant. Therefore, I quote Campbell at length:[8]

> [P]erhaps the most important ... factor in the contemporary recon-
> sideration of Dewey is the growing dissatisfaction with much con-
> temporary philosophizing, with thinking that neither grows out of the
> problems and issues of our broader society nor is able to offer any
> assistance to that society as it attempts to address its difficulties. Cre-
> ating a philosophy that was connected to society in both of these ways
> was a major concern for Dewey....
>
>   For [Dewey], we humans live our lives as natural and social crea-
> tures who have emerged from and must ever interact with our natural
> and social environment. This world is our past and our future, our
> challenge and our means. He emphasizes that we interact with this en-
> vironment much of the time—too much of the time—based on our
> unthinking desires and our untested beliefs. Yet we have the ability to
> inquire and evaluate: to move beyond the immediately good to lasting
> values, to actions and beliefs and goals that make possible human

growth and long-term fulfillment. Central to Dewey's vision is the belief that this evaluative power, which he calls intelligence, is not an individual possession but a possession of the group. The efforts of the vibrant community of cooperative inquirers are consequently our best means of addressing our collective problems. Hence my subtitle: *Nature and Cooperative Intelligence.*

As indicated by Campbell, Dewey holds that we as people are by nature social and cooperative creatures. Consequently, it is necessary to appeal to our "cooperative intelligence" to attain lasting fulfillment in life, and in addressing social and political problems. My argument is most simply that, legitimate differences notwithstanding, both Mencius and the author of chapter 16 hold a similar view to that of Dewey.

THE CONFUCIAN CONNECTION

As indicated by Watson above, perhaps the most significant interpretive difficulty associated with chapter 16 is that it "attempts to derive the Confucian virtues and concerns from the Way." That is, specifically, the chapter attempts to articulate in terms of human nature and the Way the Confucian *social* virtues or characteristics, such as love for others (*ren* 仁), appropriate conduct toward others (*yi* 義),[9] ceremonial interaction with others (*li* 禮), music in the company of others (*yue* 樂) and, thus, knowledge or understanding (*zhi* 知) among people—what I have referred to as "cooperative intelligence." Furthermore, the chapter attempts to address the major philosophical issues or concerns of the age, such as the controversial doctrine of "nonaction" (*wuwei* 無為), the character (*de* 德) of human nature or life, the "patterns" of activity and reasoning (*li* 理) that emerge therefrom,[10] the appropriate object of conscientiousness or loyalty (*zhong* 忠), and the promotion of natural-social harmony (*he* 和)—all with respect to the Way as the integral, harmonious process of life and growth. The following is my translation of the problematic passage (lines 2–5) referred to by Watson:[11]

> Those of old who promoted the Way employed tranquillity to cultivate understanding. They understood the life process, yet they did not employ this understanding to take action (*wei* 為). So they may be said to have employed understanding to cultivate tranquillity. When understanding and tranquillity are mutually cultivated, harmony and patterns emerge from our nature. Our natural character consists in the harmony, and the Way consists in the patterns. When our natural character embraces all things, we have love; and when the Way patterns all things, we have appropriate conduct. To understand appropriate conduct and to have affection for creatures is to be loyal. When there is purity and

fullness within, and a return to our true emotions, we have music. When trust is expressed in face and body, and there is compliance with culture, we have ceremony.

In his pioneering research, A. C. Graham has provided us with the clue to unlocking this "interpretive difficulty." The clue lies in the Mencian conception of human nature.[12] As indicated by Graham,

> The author surprises us by recommending the Confucian moral virtues, which like Mencius he sees as inherent in human nature. He holds that if we still the passions and achieve the equilibrium in which tranquility and awareness support and enhance each other, Goodwill [*ren*] and Duty [*yi*] become natural to us, and so do Music [*yue*] (which otherwise excites the passions) and Rites [*li*] (which otherwise are empty formalities).[13]

If we consider closely the "syncretic" intellectual attitude of the time, we find that the author's "recommendation" is not as surprising as it might initially appear.[14] Although Graham has provided us with insight into the close relationship between chapter 16 and the teachings of Mencius on human nature, Graham is reluctant to acknowledge that the author of this chapter, *like* Mencius but *unlike* Xunzi, conceives human nature as fundamentally *social* and *cooperative* with respect to "virtue" or "character" (*de*).[15] Graham's reluctance in this regard seems to stem from his following of Arthur Waley in the translation and interpretation of "*de* 德" as the "Power" of an individual substance, essence, or thing—that is, "the inherent capacity of a thing to perform its specific functions successfully."[16] Thus, the translation and interpretation of *de* as the "Power" of an individual substance, essence, or thing tends to ignore social and cooperative considerations altogether.[17]

However, if we explicitly acknowledge the social and cooperative "virtue" or "character" of human nature, then it is not at all surprising to find with the author that the Confucian *moral* or *social virtues*, such as love (*ren*), appropriate conduct (*yi*), ceremony (*li*), music (*yue*), and knowledge or understanding (*zhi*) among people are indeed inherent in human nature (*renxing*) and are, thus, naturally expressed during the course of human life (*rensheng*).[18] Furthermore, it not surprising to find with the author that the social and cooperative character of human nature or life is integral to that of "the Way" (*dao* 道), or "the Way of Heaven" (*tiandao* 天道), as the integral process of life and growth in general. In regard to the social and cooperative character of human nature and this comprehensive Way, consider the following representative remarks by Mencius:

> Love, appropriate conduct, ceremony, and wisdom are not welded in us from outside, but are originally integral to us. It is just that we never

take the time to think about it (*fusi* 弗思), that's all! (*Mencius* 6A6, reading "*wo* 我" in the original sense of "we" or "us" rather than "me")

As an exemplary person, a ruler (*junzi* 君子) regards love, appropriate conduct, ceremony, and wisdom as his nature (*xing* 性). These are rooted in his heart-mind (*xin* 心) and grow (*sheng* 生) in his expression [and are thus extended to others].[19] (7A2)

The myriad creatures are all integral to and completed by us. There is no greater joy (*le* 樂) than to realize upon reflection that one has interacted with integrity (*cheng* 誠).[20] Try your best to put yourself in the place of others (*shu* 恕) and conduct yourself accordingly.[21] You will find that there is no shorter way to love for others (*ren* 仁). (7A4)

There is a way for a person to interact with integrity. If he does not understand/express (*buming* 不明) what is socially desirable (*shan* 善), then he cannot interact with integrity.[22] Thus, integrity is the Way of Heaven (*tian zhi dao* 天之道); to direct one's thoughts towards integrity is the way of man (*ren zhi dao* 人之道). There has never been a person who achieves integrity that fails to motivate others. On the other hand, one who does not achieve integrity can never hope to motivate others. (4A12)

TYRANNY, ISOLATIONISM, ANARCHY, OR COOPERATION?: SOME DIFFICULTIES IN GRAHAM'S INTERPRETATION

Graham's reluctance to acknowledge the social and cooperative character of human nature and the Way, as conceived by Mencius and the author of chapter 16, presents its own interpretive difficulties. According to Graham, chapter 16 "is an apology for the hermit's life" and "is explicit that the sage is a hermit except in the Utopian age."[23] However, Graham's appeal to a Utopian age notwithstanding, the text seems clearly to indicate otherwise. If the chapter "is an apology for the hermit's life" and "is explicit that the sage is a hermit," why then does it "recommend" the Confucian moral or social virtues?—and why does it articulate those social virtues as inherent in human nature and the Way?

Furthermore, we find that even Confucius states that when the Way does not prevail in the world one ought to retire from public office (*Analects* 8.13)—but this hardly implies that one ought to become a hermit and attempt the suicidal task of isolating oneself from the community of social life altogether. As indicated by the author of chapter 16, a scholar (*shi* 士) can simply "deepen his roots" (line 15) and "remain in place" (line 16) in pursuit of the Way and, as such, become a teacher of others through personal example: "Rectify yourself, that's all" (line 17).[24] In regard to these social considerations, let us consider Graham's own translation of the text (lines 12–13):[25]

As long as there is no means for the Way to rise up in the age or the age
to be resurrected by the Way, even if [*sui* 雖 = although?] a sage is not
living in the mountain forests the Power in him has been obscured. It
has been obscured, therefore it is not that he has chosen his obscurity.

As for what of old was meant by [a scholar] "living in obscurity," it
was not that someone was lying low and refusing to show himself, or
keeping his words to himself and refusing to make them public, or
hoarding his knowledge and refusing to let it out. It was that the fate of
the times [*shiming* 時命] was too much awry.

Where exactly in the text, as translated by Graham, is it "explicit" that the
sage is a hermit? Graham's interpretation in this regard seems to stem from his
translation of *de* as the "Power" of an individual substance, essence, or thing and,
as such, it tends to ignore social and cooperative considerations altogether. But
even in light of Graham's own translation, Graham's interpretive remarks regarding the sage as a hermit do not seem to apply to chapter 16. They may, however,
apply to the passages that Graham gleans from the other chapters of the *Zhuangzi*,
which he then associates with chapter 16—that is, the passages that Graham
gleans respectively from chapters 20, 19, and 12.[26] But nevertheless it is strange
that Graham should associate these passages with chapter 16—in light of his own
somewhat curious remark that chapter 16 of the *Zhuangzi* is "unrelated to anything elsewhere in the book."[27]

Let us examine Graham's interpretation of chapter 16 in greater detail:[28]

> It is an apology for the hermit's life by an author of uncertain date, not
> recognisable anywhere else in the book. His style is pedestrian but he is
> interesting as the first documented instance of a true anarchist in China,
> in the sense that he conceives the ideal community as living in a spon-
> taneous oneness without any ruler at all. He dates the decline of the
> social order from the very first rulers, Sui-jen [Suiren] and Fu-hsi [Fuxi],
> and is explicit that the sage is a hermit except in the Utopian age, when
> he enters the world not to take office but to submerge in the primordial
> oneness. This anarchism is rooted in what looks like a Taoistic [Daoistic]
> variation on the doctrine of the goodness of human nature preached by
> the Confucian Mencius.

Graham's interpretive remarks are most puzzling in light of his own translation of
the chapter. First of all, as I have indicated by appeal to Graham's translation, the
chapter is not "an apology for the hermit's life" nor is it "explicit that the sage is a
hermit" except in a Utopian age or otherwise. Rather, I argue, the chapter is most
simply and unsurprisingly an apology for the familiar Daoist doctrine of *wuwei*
(lit., without action or management)—that is, "non-interference" in what Graham
calls the "wholeness" or "integrity" of "the life process" (*sheng*).[29] The author
indicates that the doctrine of *wuwei* has been violated in various ways and degrees

by the earliest, traditionally recognized rulers of China (= the known world)—such as Suiren, Fuxi, and even the "Confucian hero" Shun.[30] Consequently, we find that the author is suspicious of anyone who attempts to "take charge of the world (*wei tianxia* 為天下)"[31]—that is, literally, to manage everything under the sky (to become master of the universe so to speak). According to the author (lines 7–11), all such attempts have invariably led to tyranny over others, social hardship and intellectual confusion (*huo* 惑) and, consequently, a loss of "cooperative intelligence" or understanding (*zhi* 知) among people. Thus, Graham is quite correct to the extent that the author of this chapter, like Zhuangzi of the Inner Chapters, rejects the traditional Confucian appeal to "the way of the former kings (*xian wang zhi tao* 先王之道)." Accordingly, we find that the author holds a somewhat different political view from that of Mencius. Mencius, like Confucius, hoped for the possibility that a sage ruler of China might still arise.[32]

Still, secondly, it is not at all clear from an examination of the text that the author is "a true anarchist . . . in the sense that he conceives the ideal community as living in a spontaneous oneness without any ruler at all." What is clear, however, is that, aside from the author's obvious and justifiable suspicion of anyone who attempts to "take charge of the world," the author recommends that those who happen to find themselves in political power (those "having the caps and carriages of high office") ought to be tolerant of and defer to others (lines 5–7) and, thus, embrace the doctrine of *wuwei*, or non-interference in the naturally integral, spontaneous, and harmonious process of life/growth (*sheng*). To do so is to achieve integrity, to remain "whole" or "complete (*quan* 全)" in the company of others and, thus, to "preserve one's life in the Way." Here the author seems to make a strong appeal to the Confucian, as well as Daoist, notion of rulership (*wang* 王) by personal example through the expression of virtuous character (*de*) and the Way (*dao*)—that is, rulership by deference to and cooperation with others, as opposed to tyranny over others by "taking charge of the world" and ordering people about under threat of punishment.[33] This cooperative and deferential sense of rulership is not reducible to the conduct of any individual person, but is a natural function of community or social life, so that anyone and everyone can become a sage or sage ruler. In this regard, consider the following remarks by Mencius—bearing in mind that Mencius and the author of chapter 16 have different interpretations of the legendary sage, or sage ruler, Shun:

> When anyone told him that he had made a mistake, Zilu was delighted. When he heard others speak in a desirable manner (*shan yan* 善言), Yu bowed before the speaker. The great Shun was even greater. In order to achieve what is desirable with others, he was ready to discard his own ways and accord with theirs, and was glad to gain from others in order to achieve what is desirable (*shan*). From the time he was a farmer, a potter and a fisherman to the time he became emperor, he gained from others. To gain from others in order to achieve what is desirable is to

enable others to achieve what is desirable. Thus, there is nothing greater for a ruler (*junzi*) to do than to enable others to achieve what is desirable. (2A8)

Note that I have employed Mencius's own definition of "*shan* 善" (7B25) as that which can be consistently desired (*keyu* 可欲) without conflict or contradiction, "that which is desirable." "*Shan*" is, of course, commonly translated as "good" or "goodness." Note also that the author of chapter 16 (line 9) is suspicious of anyone who "departs from the Way for the sake of goodness (*li tao yi shan* 離道以善)." Here it would seem that Mencius and the author agree in principle if not explicitly in words, since both would agree that pursuing the Way is "desirable" or "good."[34]

Thirdly, in regard to Graham's interpretation of chapter 16, it can be argued by appeal to the text that what Graham calls the "spontaneous" or "primordial oneness" is simply the original unity (*yi* 一), natural-social harmony, or integrity of people and things inherent in the life/growth process—to the extent that it is still unspoiled by those who attempt to take charge of the world:

> Those of old lived in the midst of teeming activity, and yet with the rest of the world they attained tranquillity and tolerance. At that time the Yin and Yang were in harmony and at peace, ghosts and spirits worked no mischief, the four seasons attained their full measure, the myriad creatures were unharmed, and all that lived escaped an untimely death. Although men possessed understanding, they did not attempt to employ it for their own benefit. This was called attaining the utmost in unity with others. At that time no one stepped forward to take action (*wei* 為), so that things were continuously so of themselves (*ziran* 自然).

As indicated elsewhere by the author (lines 17–21), all attempts to take charge of and manage the world are made ultimately to further one's own individual "ambition" (*zhi* 志), and to increase one's own individual "happiness" or "joy" (*le* 樂), to the inevitable detriment of self and others. (Consider, for example, the obvious cases of Hitler, Stalin, and the self-proclaimed First Emperor of China, Qin Shihuangdi.) It is for this reason, I submit, that the author advocates cooperation with others and, thus, "cooperative intelligence" or understanding (*zhi* 知) with respect to rulership—in contrast to the political policies of tyranny, isolationism, and/or anarchy (in the sense indicated by Graham).

Lastly, in regard to Graham's interpretation of the chapter, consider what Graham calls "the doctrine of the goodness of human nature preached by Mencius": "*xing shan* 性善," translated literally as "human nature is good." As I have indicated elsewhere in regard to this "doctrine" or "theory" attributed to Mencius, it makes as little sense philosophically to say that human nature is good or bad as it does to say that the nature of oxen is good or bad—since, strictly speaking, "good" and "bad" are not characteristics of nature and the nature of things, but are terms that we employ in reference to that which we happen to desire (*yu* 欲) and dislike (*e* 惡).[35] In regard to this point, Graham makes two relevant observations:

> [E]arly expositions of the Mencian theory, such as the *Chung Yung* [*Zhong Yong*] and the appendices of the *Changes* [*Yi Jing*], never explicitly describe human nature as good. . . .[36]
>
> The word *shan* 善 is normally applied to actions and agents which accord with Heaven [*tian*] and the Way, not to Heaven and the Way themselves, so that it becomes doubtful whether Nature can be good in itself any more than the nature of water is an entity which tends downward.[37]

Furthermore, I submit, the literal translation of *xing shan* as "human nature is good" fails to capture Mencius's distinction between that which we happen to desire (*yu* 欲), and that which we judge to be desirable (*keyu* 可欲 = *shan* 善) and undesirable (*bushan* 不善) upon critical reflection or thinking (*si* 思). This distinction is implicit in Mencius's definition of the word "*shan*" (7B.25), as translated by both D. C. Lau and A. C. Graham:

> The desirable is called . . . [*shan*]. (Lau, *Mencius*, 1976, p. 199)

> It is the desirable that is meant by . . . [*shan*]. (Graham, 1986, p. 32)

The Mencian distinction between that which is desired and that which we judge to be desirable or undesirable is also emphasized by John Dewey in his "The Construction of Good":[38]

> The fact that something is desired only raises the *question* of its desirability; it does not settle it. Only a child in the degree of his immaturity thinks to settle the question of desirability by reiterated proclamation: "I want it, I want it, I want it."
>
> It is worth notice that . . . there are many other recognitions in ordinary speech of the distinction. . . . Noted and notable . . . ; remarked and remarkable; advised and advisable . . . ; blamed and blameable, blameworthy; objected to and objectionable; esteemed and estimable; admired and admirable; shamed and shameful; honored and honorable; approved and approvable. . . . The multiplication of words adds nothing to the force of the distinction. But it aids in conveying a sense of the fundamental character of the distinction; of the difference between mere report of an already existent fact and judgment as to the importance and need of bringing a fact into existence; or, if it is already there, of sustaining it in existence.

In light of the above discussion, consider Mencius's own remarks:

> That which is desirable is called "*shan*" (*keyu zhi wei shan* 可欲之謂善).
> A person who understands/expresses what is desirable (*ming shan* 明善)
> is called "trustworthy (*xin* 信)". To do so in full measure is called
> "beautiful (*mei* 美)", but to shine forth in brilliance is called "great
> (*da* 大)". To exhibit the greatness that transforms others is called "sage
> (*sheng* 聖)." The enduring influence of a sage, which is beyond one's
> ability to adequately comprehend (*buke chih* 不可知), is called "perva-
> sive (*shen* 神)." (7B25)

Note the Daoist flavor of this passage. This indicates clearly that Mencius was
influenced by the language and arguments of his Daoist-oriented critics.[39] It also
indicates the fact that Mencius was proficient in dealing with such critics on their
own terms. Consider, for example, the Mencius-Gaozi debate on human nature
(*Mencius* 6A1–4). In response to Gaozi's argument that human nature or life tends
neither to what is desirable nor undesirable, Mencius argues that

> Human nature [or life] tends to what is desirable (*renxing zhi shan* 人性
> 之善), just as water tends downward.... Although a person can be made
> to act in a way that is undesirable (*ren zhi keshi wei bushan* 人之可使為
> 不善), our social nature remains as it was [that is, tending to what is
> desirable]. (6A2)

Thus, as Mencius explains in regard to the doctrine or theory of human nature
attributed to him:

> Insofar as what is genuine in respect to people is concerned, people have
> the ability to act in a manner that is desirable (*keyi wei shan* 可以為善).
> This is what I mean by "*shan*." That a person should act in a manner
> that is undesirable (*wei bushan* 為不善) is not the fault of our natural
> ability (*cai* 才).... Love for others, a sense of community and appro-
> priate conduct towards others, ceremonial interaction with others, and
> [thus] wisdom are not welded in us from outside. They are originally
> integral to us. It is just that we never take the time to think about it,
> that's all! (6A6)

> There are gifts bestowed by Heaven (*tianjue* 天爵), and there are gifts
> bestowed by people (*renjue* 人爵). The expression of love and appro-
> priate conduct (*ren yi*), loyalty and trust (*zhong xin*), and the unfailing
> enjoyment (*le*) of what is mutually desirable (*shan*)—these are gifts
> bestowed by Heaven. (6A16)

> That which people do not have to learn, yet are able to do, is what they
> are naturally able to do (*liangneng* 良能). That which people do not

have to reflect upon, yet realize, is what they naturally realize (*liangzhi* 良知).[40] Now, there are no young children who do not realize loving their parents, and none of them as they grow do not realize respecting their elders. Loving one's parents is *ren*. Respecting one's elders is treating them appropriately (*yi*). There is nothing left to do but to extend these [*ren* and *yi*]) throughout the world. (7A15)

In short, Mencius argues that our socially oriented nature or life tends continuously to what is found to be mutually desirable upon critical reflection or thinking: community and cooperation with others—the expression of love, appropriate conduct, ceremonial interaction and, thus, "cooperative intelligence," understanding or wisdom among people. My point is that the author of chapter 16 of the *Zhuangzi* argues in a similar manner, merely verbal differences and any legitimate differences of opinion notwithstanding.

THE PROBLEM OF *SHIMING* 時命

Another interpretive difficulty associated with chapter 16 concerns the notion of *shiming* 時命. As observed by Fukunaga Mitsuji, and noted by Burton Watson, "this concept of good and bad times that are fated [*shiming*] is quite contrary to the philosophy expressed in the Inner Chapters [of the *Zhuangzi*], according to which any time is as good as any other."[41] As Watson explains, "The thinking here is in fact much closer to the ideas of timeliness and fate expressed in the Confucian *Analects* or the *Book of Changes*."[42] Considering that Confucianism and the philosophy presented in the *Book of Changes* both became intellectually prominent, Watson's explanation is largely correct. However, contrary to Fukunaga's observation as relayed by Watson, it is not altogether clear in the Inner Chapters of the *Zhuangzi* that "any time is as good as any other." Clearly the Inner Chapters recognize the importance of timeliness with respect to conduct and the completion of affairs. For example, see Watson's note (1968, p. 61, n. 12) in regard to what he takes to be a problematic passage in chapter 4, "In the World of Men," involving the notions of timely conduct and *ming*.

Consider also that the *translation* of "*ming* 命" as "fate" poses its own interpretive difficulties, if the translation presupposes the philosophical doctrine of determinism. Although *ming* may be impossible to change, this does not imply that *ming* means "fate" or "destiny" in the deterministic sense of *predetermination* by a presupposed causal agent.[43] For example, as indicated by Mencius in regard to the notion of *tian ming* (天命):

> Although no one acts and yet there is activity—this is *tian*.[44]
> Although no one directs something to happen and yet it does happen—this is *ming*. (5A6)

Although *ming* literally means "a spoken command" or "decree," such that the term carries a strong normative sense, it can be shown by appeal to a variety of textual evidence in the classical Chinese literature that, in the most general philosophical or descriptive sense, *ming* means simply "that which emerges," "issues forth," or "happens" during the course of the ongoing life/growth process.[45] Thus, that which emerges, issues forth, or does happen during the course of this process can obviously be relative to the times (= *shiming* 時命), as well as be relative to our nature (= *xingming* 性命). It is perhaps because of this ambiguity with respect to the normative and descriptive senses of the term *ming* that Mencius refers to the notion of our "correct *ming*"—in regard to facing dangerous situations that occur and punishments that have been decreed:

> There is nothing without its *ming*—according to which, if pursued, it receives what is correct (*zheng* 正) for it. Therefore, those who understand *ming* would not stand under a dangerous wall. To realize the Way unto death is our correct *ming* (*zhengming* 正命). To die in handcuffs and leg-irons is not our correct *ming*. (7A/2)

In the case of what Mencius calls our "correct *ming*," we find that "any time is as good as any other" to understand and realize the Way. Clearly, the author of chapter 16 would agree with Mencius in this regard: "Rectify yourself, that's all!"

ON THE PHILOSOPHICAL DIFFERENCES BETWEEN MENCIUS AND THE AUTHOR OF CHAPTER 16

In pointing out the similarities between Mencius and the author of chapter 16 of the *Zhuangzi* in regard to the social and cooperative character of human nature and the Way, I do not wish to minimize their philosophical differences. Some of these differences have already been indicated above.

Perhaps the major difference between these two philosophers is that, whereas Mencius tends to favor a politically pro-active approach to the Way, the author of chapter 16 emphasizes repeatedly the notion of *wuwei*, indicating a relatively "nonactive" or "quietistic" approach. Thus, whereas Mencius emphasizes, the author decidedly rejects the pro-active way of the traditionally acclaimed sage kings. This is not to say, however, that the notion of *wuwei* or non-interference in the life process does not play a significant role in Mencius's philosophy of human nature and the Way. Indeed, it does. As indicated by Roger T. Ames, the notion of *wuwei* plays a significant role in both Confucian and Daoist philosophy.[46] However, like the author of chapter 16, Mencius supplements the notion of *wuwei* with that of knowledge or understanding (*zhi* 知) among people, that is, what I have referred to as "cooperative intelligence."

A related difference is that, whereas Mencius emphasizes deliberate cultivation of our naturally social and cooperative character, the author of chapter 16 emphasizes tranquility and wishes to restrict attempts at deliberate cultivation as destroying the original "wholeness" or "completeness" of our character. Thus, whereas Mencius tends to be prospective or forward-looking in his approach, the author tends to be retrospective or backward-looking in his approach. This is not to say that Mencius is unconcerned with the natural origin of people and things, just as it is not to say that the author is unconcerned with rectifying social and political problems. The appeal to origins is a common theme throughout classical Chinese philosophy, both for making philosophical points and for establishing the legitimacy of those points. The concern to rectify social and political problems seems to be common to Chinese philosophers in general—although, of course, there are a variety of views presented on what those problems are and how those problems should be resolved.

Lastly, whereas Mencius wishes to honor the traditional sages and their institutions, the author of chapter 16 does not. The author views the institutions of the traditional sages as a primary cause of social confusion and disorder. As such, the author tends to be critical of customary conventions and conventional learning. In this respect, the author's view is consistent with the free-wheeling spirit of the *Zhuangzi* and the unconventional or nonconventional views presented throughout the book.

Thus, we find that whereas Mencius tends to be politically optimistic, proactive, and traditional in his approach to the Way, the author tends to be politically pessimistic, skeptical, and nonconventional. For the author, it seems, the attempts to improve a corrupt social or political situation by appeal to customary conventions only tend to worsen it. Furthermore, it seems that in such situations the temptation to benefit oneself at the expense of others is too great.

In spite of these philosophical differences, it is important to bear in mind that both Mencius and the author of chapter 16 strongly emphasize "happiness" or "enjoyment (*le* 樂)" in the naturally social and cooperative character of human nature and the Way—and, thus, enjoyment in the naturally cooperative intelligence or understanding among people. Neither philosopher seems to indicate a greater overriding value. It is for this reason primarily that I have appealed to the socially oriented philosophy of John Dewey for purposes of elaboration, and for purposes of resolving the outstanding interpretive difficulties associated with chapter 16 of the *Zhuangzi*. In this regard, consider the following remarks by Dewey from *Experience and Nature*:[47]

> Human experience in the large ... has for one of its most striking features preoccupation with direct enjoyment, feasting and festivities; ornamentation, dance, song, dramatic pantomime, telling yarns and enacting stories. In comparison with intellectual and moral endeavor, this trait of experience has hardly received the attention from philosophers that it demands.

Nothing but the best, the richest and fullest experience possible, is good enough for man. The attainment of such an experience is not to be conceived as the specific problem of "reformers" but as the common purpose of men. The contribution which philosophy can make to this common aim is criticism. Criticism certainly includes a heightened consciousness of deficiencies and corruptions in the scheme and distribution of values that obtains at any period.

SUMMARY AND CONCLUSION

In this paper I have tried to show how some of the outstanding interpretive difficulties associated with chapter 16 of the *Zhuangzi* can be resolved by considering more closely the historical, political, intellectual, and textual context in which the chapter was written. In particular, I have appealed to the teachings of the Confucian philosopher Mencius, and have argued that both Mencius and the author of chapter 16 conceive human nature and the Way as fundamentally social and cooperative with respect to "virtue" or "character." Consequently, I argue, both philosophers appeal to the cooperation and "cooperative intelligence" of people as the only means or "Way" to attain lasting fulfillment in social life, and to address and resolve adequately any social and political problems that arise. For purposes of elaboration, I have appealed to the socially oriented philosophy of John Dewey.

The interpretation of chapter 16 that I have presented differs in significant respects from that of Burton Watson and A. C. Graham. To the extent that my interpretation is useful in resolving the interpretive difficulties associated with the chapter, I leave it for the reader to consider and decide. In what follows, I present a complete, annotated translation of this somewhat problematic and neglected chapter.

ZHUANGZI, CHAPTER 16: "REPAIRERS OF NATURE (*SHAN XING* 繕性)"

Those who attempt to repair their nature through conventional learning, in hopes of recovering what they were originally; those who attempt to smooth over their desires through conventional thinking, in hopes of attaining enlightenment—we may call them the blinded and benighted people.[48]

Those of old who promoted the Way employed tranquillity to cultivate understanding. They understood the life process, yet they did not employ this understanding to take action. So they may be said to have employed understanding to cultivate tranquillity.[49] When understanding and tranquillity are mutually cultivated, harmony and patterns emerge from our nature.[50] Our natural character consists in the harmony, and the Way consists in the patterns.[51] When our natural character embraces all things, we have love; and when the Way patterns all things, we have appropriate conduct. To understand appropriate conduct and to have affection for creatures is to be loyal. When there is purity and fullness within, and a return to our true emotions, we have music. When trust is expressed in face and body, and there is compliance with culture, we have ceremony. But if emphasis is placed *exclusively* on the practice of ceremony and music, then the world becomes disordered.[52] If that is the manner in which one attempts to rectify, then he draws a cloud over our natural character. Our natural character is not to be put at risk. If it is put at risk, then things will invariably lose their nature [or life].[53]

Those of old lived in the midst of teeming activity,[54] and yet with the rest of the world they attained tranquillity and tolerance. At that time the yin and yang were in harmony and at peace, ghosts and spirits worked no mischief, the four seasons attained their full measure, the myriad creatures were unharmed, and all that lived escaped an untimely death. Although men possessed understanding, they did not attempt to employ it for their own benefit. This was called the utmost in unity with others. At that time no one attempted to take action, so that things were continuously so of themselves.[55]

However, a time came when our naturally harmonious character deteriorated to the point that Suiren and Fuxi stepped forward to take charge of the world [lit., to manage everything under the sky]. As a result, there was compliance but no unity. Our natural character then further deteriorated to the point that Shennong and the Yellow Emperor stepped forward to take charge of the world. As a result, there was stability, but no longer any compliance.[56] Our natural character continued to deteriorate to the point that Yao and Shun stepped forward to take charge of the world.[57] They started the trend of reformation through government and, consequently, introduced artificiality [lit., rinsed the clean and scattered the simple], departed from the Way for the sake of goodness, and thereby endangered our natural character for the sake of conducting affairs.[58] As a result, they abandoned our nature in order to follow after their heart-minds. Although heart-minds distinguished and recognized one another, this was insufficient to settle the world, so that cultural conventions were tacked on, and information thereby accumulated.[59] Cultural conventions destroyed what is basic to us, and information swamped our heart-minds, so that for the first time people became confused and disordered. They could not return to their nature and true emotions, nor recover what they were originally.

From this we can see that the world had lost the Way and the Way had lost the world. The world and the Way had lost each other. From what source then could a man of the Way arise in the world? From what source then could the world arise in the Way? If the Way does not arise in the world and the world does not arise in the Way, then, although the sage does not retire to the mountains and forest, his natural character is obscured. It is obscured, so that he does not choose to obscure it.[60]

Thus, regarding what was of old meant by a scholar "living in obscurity," it was not that he hid and refused to show himself, nor that he kept his words to himself and refused to speak out, nor that he stowed away his understanding and refused to share it.[61] It was simply that what had emerged [or what had been decreed] at the time was greatly awry.[62] If what had emerged at the time was fortunate in that it allowed him the opportunity to perform great deeds in the world, then he would have returned to the unity without leaving a trace. If what had emerged at the time was unfortunate in that it afforded him only great hardship in the world, then he would have deepened his roots to secure what was ultimate, and attend upon that. This was called preserving one's life in the Way.

Those of old who sought to preserve their lives did not engage in disputation to ornament their understanding.[63] They did not employ their understanding to trouble the world, nor employ their understanding to trouble our natural character. Undaunted, they simply remained in their places and returned to their nature. What more could they have done? It is not inherent in the Way to engage in petty actions. It is not inherent in our natural character to make petty distinctions. Petty distinctions harm our natural character. Petty actions harm the Way. Therefore, it is said, "Rectify yourself, that's all!"[64] To be happy in completeness is what it means to achieve one's ambition.[65] When those of old spoke of achieving their ambition, it was not a matter of having the caps and carriages of high office. They meant simply that nothing could be added to their happiness.[66] But nowadays what is meant by achieving one's ambition is a matter of having caps and carriages. That caps and carriages happen to belong to one's person is not a result of what emerges from our nature. A thing that arrives by chance is a lodger with us, and we who give it lodging can neither prevent it from coming nor stop it from departing. The men of old did not for the sake of caps and carriages pursue their ambition, and did not because of poverty and need try to conform to convention. It was simply that they were as happy in one condition as in the other—and, therefore, they had no worries. Nowadays when our lodgers depart we are unhappy, from which it can be seen that we tend to ruin the happiness we have. Therefore, it is said, "Those who abandon themselves in things and lose their nature in convention may be called the wrong-way-around people."

NOTES

1. Watson 1968, p. 172n2. Brackets mine. Line numbers refer to those in the *Harvard-Yenching Sinological Index*. Cf. chapter 38 of the *Laozi* or *Dao De Jing*. According to this chapter, the Confucian virtues and concerns mark a departure from the Way (*dao* 道).
2. Watson 1968, p. 174n5.
3. Graham 1989a, p. 28.
4. Here it is especially important to consider the "hundred schools" of philosophy that emerged during the Warring States period (463–222 B.C.E.) of classical China, and the "syncretic" intellectual attitude that was necessary to establish and maintain social reunification and harmony. For discussion on

the historical, political, and intellectual context of Confucianism and Daoism, see, for example, Roger T. Ames (1983). Ames's discussion of *wuwei* ("non-action" or "non-interference") as a political policy in these traditions is particularly relevant.

In regard to the textual context of the *Zhuangzi* itself, I submit that chapter 16 should be read at least in light of the other Outer Chapters, particularly those that A. C. Graham describes as "Syncretist"—that is, chapters 13 ("The Way of Heaven") and 15 ("Finicky Notions"). As indicated by Graham (1986, p. 319), the contemporary Chinese scholar Kuan Feng groups chapters 15 and 16 together in the traditional manner. Graham disagrees with Kuan Feng in this regard. However, the interpretation I shall present tends to agree with the traditional grouping of the chapters presented by Kuan Feng.

It seems that Graham's method of grouping the chapters is based largely on grammatical considerations for the purpose of determining specific authors and, thus, tends to ignore some rather important considerations of relative content. According to Graham, chapters 15 and 16 of the *Zhuangzi* constitute "single essays." But Graham describes the former as "Syncretist," and the latter as "Primitivist in tone" (1986, p. 319) and (grammatically?) "unrelated to anything elsewhere in the book" (1989a, p. 28). Nevertheless, Graham points out that, like all homogeneous blocks of text, both essays/chapters "must be presented complete" (1989a, p. 31).

5. That the chapter resonates with the teachings of Mencius should not be surprising. As indicated by Arthur Waley (*The Way and Its Power*, p. 49), "The branch of Confucianism founded by Mencius was profoundly influenced by the [Chi]-country [D]aoism," which focused on achieving a quiet heart-mind (*xin*), tending of the vital spirit (*shen*), as well as promoting natural harmony (*he*). "In this there is nothing surprising, for Mencius spent much of his life in the country of [Chi]."

Note that the chapter also bears resemblance in both content and style with the opening passages of the Confucian classics, *Great Learning* (*Da Xue* 大學) and the *Doctrine of the Mean* (*Zhong Yong* 中庸), which were originally chapters in the *Book of Ceremony* (*Li Ji* 禮記). These passages emphasize the naturally social and cooperative character of people and things—in addition to exemplary conduct on the part of particular persons.

6. See *Xunzi*, "Our Nature Is Bad [*Xing E* 性惡]". "Artifice" is A. C. Graham's translation of "*wei* 偽." As Chung-ying Cheng has indicated to me in conversation, *wei* 偽 literally means that which is the result of "human making" or "action" (*wei* 為). For discussion of Xunzi's criticism of Zhuangzi, see Fung Yu-lan 1952, p. 279f.

7. See, for example, Dewey's *Human Nature and Conduct: An Introduction to Social Psychology* (1922), *Experience and Nature* (1925), *The Quest for Certainty: A Study of the Relation between Knowledge and Action* (1929), and

Philosophy and Civilization (1931). In the latter work, pp. 79–80, Dewey proposes "the social" as the all-inclusive philosophic category:

> There are at the present time a considerable number of persons who habitually employ the social as a principle of philosophic reflection.... There are others, probably a greater number, who decline to take "social" seriously as a category of description and interpretation for purposes of philosophy, and who conceive any attempt so to take it as involving a confusion of anthropology and sociology with metaphysics. The most they would concede is that cultural material may throw light on the genesis and history of human beliefs.... Denial of opposition between the social and natural is, however, an important element of the *meaning* of "social" as a category.... A denial of the separation is not only possible to a sane mind, but is demanded by any methodological adoption of the principle of continuity.... Upon the hypothesis of continuity—if that is to be termed a hypothesis which cannot be denied without self-contradiction—the social ... furnishes philosophically the inclusive category.

The general philosophical point made by Dewey is that the category of social phenomena is *continuous with*, but *irreducible to*, other categories of natural phenomena—for example, phenomena that are predominately mechanical or mechanistic in character. A related point made by Dewey is that people and things exist (= act-react, interact or "transact") only *relative* to one another—and not as absolute individuals or things-in-themselves.

8. Campbell 1995, pp. ix–x.
9. "Appropriate conduct" or "a sense of appropriate conduct" is Roger Ames's translation of "*yi* 義."
10. "Pattern" or "patterns" is A. C. Graham's translation of "*li* 理."
11. Unless explicitly indicated otherwise, all translations are my own. Note that, as indicated by both Watson and Graham, the last line of this passage involves textual corruption.

    Note also the striking resemblance of this passage with the last section of chapter 11, the title of which is translated by Watson as "Let it Be, Leave It Alone." As indicated by Watson (1968, p. 124n17) , the last section of that chapter, "with its recognition of the necessity for benevolence, righteousness, law, ritual, etc., seems to clash violently with what has gone before. Some commentators interpret it as a description of the kind of compromise even the perfect [Daoist] ruler must make if he is to rule effectively. Others regard it as an interpolation or a passage misplaced from some other section. See the similar passage on p. 79."
12. See Graham's "The Background to the Mencian Theory of Human Nature," in Graham 1986.

13. Graham 1989a, p. 171. Compare with Mencius's remarks in regard to Gaozi on "achieving a quiet heart-mind," *Mencius* 2A2.

14. As indicated above, Graham does not acknowledge the syncretic character of chapter 16, although he explicitly does so in regard to chapters 13 and 15.

15. In contrast to Mencius, Xunzi argues that people are by nature selfish and disgusting (*e* 惡), so that it necessary to "transform" our nature by way of *ren, yi,* and *li.* See *Xunzi,* "Our Nature is Bad (*Xing E*)."

16. See Graham 1989a, p. 7. See also Waley, *The Way and Its Power* (n.d.).

17. This philosophical criticism is reflected in the contemporary communitarian critique of classical liberalism, in regard to the latter's emphasis on *individualism* and *individual* liberty or freedom. See, for example, Michael Walzer's "The Communitarian Critique of Liberalism" in David Theo Goldberg, ed. (1995), pp. 198–211, originally given as the John Dewey Lecture at Harvard Law School in September 1989, also found in *Political Theory* 18.1 (Feb. 1990): 6–23. Note that Walzer's communitarian critique in no way denies what is of obvious value in classical liberal theory—namely, individual liberty or freedom. Walzer's point is simply that classical liberals tend to forget that people are by nature *social creatures* who gain identity as people only in the context of a social environment or tradition. Accordingly, social obligations as well as individual liberties should obtain. This point is also made in Alasdair MacIntyre's *After Virtue* (1984). In regard to Aristotle's virtue-based ethical theory, MacIntyre redefines "virtue" to include a personal narrative set against the background of a social tradition.

    With respect to classical Confucian philosophy, Herbert Fingarette puts forth his own communitarian critique of liberalism in his general introduction to Mary I. Bockover, ed. (1991). There Fingarette focuses on the tension between *individual rights* and *social obligations.*

18. See Graham's discussion (1986) on the interchangeability of the terms "*xing* 性" (nature) and "*sheng* 生" (the life process) in "The Background to the Mencian Theory of Human Nature."

19. "Exemplary person" is Roger Ames's translation of "*junzi* 君子*.*"

20. "Integrity" is A. C. Graham's (1986, p. 55) translation of "*cheng,*" also commonly translated as "sincerity." As indicated by Graham,

    > Each thing has its nature, and 'becomes complete' (成 *ch'eng* [*cheng*]) by fulfilling the capacities of its nature. In man this state of maturity, by which we act wholeheartedly according to our nature and become in the full sense men, is 誠 *ch'eng* [*cheng*]) … "wholeness, integrity," defined in the *Chung Yung* [*Zhong Yong*] by "Integrity is self-completion."

    It should perhaps be added that, for Mencius, people achieve wholeness or integrity only in the context of others, and only by treating themselves and others appropriately (*yi*).

21. Note that "putting yourself in the other person's place" is Roger Ames's interpretive translation of "*shu* 恕."
22. Note that "*shan* 善" is commonly translated as "good."
23. Graham 1989a, p. 171.
24. Note that chapter 15 discusses five types of scholars (*shi*), which, as indicated by Graham (1986, p. 319), include:

    1. Moralists who disapprove of the regime
    2. Moralists who prefer teaching and self-improvement
    3. Politicians concerned only with personal ambition and organizational issues
    4. Hermits who sit fishing by the river (Zhuangzi himself would be a good example)
    5. Cultivators of longevity

    In regard to these five types of scholars, Graham indicates, "Only one of the types criticized does take office; public life is if anything even more important for the Syncretist than for a Confucian, who can at least withdraw from it on moral grounds." Elsewhere Graham (1989a, p. 264) indicates, "After declaring that all five can fulfil their aims by following the comprehensive Way of Heaven and Earth, the writer proceeds to an exposition, much of it in the same words as in [chapter 13] 'The Way of Heaven'." Here I would argue that both chapters 15 and 16 should be read in light of chapter 13, "The Way of Heaven."

25. Graham 1989a, p. 172.
26. Ibid., pp. 173–75.
27. Ibid., p. 28.
28. Ibid., pp. 170–71.
29. See Graham 1986, pp. 9–17, 55.
30. Compare with chapter 11.
31. "Take charge of the world" is Watson's (1968) translation of "*wei tianxia.*"
32. See, for example, *Analects* 6.30; and *Mencius* 2A1, 7B38.
33. Note that deference to others is a common underlying theme in the writings of Roger T. Ames and David L. Hall on classical Chinese philosophy. See Hall and Ames 1987 and 1995.
34. For discussion on discarding the concept of good (*shan*), see chapter 10 (Watson 1968, p. 113).
35. Skaja diss., (Ph.D. University of Hawaii, 1992), pp. 22 and 108.
36. Graham 1986, p. 57.
37. Graham 1986, p. 58.
38. Chapter 10 of Dewey's *The Quest for Certainty* (1929), p. 260.
39. See note 5 above.
40. Here it important to bear in mind that *liangneng* and *liangzhi* also carry the connotation of excellence. Thus, *liangneng* can be construed as the natural or

instinctive ability to excel in the Way; and *liangchih* can be construed as the natural or instinctive ability to excel in understanding or realizing the Way (in practice).

41. Watson 1968, p. 173n4.

42. Watson 1968, p. 173n4.

43. See Hall and Ames 1987, chapter 5, for discussion on the notion of *ming* 命.

44. Note that, depending on context, "*tian* 天" can be translated as "Heaven" or "Nature."

45. Thus, for example, *tianming* 天命 is that which emerges or issues forth from *tian* (the heavens, sky, or Nature as the process of life/growth)—which, as indicated in the first line of the *Zhong Yong*, is our nature or *xing*: "*Tianming zhi wei xing*" 天命之謂性. Accordingly, *xingming* 性命 is that which emerges or issues forth from our nature or *xing*. Note that a number of passages in the Outer Chapters of the *Zhuangzi* involve the notion of *xingming*. In line with this general interpretation of *ming*, the author of chapter 16 indicates that harmony and patterns of activity "emerge from our nature (*qu qi xing* 出其性)."

46. See Ames 1983, chapter 1.

47. Dewey, *Experience and Nature*, pp. 78, 412.

48. Note that both Watson and Graham translate *suxue* 俗學 as "vulgar learning," and *susi* 俗思 as "vulgar thinking." It is difficult to determine precisely the subjects of the author's criticism. As indicated by Watson 1968, p. 171n1, "The writer is attacking the Confucian and Mo-ist ideals of moral training, and those schools of thought that advocated the lessening or elimination of desire."

 However, it is clear that, like the author, the Confucian Mencius was not concerned with "repairing our nature." On the other hand, as I have indicated, the Confucian Xunzi advocated in "Our Nature Is Bad" that the nature of people needs to be "transformed" or "repaired" by those versed in the Way. Note that, in the *Zhuangzi*, discussions of our nature (*xing*) begin only with chapter 8.

 Here I would argue that the author is, in general, critical of those who are compelled to "take action (*wei*)." All such attempts violate the doctrine of *wuwei*, or "non-interference" in the life/growth process (*sheng*) that constitutes our nature (*xing*). The reference to "vulgar" or "conventional" learning and thinking seems to indicate that this chapter was presented as a scholarly plea intended to influence the various rulers of state in adopting a political policy of *wuwei*. Cf. chapter 11, "Let It Be, Leave It Alone" (Watson's translation).

49. Here the author's dual emphasis on attaining understanding and tranquillity indicates clearly the philosophy of *wuwei*. Cf. chapter 13, "The Way of Heaven," on the tranquillity and understanding of the sage. Cf. also Mencius's remarks (2A2) on the way of "attaining a quiet heart-mind."

50. See the above discussion on the notion of *ming*.

51. I have translated "*de* 德" as "our natural character," which the author indicates is one of social and cooperative harmony. Note that the reference to *de* (virtue or character) is made before the reference to *dao* (the Way), which is consistent with the ordering of these notions in the *Mawangdui* version of the *Laozi*.

    Cf. chapters 5 and 9 on the notion of complete character (*quan de* 全德), and chapter 11 on the notion of great character (*da de* 大德).

52. Contrast with *Xunzi*, chapters 19 and 20, "On Ceremony" and "On Music."

53. This is the problematic passage indicated by Watson (1968, p. 172n2), discussed above. As indicated by both Watson and Graham, line 4 is corrupt.

    Note that the author is not critical of ceremony (*li*) and music (*yue*) as such, since these are an expression of our naturally social and cooperative character. Rather, he criticizes attempts to rectify *exclusively* by means of ceremony and music. As indicated by the author, such attempts fail to do justice to what is *basic* to the practice of ceremony and music—namely, our naturally social and cooperative character, and the Way. Cf. the last section in chapter 12, which endorses the practice of love, appropriate conduct, and ceremony in respect to our natural character and the Way.

54. Note that Watson translates *hun mang* 混芒 as "crudity and chaos," whereas Graham translates it as "the merged and featureless."

55. This passage indicates clearly the naturally social and operative character of people and things inherent in the life process.

56. For critical discussion of the legendary Yellow Emperor's attempt to "govern the world," see chapter 11 (Watson 1968, pp. 118–19). Note that the Yellow Emperor, like the legendary Laozi, is commonly considered to be a Daoist hero, as indicated by the conjunctive term "Huang Lao."

57. As indicated by Watson (1968, p. 172n3), "All these figures are mythical rulers or culture heroes".

58. For a contrasting account of Yao and Shun on rulership, and the deterioration of our natural character, see chapter 12 (Watson 1968, p. 131). There the subject of attack seems to be the Legalists (*fajia* 法家), who advocated rulership strictly by means of rewards and punishments.

59. Note that "*wen* 文" is usually translated as "culture." However, in light of the previous remarks by the author, I have translated the term as "cultural conventions." Note that the author is not critical of culture as such, that is, in the Deweyian sense of community. Here the author seems to be referring to the cultural conventions instituted by the various legendary rulers indicated above.

60. Here the author's point seems to be that the natural character of the sage has been obscured by the people of the world having lost the Way as the result of tyrannical rulers—and *not* that the sage retires to the mountains and forests as a hermit. Indeed, the lines that follow seem to indicate explicitly that a scholar or sage is not a hermit, which is consistent with my basic argument in regard to interpreting this chapter. Cf. *Mencius* 7A9.

61. Cf. the five types of scholars discussed in chapter 15.
62. See the above discussion on the notion of *shiming*.
63. This seems clearly a derogatory reference to the Mo-ists—and to the rhetoricians or so-called "logicians" (*mingjia* 名家) such as Hui Shi, who dispute about the meaning of "hard" and "white."
64. The author's advice, it would seem, is simply that one should accord with our nature, natural character, and the Way.
65. Cf. chapter 5, "Signs of Character Complete." Also, see chapter 12 for further discussion on the completeness of our natural character. There Confucius's student Zigong is made to say:

> Those who grasp the Way are complete in character; being complete in character, they are complete in body; being complete in body, they are complete in spirit; and to be complete in spirit is the way of the sage. Such a person is content to live among people and walk by their side, never knowing where it will lead.... The praise and blame of the world are no loss or gain to him. He may be called a man of complete character. (cf. Watson's 1968 translation, pp. 135–36)

66. Cf. chapter 13 on "Heavenly Joy," "Great Peace" in government, and the "Great Way." Cf. also Mencius's emphasis on delighting in the Way (7A8).

REFERENCES

Ames, Roger T. 1983. *The Art of Rulership: A Study in Ancient Chinese Political Thought.* Honolulu: University of Hawaii Press.

Bockover, Mary I. ed. 1991. *Rules, Rituals, and Responsibility.* La Salle, Ill.: Open Court.

Callicott, J. Baird, and Roger T. Ames, eds. 1989. *Nature in Asian Traditions of Thought: Essays in Environmental Philosophy.* Albany: State University of New York Press.

Campbell, James. 1995. *Understanding John Dewey: Nature and Cooperative Intelligence.* Chicago: Open Court.

Chan, W. T. 1963. *A Source Book in Chinese Philosophy.* Princeton, N.J.: Princeton University Press.

Dewey, John. 1922. *Human Nature and Conduct: An Introduction to Social Psychology.* New York: Henry Holt.

———. 1939a. *Freedom and Culture.* New York: G. P. Putnam.

———. 1939b. *Intelligence in the Modern World: John Dewey's Philosophy.* Edited with introduction by Joseph Ratner. New York: Random House.

———. 1946. *Problems of Men.* New York: Philosophical Library.

———. 1958 [1925]. *Experience and Nature,* 2nd ed., revised. New York: Dover Publications, 1958 (first published in 1929).

————. 1963 [1931]. *Philosophy and Civilization.* New York: Capricorn Books.

Duyvendak, J. L. 1947. "The Philosophy of Wu Wei." *Études Asiatiques* 3/4 (1947).

Fung Yu-lan. 1952. *A History of Chinese Philosophy,* trans. Derk Bodde. 2 vols. Princeton, N.J.: Princeton University Press.

Goldberg, David Theo. 1995. *Ethical Theory and Social Issues: Historical Texts and Contemporary Readings,* 2nd ed. Ft. Worth, Texas: Harcourt Brace.

Graham, A. C. 1986. *Studies in Chinese Philosophy and Philosophical Literature.* Singapore: Institute of East Asian Philosophies.

————. 1989a. *Chuang-Tzu: The Inner Chapters.* London: Unwin, rpt.

————. 1989b. *Disputers of the Tao.* La Salle, Ill.: Open Court.

Hall, David L., and Roger T. Ames. *Thinking Through Confucius.* 1987. Albany: State University of New York Press.

————. 1995. *Anticipating China: Thinking Through the Narratives of Chinese and Western Culture.* Albany: State University of New York Press.

Ivanhoe, Philip J. 1990. *Ethics in the Confucian Tradition: The Thought of Mencius and Wang Yang-ming.* Atlanta, Ga.: Scholars Press.

Knoblock, John. 1988, 1990, 1994 *Xunzi: A Translation and Study of the Complete Works.* 3 volumes. Stanford; Stanford University Press.

Lau, D. C. 1963. *Lao Tzu: Tao Te Ching.* Harmondsworth, U.K.: Penguin.

————. 1976. *Mencius.* Middlesex, U.K.: Penguin, rpt.

————. 1982. *Confucius: The Analects.* Middlesex, U.K.: Penguin, rpt.

MacIntyre, Alasdair. 1984. *After Virtue: A Study in Moral Theory,* 2nd ed. Note Dame, Fnd.: University of Notre Dame Press.

Mair, Victor H., ed. 1983. *Experimental Essays on Chuang-tzu.* Honolulu: University of Hawaii Press.

Rosemont, Henry, Jr., ed. 1991. *Chinese Texts and Philosophical Contexts: Essays Dedicated to Angus C. Graham.* La Salle, Il.: Open Court.

Schwartz, Benjamin I. 1985. *The World of Thought in Ancient China.* Cambridge, Mass.: Harvard University Press.

Skaja, Henry. 1992. "Getting Clear on Confucius: Pragmatic Naturalism as a Means of Philosophical Interpretation." Ph.D. diss., University of Hawaii.

Waley, Arthur. 1964 [1938]. *The Analects of Confucius.* London: George Allen & Unwin.

————. n.d. *The Way and Its Power.* New York: Grove Press.

Watson, Burton, trans. 1963. *Hsün Tzu: Basic Writings.* New York: Columbia University Press.

————. 1968. *The Complete Works of Chuang Tzu.* New York: Columbia University Press.

5

Living Beyond the Bounds

Henry Miller and the Quest for Daoist Realization

RANDALL P. PEERENBOOM

One of the central themes of Zhuangzi is self-realization. His world is populated with extraordinary individuals who find the way, and having found the way, ascend to heaven in broad daylight, enter water without getting wet, walk on fire without getting burnt; trusting to the great *dao* 道, they throw off the shackles of conventional morality and live freely, beyond the cares of the everyday world, even death, as in the following tale of Master Sanghu, Mengzi Fan, and Master Qin Chang. One day the three were having a conversation about who could climb up to heaven and wander in the mists, roam the infinite, and forget life once and for all. Finding no disagreement among them, the three became fast friends. The story continues:

> After some time had passed without event, Master Sanghu died. He had not yet been buried when Confucius, hearing of his death, sent Zigong to assist at the funeral. When Zigong arrived, he found one of the dead man's friends weaving frames for silkworms while the other strummed a lute. Joining their voices, they sang in unison:
>
> > Ah, Sanghu,
> > Ah Sanghu,
> > You have gone back to your true form,
> > While we go on being human, O!
>
> Zigong hastened forward and said, "May I be so bold as to ask whether it is in accordance with the rites to sing with the corpse right in front at your feet?"

125

The two men looked at each other and laughed. "What does this man know about the meaning of the rites?"

Zigong returned and reported to Confucius what had happened. "What sort of men are they anyway?" he asked. "Decencies of conduct are nothing to them, they disregard their personal appearance, and sing in the presence of a corpse without the slightest change of expression on their faces!"

"Such men as they," said Confucius, "wander beyond the bounds. As for me, I wander within them. Beyond and within are worlds apart. It was stupid of me to send you to offer condolences. They are at the stage of being fellow men with the maker of things, and go wandering in the single breath of heaven and earth. They look upon life as a swelling tumor, a protruding wen, and upon death as the draining of a sore or bursting of a boil. To men such as these, how could there be any question of putting life first and death last? They borrow the forms of different creatures and house them in the same body. They forget liver and gall, cast aside ears and eyes, turning and revolving, ending and beginning again, unaware of where they start or finish. Idly they roam beyond the dust and dirt; they wander free and easy in the service of inaction. Why should they fret and fuss about the rites of the vulgar world or give a hoot for the eyes and ears of the common herd."

Zigong said, "Well then, Master, why do you stay within the bounds?"

"Alas, I am one of those men condemned by Heaven.[1]

The realized ones in whom the power (*de* 德) is complete[2] live beyond the bounds, unencumbered by the usual social constraints that keep most shackled to their dreary jobs, stuck in unhappy marriages, slaves to the moral commandments drummed into all schoolchildren as part of their daily educational diets along with the names of civil war generals, the esoterica of irrational numbers and square roots, the abbreviations of iron and oxide, and all the rest of the vast wealth of trivia deemed necessary to be a productive member of society by the likes of Bill Bennet and his fellow pundits. But not everyone has what it takes to live beyond the bounds. Some, like Confucius, duly imbued with a firm sense of social responsibility and above all the seriousness of life—or, as Zhuangzi puts it, tattooed by *ren* 仁 (benevolence) and *yi* 義 (moral righteousness), their nose cut off by right and wrong—are destined, or sentenced, as the case may be, to be pillars of society, the great bulk of humanity whose primary function is to ensure that the trains run on time and everyone's toaster works in the morning.[3]

Zhuangzi is far from alone in depicting the battle between individual self-realization and the conforming pressure of socialization as the great epic of life.

The idea that society corrupts, that we must break through the bondage of social convention to our true self, to a life of personal freedom, is an eternal and ever popular theme, linking the struggle of the Nietzschean superman in overcoming the slave mentality of the herding masses to the Romantic search for truth and authenticity in subjective experience and the immediacy of felt emotions to Thoreau's attempt to escape the damning and distorting life in modern societies by retreating to the freedom of Walden Pond to, ultimately, the metaphysically tinged, sex-filled ravings of Henry Miller.

The struggle for freedom and the need to resist the hobbling pressures of conventional mores and life-patterns if one is to be free and uniquely oneself is the central theme of Henry Miller's life and, since Miller sought to turn his life into art by writing autobiographical novels starring Henry Miller in the lead role, the subject of his writings as well. Miller firmly believes that because we come into this world filled with curiosity and nonjudgmental awe for even the mundane, free from the concerns that dominate the socially indoctrinated adult, adulthood represents a descent from childhood. While in some ways we are more restricted as children,

> this thoroughly restricted life of early boyhood seems like a limitless universe and the life which followed it, the life of the adult, a constantly diminishing realm. From the moment one is put in school one is lost; one has the feeling of a having a halter put around one's neck. The taste goes out of the bread as it goes out of life. Getting the bread becomes more important than the eating of it. Everything is calculated and everything has a price upon it.[4]

Trapped by materialism and social mores that emphasize the need for security, a job, marriage, family, adulthood is enslavement; innocence is lost, as is curiosity, joy—life loses flavor. The challenge then is to find a way to maintain the innocent curiosity and wonder of the child, to avoid the entrapment of materialism, the quest for power and fame, and the burdensome nature of social obligations. The challenge, in Zhuangzi's terms, is self-realization, to be one of the singular persons who live beyond the bounds of the everyday humdrum, content in one's own being, without the need for the affirmation of others.

Interestingly, Miller was not only familiar with Nietzsche, Thoureau, and the Romantics but with Laozi and Zhuangzi. He claims to have read the *Daodejing* as a teenager, and counted it as one of the hundred most influential books in his life.[5] He was fascinated with Daoist ideas and ideals, in particular, the notion of freedom, of free and easy wandering, and the self-realization that comes through acceptance of all aspects of life; the relativity and interdependence of value terms such as good and bad, pretty and ugly; the open embracing of inconsistency and contradiction; the lack of dogma and rejection of rule ethics; the disdain for social conventions; the *wuwei*-like faith in the underlying harmony of the universe and that all will work out if one simply follows one's natural inclinations combined with the anarchistic belief that people can govern themselves without need for political or moral authority. So captivated was he by Daoism that he took to calling himself the Happy Rock, evoking images of the Uncarved Block and the Great Clod.[6] Later in life, he seemed to delight in playing the enlightened guru to the many spiritual seekers, children of the '60s, who made the pilgrimage to Miller's Big Sur hermit retreat to pay homage to the Daoist sage depicted in the great autobiographical works *Tropic of Cancer*, *Tropic of Capricorn*, and *The Rosy Crucifixion*.

While some of Miller's biographers and critics have taken issue with Miller's cultivated image as a Daoist sage, Miller did lead, by all accounts, a singular life.[7] He grew up in New York, an intelligent boy with a talent for music. After high school, he enrolled in college, but dropped out after just two months, taking up with a woman old enough to be his mother, and embarking on the first in a long series of jobs, none held for very long, between which were interspersed extended periods of unemployment. At twenty-six, he split with the older woman to marry Beatrice Wickens, with whom he had a daughter. The cycle of endless short-term jobs followed by unemployment continued, until at twenty-nine, having falsified his resumé by claiming a Ph.D. from Columbia, he applied for a job as a messenger. Finding himself rejected for even that lowly job notwithstanding the bogus Ph.D., Miller demanded a meeting with the president of the company. He finally managed to get the ear of the general manager and, being a gifted talker, persuaded the general manager to give him a job. Indeed, the general manager was so impressed with Miller that he promised him the position of employment manager after a brief stint as messenger. Miller wore a tie to work every day, supported his wife and child in relative comfort, and was deeply unhappy with every aspect of his life. Quickly tiring of his wife, whom he found dull and sexually repressed, and feeling himself not suited to be a father, he spent hours wandering the streets of New York sponging money off his friends for meals and trips to the dance halls. During this time, he had numerous affairs with a variety of women, from dance hall girls to job applicants to the wives and lovers of his best friends.

During one of his trips to a dance hall, Miller met June, aka Mona, a deeply mysterious and singular person in her own right. Miller soon divorced Beatrice, married June, walked out on his job without collecting his severance pay, and began the life of torment and anguish so vividly portrayed in *The Rosy Crucifixion*. For the next several years, Henry and June lived a hand-to-mouth existence, depending primarily on the ability of June to extract money from male admirers, her "victims," as she and Henry referred to them, although for a time they did try to sell some of Henry's short stories in the Village cafés and even tried their hand, none too successfully, at running a speakeasy. At about this time, June began what appears to have been a lesbian relationship with Mara Andrews, aka Stasia. Soon, the three of them were sharing one tiny apartment.

Eventually, Miller made it to Paris, where, approaching forty, he began to write in earnest while assuming his place in the Paris bohemian expatriate scene. Despite living hand to mouth, often sleeping on park benches, and touching up friends for food and a place to stay, he somehow managed to write *Tropic of Cancer* and *Tropic of Capricorn*, among other works. With his marriage to June on the rocks, he also began an affair with Anais Nin, who showed an interest in both Henry and June, resulting in another emotionally complicated love triangle.

As World War II approached, Miller abandoned Paris, returning to the United States via Greece, where he stayed with Lawrence Durell. After touring around America for a year (captured in *The Air-Conditioned Nightmare*), he settled in California, eventually ending up in an isolated house in Big Sur overlooking the sea, where he married his third wife, Lepska, with whom he had two more children. Miller's marriages never seemed to last more than seven years, and this one was no exception. After divorcing Lepska, Miller married Eve, and once that relationship ended, he married, in his seventies, a young Japanese woman who was primarily interested in obtaining a green card. Much to Henry's chagrin, the relationship was never consummated, finally ending, like all previous marriages, in divorce.

During his early years back in the States, when Miller was in his fifties and sixties, Miller's books were banned in the United States. As a result, he was relatively unknown in his own country and, cut off from his royalties abroad that could not be repatriated, relatively hardpressed financially.[8] Miller quickly became a hero to the liberal establishment that championed the cause of free speech. He also became a cult hero to those seeking sexual liberation, to struggling writers in need of role model, and a sage guru to those searching for the key to the mystery of life, who saw in Miller the free and easy wandering Daoist sage of the *Laozi* and *Zhuangzi*.

ART AS LIFE, LIFE AS ART: THE *DAO* OF WRITING

Miller saw writing and life in terms of the Romantic project of self-discovery, self-creation, and ultimately self-liberation. As an artist, Miller had to strip away the layers of social convention to discover his authentic self and unique voice. The years spent as a struggling artist, sleeping on benches, wandering the streets, provided Miller the opportunity to experience first hand and intimately a wide range of humanity. These encounters proved invaluable, but not only as subject matter in themselves, a seemingly endless source of entertaining stories of intriguing characters. They also served as a mirror, allowing Miller to gain a better view of himself through examining his experiences with others. The ultimate subject of all of Miller's work is Miller himself, or perhaps life itself, as experienced by Miller. As a result, everything and everybody in his life is seen through the prism of

Miller's self-directed, quasi-psychoanalytic, quasi-metaphysical scrutiny. All become grist for the mill of self-discovery.[9]

When art becomes life, self-discovery is not the ending point but merely the first step, to be followed by self-creation and ultimately self-realization and liberation.[10] Having discovered one's true self, the artist seeks to reveal and give expression to one's self and one's world through art, and in the process to recreate them. But whereas most writers reveal themselves indirectly through their art, Miller took himself as subject. In writing "autonovels," Miller engaged in the ultimate act of recreation. He recreated his world with himself as protagonist, turning his life into myth, a book, and himself into a character in a never-ending story, thus blurring the line between truth and fiction. But then Miller always had a tenuous grasp of the distinction between truth and fiction. From an early age, Miller felt particularly keenly that books were more real than life itself: "I used to think then that all the tragic events of life were written down in books and that what went on outside was just diluted crap."[11]

Art for Miller serves as a vehicle for transcendence and self-realization in that in the process of creating one's self, of turning one's life into myth, the artist seeks to transcend the boundaries of everyday life, of traditional morality, eventually bursting forth in a new realm of freedom where conventional rules no longer apply:

> [F]or the artists there is nothing but the present, the eternal here and now, the expanding infinite moment which is flame and song.... Obedient to every urge—without distinction of morality, ethics, law, customs, etc. He opens himself to all influences—everything is gravy to him.[12]

Writing allowed Miller to take the experiences of life and transmute them into art, and then to transmute art into a new life. Somewhat paradoxically, the key to the recreated life is acceptance—having struggled down the path, one discovers that there is nowhere to go, that one had everything one needed all along but just didn't realize it. Like Laozi and Zhuangzi, Miller repeatedly encourages one to abandon the socially overdetermined categories of good and bad, beautiful and ugly, worthy and unworthy, and embrace life in its many manifestations to the fullest. Along the way, we must learn to accept rather than fight against our subconscious urges and desires because repression results in calamity: "Every aspect or aspect of life is necessary and inevitable, and capable of conversion at different levels. But it is not possible to eliminate, which is the hobby of moralists. One may succeed in repressing, but the results, as we know, are disastrous. To live out one's own desires and, in doing so to subtly alter the quality of desire, is, it seems to me, the great purpose of living."[13]

Ultimately, through the process of self-discovery, self-creation, and self-realization, art and life merge: "when my writing becomes absolutely truthful there will be no discrepancy between the man and writer, between what I am and what I do or say. This, I say without hesitation, is the highest goal a man can set himself; it is the goal of all religious teachers."[14] When art and life merge, one experiences harmony, an organic unity to the cosmos, ecstasy, and peace: "the men who are thoroughly wide-awake and completely alive are in reality, and for these reality has always been close to ecstasy, partaking of a life of fulfillment which knows no bounds. Of them only may it be said that they live in the present. Through them it is permitted us to grasp the meaning of timelessness, of eternity which is victory."[15] But once art and life merge, there is no longer a need for art as a vehicle to life: "Art is only a means to life, to the life more abundant. It is not in itself more abundant. It merely points the way."[16] From then on, in Zen-like fashion, life itself becomes art.

THE *DAO* OF SEX

Miller's writings are often dismissed as pornography—repetitive, boring, infantile. There is no denying that Miller's writings are drenched in sex. But the role of sex must be understood in terms of the goal of self-liberation and the need to transcend personal and social limitations. Sex plays the same symbolic and substantive role for Miller as death and funerals for Zhuangzi (or god and morality for Nietzsche, or the nature-society conflict for Thoureau). Funerals, for Zhuangzi, were the epitome of the kind of artificial social and moral conventions that prevent the individual from living freely, from accepting life—and death—as it is. Funeral ceremonies were the centerpiece of the Confucian system of *li* 禮—the elaborately prescribed network of rituals or proprieties that set the rules for human interactions. They were heavily scripted events, with all details choreographed from the clothes one wore to the manner and duration of wailing to the period for mourning (three years for the death of a parent). Little surprise then that Zhuangzi chose a funeral scene and the different reactions to it by Confucius and his Daoist counterparts to illustrate the chasm between those who live within the bounds and those who live beyond.

Miller's America was very puritanical and inhibited, particularly with regard to public descriptions of sex. Today, when one can pick up a copy of *Hustler* or the five-star video Anal Delinquents at the corner liquor store or dial 900-oral-sex to indulge in aural fantasy twenty-four hours a day, Miller's books have lost much of their ability to shock. But at the time, when *Lady Chatterly's Lover* was banned as pornographic, they were explosive. And they were intended to be. Sex was the great taboo. Miller used sex to challenge social conventions and thus to liberate:

> In the world of hero-Miller any act associated with the free and uninhibited release of sexual feeling is not only permissible, it is admirable. He concentrates on the most uninhibited activities, activities which the

ordinary man of middle-class American culture would be likely to find most reprehensible (that is, about which he would be most fearful), activities of a kind or under circumstances which he is most unwilling to admit to himself that he desires. What is most censorable, then, is what is most desirable and vice versa. Miller picks unerringly what in the American culture has been least acceptable. In the Victorian world it has always been considered normal (to the extent that sex was considered at all) to have intercourse in only one position, in a bed with the man on top. Miller is careful to describe every other position and every other location. Most frequently the woman jumps onto his lap in a straddling position. Such a position de-emphasizes the traditional active-passive relationship and makes both partners active. He varies the locale for sex, takes it outdoors and indoors, in public and private places. He breaks the rule of privacy by having more than one couple present, or having several women, or several men and one woman. He varies sexual practices widely, and goes far outside professed norms of his culture, especially lower class culture. Mouth-genital contacts even to emission are quite the rule in any prolonged contact with a woman.... Many complex and even athletic positions are used. In one scene in *Sexus*, Miller and two women seem to re-enact most of the basic positions of Hindu mythology.[17]

Raised by Puritanical parents, Miller was aware that he too was a product of his age.[18] Part of the process of self-discovery and self-liberation was overcoming his own inhibitions. As an artist and as a person, he needed the courage to strip himself naked, to expose himself, even when doing so showed him in a less than positive light. Indeed, almost masochistically, Miller seemed to feel the need to flaunt his least attractive side, those aspects most likely to not only shock but repulse. Many friends and biographers have noted that Miller the man was much less sexually predatory, more caring and warm, than the autobiographical Miller who coldly, machinelike, consumed whatever came his way, all the while plotting his next conquest or his next meal.

Miller's philosophy of acceptance also led him to emphasize the unseemly side of sex, the brute physical aspects and the amoral quality of our natural urges and instincts. Rather than glorifying sex, treating it as a subject of poetry, he insisted that we come to accept it for what it is. Believing that repression inevitably results in disaster, Miller stressed acceptance of our natural urges and instincts as revealed in dreams:

It is the potential, indestructible man who comes to life in the dream. For his being there is no longer a censorship; taboos, laws, conventions, customs are annihilated. In the realm of sex it is the only true freedom he knows. He moved toward the object of his desire unimpeded by time, space, physical obstacles, or moral considerations. He may sleep with his mother as naturally and easily as with another woman. He may take an animal in the field and satisfy his desires without the slightest revolt. He may fuck his own daughter and find it extremely pleasurable. In the waking world, crippled and shackled by all kinds of fetters, everything is wrong or evil except that which has been prescribed by fear. The real inner being knows that these things are not wrong, not evil; when he closes his eyes he gives himself up to all these practices and pursuits which are prohibited.[19]

One must learn to act on the urges that society tries to suppress if one is to become authentic and to "complete one's potential (*de*)." But such urges are not always pretty. Even today we are brought up on the sanitized accounts of romantic love portrayed in Hollywood movies where the starlet remains perfectly coiffed even after a vigorous tumble in the sheets or on romance novels with hunks like Fabio gracing the cover. In this fantasy world, everything is safe and clean. Or we learn about sex in classes that speak of "penis" and "vagina" and make the act of intercourse sound like a high-school science experiment to be carried out wearing white laboratory coats and rubber gloves (and now, definitely, in this age of AIDS and "safe sex," condoms!). As a result, the real thing sometimes appears too real. Miller forces us to confront the reality of sex by dwelling on the physical aspects. He is obsessed with genitalia: "he dwells upon them, inspects them, describes them in detail, their parts, colors, textures, and compares them with others."[20] Moreover, he does so not in the language of textbooks or euphemisms found in the literature of the time but in the coarse language of the street, of real life. Miller uses language in the way the Zen master uses language, or a slap in the face—to shock, to cause one to break out of the bounds of the everyday to a deeper reality, to become enlightened. As a result, he puts together combinations of words "calculated to be as disturbing as possible to the sensitive reader."[21]

MILLER AS MYTH: THE HAPPY ROCK

Having failed at everything else, Miller turned to art for salvation. Writing was the only means left to discover his true voice, his authentic self. To free himself from the shackles that kept him within the bounds, he had to die and be reborn, re-created, through literature. Miller's early years were a time of frustration and despair. At one point, he even tried to commit suicide. He felt hemmed in, stuck. To break free, he needed to give up his job, his wife, his kids, even June, his muse and the great love of his life. As a result, his early works are filled with destruction and violence; they are the traumatic, cathartic rebirth necessary to reach the peace and harmonious acceptance of life that dominate his later works.[22]

In contrast, there is less evidence of a struggle in Zhuangzi. While many of the Daoist sages described by Zhuangzi seem to have come to the way through some type of meditation,[23] others seem to have been born knowing,[24] or to have discovered the way through repetitive mundane activities, as in the case of Butcher Ding.[25]

Whatever the differences in paths, the results are in many ways similar. First and foremost is the joyous acceptance of life, warts and all:[26]

> I have always insisted that life is good, even when it is bad; that men are failures, washouts, but life is good. Once again we're getting back to that broad discrimination which characterizes Chinese philosophy; there's only one life and it is always good ... more than good, much more. It is man who is mad, and unequal to the situation. One does not have the right to speak of good or evil when talking about life. Life is energy—tremendous energy. What do morals and ethics have to do with it? Isn't it almost a questions of health, of well-being? Vital energy, that's what life is. I have no hesitation in saying that, even if it gives "intellectuals" a laugh. Man sets up religions, ethical systems and moral values that contravene life, go against its meaning, against what I call well-being. Actual good health is just the opposite.[27]

Zhuangzi expresses acceptance of life by populating his world with a collection of misfits, hunchbacks, and cripples who turn out to be charismatic sages, capable of attracting the attention of the ruler despite their humble position and the affection of the most beautiful women despite their ugly countenance and physical deformity.[28] Miller achieves the same effect in his many descriptions of prostitutes, bums, and the average unheralded everyday Joe. Throughout his life, Miller maintained a childlike naiveté. He found everybody and everything interesting, read broadly, some would say indiscriminately, and made friends easily with an astonishingly wide range of people, including often the down and out, with whom he seemed to have a special affinity:

> Basically, you see, when all's said and done, I really like the bums, the no-goods. I even adore them because I'm pretty ... sick, yes, sick, of good people, you see? The good people, good consciences, right? That kind of person does more harm than bad people.... Because generally, those who are well-to-do and say they lead the good life, who say they care about other people are nothing but hypocrites, and they make me puke. I can't stand people like that.... I like everything human. To be human is perhaps the nearest thing to being an angel.[29]

Zhuangzi and Miller share a common belief in an underlying harmony to the world, a faith that life is good and abundant, and all will work out if one is true to oneself and accepting of life.[30] Miller's motto was "always merry and bright." Finding himself destitute in Paris, he reportedly declared: "I have no money, no resources, no hopes. I am the happiest man alive."[31] Whatever the truth of that assertion, Miller's friends and biographers, indeed Miller himself, were often struck by his unshakable faith that he was destined for great things, even when he was stuck in an unhappy marriage and job, or when, approaching middle age with nothing written, he was sleeping on Paris benches, penniless.

For both Zhuangzi and Miller, stripping away social conventions and accepting life as it is will lead to the discovery on one's own path.[32] "Every man has his destiny: the only imperative is to follow it, to accept it, no matter where it leads him."[33] Life and art merge, one lives in harmony, and in the process one discovers "the organic relatedness, the wholeness, the oneness of life."[34] The experience is akin to religious ecstasy. One is at peace. Externally, the experience is manifest in freedom, a freedom of the soul, and a generosity of spirit. One of the most striking features of Henry Miller was his generosity. He was notoriously free both with his time and with what money he had. Shortly after coming into a large sum of money, Miller was often broke, having spent it on a good time or given it away to those in greater need. His correspondence was similarly free-flowing. He seems to have responded to virtually anyone who wrote to him. Remarkable that someone could write so many letters and still find time to write.

HENRY MILLER: SAGE OR POSER?

Although one would expect reactions to a singular individual such as Henry Miller to be strong, the vehemence of the reactions to him still surprises. Few seem capable of evaluating Miller as a person or as an author in a detached and balanced way. On the one hand, there are the awe-struck homages of his spiritual followers who see him as Zhuangzi incarnate. On the other hand, there are those who dismiss his writings as tedious, formless smut, accuse him of being a poser, a fake, a charlatan, or criticize his "philosophy" as simplistic and irresponsible.

One of the problems in critically evaluating Miller's, or for that matter Zhuangzi's, "philosophy" is that neither was a systematic philosopher, and both possessed an anti-intellectual streak that caused them to mock the world of ideas and learning and celebrate its opposite. And yet, familiar with the leading thinkers of their times, they lived in the realm of ideas, regularly taking other philosophers as the subject of their verbal sword-play. But their ruminations most often were presented in a nonlinear, nondiscursive form. Ideas, thoughts, words, often inconsistent and contradictory, gushed forth in an endless stream. Both Zhuangzi and Miller are characterized by excess, by a great exuberance that leads to wild flights of fancy, accounts of supernatural beings who, in Zhuangzi's case, ride the winds and live on dew and air, make no plans and draw no distinctions, and who seem confused as to whether they are awake or dreaming; in Miller's case, equally fantastic accounts of sexual encounters that challenge the limits of the human anatomy or hard-to-swallow assertions as to the glories of suffering, of being homeless and hungry, and the joys of sleeping on frigid benches in the cold Paris winters. It is almost as if both Zhuangzi and Miller deliberately set out to merge content and form—their liberated, flowing, excessive prose itself beyond the bounds of literary convention and everyday truths.

The problem is exacerbated in Miller by his fascination with the subconscious, which he attempts to capture in dream sequences and fantasies written in a stream-of-consciousness fashion. But he stands out even among stream-of-consciousness writers for his flights of fantasy and wildly careening collage of images. So excessive is his prose that he is often accused of literary buffoonery, a charge that he did not entirely deny, as, in typical Miller fashion, he thought buffoonery more direct and capable of greater truths than the stylized, crafted prose of conventional literature.[35]

While the style of writing and lack of consistency caution against an overly literal or analytical reading of isolated passages, when Miller's (or Zhuangzi's) works are considered in total, enough of a picture emerges to make some critics worried. Miller shared the Daoist inclination toward anarchy, and the belief that if left alone, people will be able to govern themselves without the need of the state or the coercive force of law.[36] Toughminded moral philosophers find such a view absurdly naive. They also worry about whether one can be both liberated and part of a community. One of the criticisms of Daoism is that while it may be appropriate for hermits or those who, like Zhuangzi, prefer to leave the world behind and drag their tails in the mud,[37] it is too passive for those who wish to live among others. Similarly, while immediacy and acceptance may be fine for the artist, one wonders what would happen if everyone followed their natural inclinations.

But even if Miller and Zhuangzi are wrong that the result of everyone following their natural inclinations would be harmony rather than chaos, the fact is that not everyone will. As most people are condemned—and content—to live within the bounds, the moralist's worry is unnecessary. Society can tolerate the occasional artist or anarchist. At the same time it would be wrong to assume that self-realization is reserved for artists, hermits, and anarchists, or that those who live beyond the bounds have nothing to contribute to others. "Beyond the bounds" is not to be taken too literally. Many of the realized persons portrayed in the Zhuangzi are ordinary men, and several are craftsman. And while art was the only path for Miller, he is aware that others have their own way to the same end. Both Zhuangzi and Miller believed that it is not so much what one does as how one does it. One's attitude toward life, toward experience, is the key.[38] Similarly, while both Zhuangzi and Miller believed that there were limits to how much the individual can affect social change, they nevertheless felt that the realized person made an invaluable contribution to society by living an exemplary life: "I am fatuous enough to believe that in living out my own life in my own way I am more apt to give life to others (even though it is not my chief concern) than I would if I simply followed somebody else's idea of how to live my life and thus become a man among men."[39]

But is it really possible to live the life of acceptance and reconciliation of opposites? Can one really be indifferent to good and bad? Isn't it a waste of time to treat all books as equally worthy? All people as equally interesting? And can one truly be as giving as a Daoist sage? Won't others continue to take until there is nothing left, of your time if not material possessions? And, perhaps most importantly, while it is easy to say that one benefits others by being true to oneself, how does one know that one is being true to oneself as opposed to simply self-indulgent?[40] Artists in particular are notoriously narcissistic, trampling over the feelings and needs of others in the name of art.

One will never know whether Zhuangzi the person resembled the Daoist sage of the Zhuangzi, given the dearth of historical information. But whereas Zhuangzi lived and died more than 2,000 years ago, Henry Miller is a contemporary figure who died only recently. Many people who knew him well are still alive. Moreover, given the nature of his work, his recreation of himself as Daoist sage, and his attempt to blur the distinction between Henry Miller the person and Henry Miller the author/character, it was inevitable that his biographers would focus on the truth of his writings and the discrepancy between Miller the person and Miller the myth. Miller has always insisted that his autonovels are true in spirit, and often more true than factual truth: "For years I have been trying to tell this story and always the question of the truth has weighed upon me like a nightmare. Time and again I have related to others the circumstances of our life, and I have always told the truth. But the truth can also be a lie. The truth is not enough. Truth is only the core of a totality which is inexhaustible."[41] Needless to say, such statements have only thrown fuel on the fire.

Inevitably, there are discrepancies between Miller the person and Miller the myth. In some instances, Miller the person is actually superior. As noted earlier, his friends generally found him much warmer, more caring, and less sexually aggressive than Miller the character (which is not to deny the charges of sexism raised by feminist critics). But at other times Miller cannot live up to the ideal created in his books. For instance, Miller the character, upon hearing of his fourth wife Eve's death, sobbed all morning before going off to play ping pong, and then "began an afternoon and evening in which I was as gay as I have ever been. I ended up in a restaurant with four Canadian girls at my table and one on my lap. Still merry, more alive than ever."[42] But according to a friend who was at Miller's house at the time, Miller's reaction was decidedly less sagelike. According to the friend, Miller collapsed on the floor and had to be helped to bed, where he remained for days.

Miller was also capable of great self-promotion. Upon publication of *Tropic of Cancer*, he wrote letters to the leading literary figures of his days and sent them copies of the book, and even went so far as to visit booksellers in Paris to plug his work. Later in life, he orchestrated a campaign to have himself nominated for the Nobel Prize. Such blatant fame-seeking is difficult to square with Zhuangzi's celebration of the useless and unknown. On the other hand, some have pointed out that Miller clung to the image of a penniless artist even after he had a considerable royalty income,[43] while others criticized him for buying a home in the suburbs of Los Angeles and mingling with movie stars once he became famous and rich—apparently, you are damned if you do and damned if you don't.

Miller's insistence on immediacy, on throwing himself headfirst into the torrent of life, is also at odds with his need to detach himself from the moment, to observe with the artist's eye, to record, and then to relive the moment later, more fully, in his writings.[44] Indeed, Miller often seems detached, particularly in his many sexual escapades. In the midst of sex, his mind is often on roast beef sandwiches, loose change laying on the floor that he must remember to scoop up, other women, books he is going to write, even future descriptions of the scene taking place—anything, in short, but the matter at hand.

But the most serious criticism perhaps is that while Miller was tremendously giving in terms of both money and time, he was nevertheless self-centered and egotistical. Of course, no one could write as much as he did unless he reserved some time for himself. But Miller's need for independence and space to recreate himself may have been the cause of his many failed marriages. At the end of day, he may not have been able to give himself totally to another but rather remained always the narcissistic author-child, wrapped up in the overwhelming importance of the drama of his own life.

No doubt Miller fell short of the ideal of the Daoist sage portrayed in his autonovels. Surely, on occasion, finding it difficult to accept the hardness of the bench he was sleeping on and the hunger in his stomach, he must have longed to be sitting before a fireplace, belly full, sipping cognac. But when all is said and done, Henry Miller seems to have lived a particularly singular and courageous life. How many, approaching forty, would dare to throw it all off and depart for a foreign country with only a few dollars in one's pocket to try to become a writer? Much of the criticism of Miller as a person strikes me as the carping of those caught within the bounds who want to drag down those who live outside the bounds in order to maintain their sense of superiority and reassure themselves that their own lives have not been wasted. The portrait that emerges of Henry Miller both in his own writings and in the descriptions of those who knew him is, in broad strokes, that of someone who did exhibit many of the traits of a realized person. He seems to have avoided the danger of becoming trapped by possessions, gave freely to those in need, befriended a wide range of people, and most importantly, thoroughly enjoyed himself right up to the end, riding his bike, delighting in good food, drink, and conversation, and playing ping pong well into his 80s, when, at the age of 89, he died peacefully in his sleep. All in all, a life well-lived.

CODA

I met Professor Yang Yu-wei for the first time when I went to Taipei to read classical Chinese texts as part of my Ph.D. studies in Chinese philosophy. I had been warned in advance that he was a singular character, and that not all found his unique approach to teaching to their liking. I was particularly concerned because Professor Yang had kindly offered, sight unseen, to put me up gratis for the many months I would be in Taiwan. What would happen if we didn't get along? But I was reassured that if I found either Yang or the accommodations unsuitable, I could simply tell him so, and that would be that, no hard feelings.

Not knowing where Professor Yang lived, I made my way to Taiwan Normal University, where I gave him a call. He immediately volunteered to walk over and meet me. I described myself but realized after hanging up that I had failed to get his description. That was not to be a problem. A few minutes later, I heard someone frantically calling out my Chinese name. I looked around and saw this skinny, bare-chested fiftyish man dressed in khaki shorts and white knee socks, with a red, white, and blue headband holding back his wavy, blow-dried and recently permanented, slightly greying hair. He darted across the busy main street, dodging traffic, all the while calling out my name in a booming voice sure to attract the attention of the wandering undead and waving his arms in whirlwind fashion, managing somehow to evoke simultaneously images of Don Quixote and Sancho Panza, Jack Nicholson in *One Flew Over the Cuckoo's Nest*, and the Bodhidharma. Welcome, I thought, to the wonderful world of Oz.

Much of the first day was spent tidying up a room barely big enough to hold a bed and desk but filled nonetheless with everything from dust-covered books to ten-year-old calendars to empty scotch bottles left, I was told, by previous students. Lessons began the following day. Professor Yang would read a passage, explain the meaning, analyze the grammar, comment on ideas, or point out similar passages in other classical texts, which he had memorized as a precocious child. We would then move on to the next passage. But inevitably, sooner or later, he would come across a word, phrase, or idea that would get his juices flowing. Enthusiasm growing, he would lean over, closer and closer, his face inches from mine, spraying me with spit as the words gushed forth, overwhelming. Soon he would be associating freely—Zhuangzi, JFK, the idiots at Harvard, violence on TV, the price of fish. Unable to contain himself, he would leap up, arms flailing, and pace the room, his voice roaring, the veins in his neck bulging, on the verge, surely, of a massive coronary stroke. Alarmed, I would sometimes try to calm him down, get him back seated, return his attention to the text. Other times, it was hopeless. Any attempts to dam the dike, to interject a comment or take issue with the endlessly flowing opinions, went unheeded or, better yet, met with curses, insults, personal attacks. Had I the temerity to question the grammatical basis for a particular reading, Professor Yang, nostrils flaring, would often as not dismiss me with the summary comment, delivered at maximum voice, with a dollop of spittle for good measure, "*Ni de wenfa shi goupi de wenfa*"—roughly, "Your grammar is good for shit!"

But at some point, either that day, perhaps the next, perhaps a week later, Professor Yang would return to my objection, assuming there was any merit to it. He might casually mention over dinner or while watching TV that a certain passage could be interpreted in a certain way, that he had encountered uses of a term in other texts not unlike the one I had suggested. Or he might simply explain the passage the next day along the lines I had suggested without further comment, as if he had read it that way all along. Of course, more often than not, he was right in his reading of the text (and his assessment of my grasp of grammar), but it was nonetheless gratifying to know that even in the midst of his wildest tirades he was listening.

At the end of the day, I learned much from Professor Yang, the least important of which was classical Chinese grammar. He, like Henry Miller and Zhuangzi, is a singular person, and my life is infinitely richer for having know him.

NOTES

1. *Zhuangzi*, Concordance of Philosophers (Taipei: Nanyu Press, n.d. [reprint of Harvard-Yenching Concordance, 1947]), vol. 2, pp. 17–18. The translation follows that of Burton Watson, *Chuang Tzu: Basic Writings* (New York: Columbia University Press, 1964), pp. 82–84, and Angus Graham, *Chuang-tzu: The Inner Chapters* (London: George Allen & Unwin, 1981), pp. 89–90.
2. "Signs of fullness of power" is the title of one of the Inner Chapters, a chapter about misfits, hunchbacks, cripples, and the seriously ugly who, despite their physical deformities, are charismatic individuals on the basis of the fulfillment of the *de* within them.
3. Watson, *Chuang Tzu*, p. 85.
4. *Tropic of Capricorn* (New York: Grove Press, 1961), p. 129.
5. *Face to Face with Henry Miller: Conversations with Georges Belmont* (London: Sidgwick & Jackson, 1970), pp. 41–42 (hereafter, *Conversations*). Miller's claim to have read Laozi as a teenager is challenged by Robert Ferguson based on a statement in *Sexus* that seems to indicate that at thirty-three Miller had not yet read the *Daodejing*. See Ferguson, *Henry Miller—A Life* (New York: W. W. Norton, 1991), p. 35 (hereafter, *Henry Miller*). Ferguson also notes that Miller read Herbert Giles, Richard Wilhelm, Herbert Hesse, and others who wrote on Chinese philosophy, Daoism, and Zen, and that he consciously strove to become the kind of Daoist sage depicted by Laozi and Zhuangzi.
6. For the Uncarved Block, see the *Daodejing*, chapters 1, 37; for the Great Clod, see Watson, *Chuang Tzu*, p. 80.
7. See, for example, Ferguson, *Henry Miller*. Ferguson is particularly dismissive of the sycophantic accounts of Miller by his friends and acquaintances in *The Happy Rock* (Philadelphia: Walton Press, 1945) (hereafter, *Happy Rock*).
8. Ferguson argues that Miller could have figured out a way to repatriate his royalties if he wanted to and that the problem was not so much the lack of income but financial irresponsibility and mismanagement of funds. Miller's ability to spend or give away large sums of money is legend. Ferguson believes

Miller resisted financial security because it conflicted with his image of the starving artist struggling to make ends meet. *Henry Miller*, p. 348.

9. Miller often dismissed psychoanalysis on the grounds that it created more problems than it solved. Given how impressionable most people are, mention the Oedipal complex and they will find a way to feel conflicted about sleeping with their parents, or at least to worry and feel guilty about suppressing the inclination to do so, which they know must be lurking just below the surface in their subconscious. See *Conversations*, p. 23. Yet despite his avowed antipathy, Miller apparently practiced psychoanalysis for a period when Anais Nin was working with Otto Rank in New York. More importantly, his works are dominated by the same kind of inner directed gaze, and many of his wildest passages are subconscious dream-state fantasies.

10. Miller's views on art seem to have been influenced by the writings of Otto Rank, in particular Rank's *Art and Artist* (New York: Tudor Publishing, 1932); see William Gordon, *The Mind and Art of Henry Miller* (Baton Rouge: Louisiana State University Press, 1967), pp. 47–84.

11. *Black Spring* (New York: Grove Press, 1963), p. 107.

12. Henry Miller, "Creative Death," in *The Wisdom of the Heart* (New York: New Directions, 1941), p. 3.

13. Quoted in Knud Merrild's essay on Miller in *Happy Rock*, p. 88.

14. Ibid.

15. Henry Miller, "A Salute Collective," in *The Wisdom of the Heart*, p. 89.

16. "Reflections on Art," in *The Wisdom of the Heart*, p. 23.

17. Gordon, *The Mind and Art of Henry Miller*, pp. 25–26.

18. *Conversations*, p. 83.

19. *The World of Sex* (New York, 1940), p. 78.

20. Gordon, *The Mind and Art of Henry Miller*, p. 27.

21. Ibid., p. 27.

22. Rebirth is an explicit and recurrent theme for Miller: "I had two beginnings really, one here in America, which was abortive, and the other in Europe. How was I able to begin again, one may well ask? I should answer truthfully—by dying. In that first year or so in Paris I literally died, was literally annihilated—and resurrected a new man." *The World of Sex*, p. 10; see also *Conversations*, p. 44.

23. See, for example, Watson, *Chuang Tzu*, pp. 57–58, 82–83, 90–91.

24. Ibid., pp. 77–81, 88.

25. Ibid., pp. 50–51.

26. In addition to the opening tale of Master Sanghu and friends, see for example, Watson, *Chuang Tzu*, pp. 46–48, 73–74, 83–85.

27. *Conversations*, p. 63.

28. See, for example, Watson, *Chuang Tzu*, chapter 5, "The Sign of Virtue Complete."

29. *Conversations,* p. 107.
30. Whereas Laozi seems confident that finding the way will lead to social harmony, Zhuangzi appears more skeptical. Indeed, even on a personal level, obtaining the way is no guarantee that one will live a life of riches and comfort. Rather, the point seems to be that harmony and peace are to be found in acceptance of life in its many manifestations, as in the stories of the cripples who, despite their deformities, lead a life of contentment.
31. *Tropic of Cancer* (New York: Grove Press, 1961), p. 1.
32. See, for example, Zhuangzi's description of "sitting and forgetting," Watson, *Chuang Tzu,* pp. 90–91.
33. "Reflections on Art," p. 22.
34. "Creative Death," in *The Wisdom of the Heart,* p. 10.
35. See, for example, Anais Nin, *The Diaries of Anais Nin,* vol. 1 (New York: Swallow Press, 1966), p. 198.
36. See *The World of Sex,* p. 78. Ferguson attributes Miller's early enthusiasm for anarchism to the writings of Emma Goldman and Peter Kropotkin rather than Daoism, although Kropotkin's belief that a viable social order if people are left to follow their own natural inclinations is similar to the Daoist view of *wuwei.* Ferguson, *Henry Miller,* pp. 34–35.
37. Watson, *Chuang Tzu,* p. 188.
38. As Watson notes, *fang* 方 means not only "bounds" or "realm" but "method". Watson, p. 83 n18.
39. *The Cosmological Eye* (New York: New Directions, 1939), p. 157.
40. While Zhuangzi seems to have been relatively unconcerned with truth in the sense of correspondence between our ideas and reality, he was very concerned with the issue of authenticity, of determining what was *tian* 天—heaven, nature—and what was human. Although Miller uses the language of truth, he does so in the sense of being true to oneself, of being authentic.
41. *Tropic of Capricorn,* p. 333.
42. *Letters by Henry Miller to Hoki Tsukuda Miller,* ed. Joyce Howard, p. 23, quoted in Ferguson, *Henry Miller,* p. 356.
43. Ferguson, *Henry Miller,* p. 348.
44. Zhuangzi the philosopher-author presumably would have felt the same conflict, as philosophy requires a self-reflective detachment. Perhaps the style of writing, less analytical, more free-flowing, is an attempt to reduce the conflict by catching some of the flavor of the immediacy of life.

6

On Hui Shi

LISA RAPHALS

Tian xia, the last chapter of the *Zhuangzi*, ends on an unlikely note—a list of the paradoxes of Hui Shi 惠施, minister of the state of Wei. The *Zhuangzi* concludes with the words:

> What a pity that Hui Shi's talents were wasted and never came to anything, that he would not turn back from chasing the myriad things! He had as much chance of making his voice outlast its echo, his body outrun its shadow. Sad, wasn't it?[1]

Hui Shi continues to provoke interest and curiosity. "The sparseness of the remains of Hui Shi is perhaps the most regrettable of all the losses in ancient Chinese literature," remarks A. C. Graham, "for everything recorded of him suggests that he was unique among the early thinkers for his breadth of talents, and interests, a true Renaissance man."[2]

Most of our received images of Hui Shi come from the oldest texts that mention him, the *Zhuangzi* and the *Lüshi chunqiu*. Both portray him, sympathetically or not, as a sophist: as Zhuangzi's logical opponent, or as a master of fine distinctions, unwilling or incompetent to engage in real statecraft.[3]

The oldest layers of the *Zhuangzi* and the *Lüshi chunqiu* date from the late fourth and third centuries B.C.E.[4] Later texts also discuss and quote his arguments and exploits: the *Xunzi* and *Han Feizi* (third century), the *Hanshi waizhuan* and *Huainanzi* (second century), and the *Shuo yuan* and *Zhanguo ce* (first century). In this paper I use this range of portrayals to present four distinct images of Hui Shi, beginning with the received view of a sympathetic sophist, Zhuangzi's maladroit but likeable "sidekick." Next I turn to three distinct third-century views of Hui Shi. The maladroit sophist of the *Lüshi chunqiu* emerges from several debates in which Hui Shi engages at the court of King Hui of Wei. The Hui Shi of the

Xunzi is a dangerous heterodox philosopher who wants to introduce laws instead of relying on the *li*. The Hui Shi of the *Han Feizi*, by contrast, is both a skilled analogist and an effective minister. These four images reappear in the second- and first-century accounts of the *Huainanzi*, *Zhanguo ce*, and *Shuo yuan*.

THE SYMPATHETIC SOPHIST OF THE *ZHUANGZI*

The relationship between Zhuangzi and Hui Shi in the *Zhuangzi* has been widely commented on.[5] The *nei pian* contains relatively few encounters: debates about the "uselessness" of the calabash and the tree of heaven (chapter 1), a passing reference to Hui Shi leaning on his stericula (chapter 2), and the debate about essential qualities (chapter 5).[6] Most of the better-known vignettes are in the outer and miscellaneous chapters: Zhuangzi's disinterest in Hui Shi's office (chapter 17), the happiness of fish (chapter 17), Zhuangzi's mourning his wife (chapter 18), a debate about names (chapter 24), the death of Hui Shi (chapter 24), the "snail" dialogue (chapter 25), another discussion of uselessness (chapter 26), a discussion of Confucius (chapter 27), and Hui Shi's paradoxes (chapter 33).[7] Yet all these stories, with the exception of the syncretist *Tian xia* chapter, are either in the Inner Chapters, conventionally attributed to the historical Zhuangzi, or in chapters considered by Graham and Guan Feng to be closely related to him.[8]

In these stories, Hui Shi inevitably gets the worst of the argument, but, as Shuen-fu Lin points out in his review of Graham's emendations of the *Zhuangzi* text, the debates between Zhuangzi and Hui Shi are central to the structure of the text: "the more carefully we read the six seemingly random pieces of prose [at the end of *Zhuangzi* 1], the more we feel that there is an intricate kind of unity within them. There is clearly an 'inner logic' to its organization."[9] That "inner logic" may help to explain Hui Shi's place of prominence at the end of the text.

THE MALADROIT SOPHIST OF THE *LÜSHI CHUNQIU*

Overall, the *Lüshi chunqiu* portrays Hui Shi as a man of clever arguments who cannot or will not put them to practicable use. The section of chapter 18 titled "Unstable Words" (18.5) presents a series of clever arguments with no basis in good judgment. This series ends with the story of Hui Shi's creation of a law code for King Hui of Wei:

> Master Hui created a law code for the state of King Hui. When he had completed it, he showed it to the people, who all thought it excellent. He presented it to King Hui, who was much pleased by it, and who showed it to Di Jian, who said: "Good." King Hui said: "It's good, but is it practicable?" Di Jian said: "It is not." King Hui said: "How can it be good (*shan* 善) but impracticable?"

King Hui asked how something can be efficacious but impractical. Di Jian answers by analogy:

> Now if there are men raising a great tree, and those in front sing "*Ya xu*" and those in back answer in response, this song is strong enough to raise a heavy log. It's not as if the tones of Zheng and Wei are not stirring, but in the end, this sort of thing would not be useful, and they would not be as appropriate as this.

According to this analogy, the simple "*ya xu*" call and response harmonizes the loggers sufficiently to lift a great tree. The *Shi jing* airs from Zheng and Wei are not strong enough stuff for this limited purpose, and, as the *Lüshi chunqiu* version of the story points out, there is no greater log than the state. The criticism of Hui Shi's law code, then, seems to be that it is too "good." In other words, it lacks the necessary grit to do the job of creating lawfulness in a state. This story also appears in *Huainanzi* 12 but with a slightly different ending (discussed below).[10] Several other scattered references in the *Lüshi chunqiu* describe Hui Shi's words as impracticable.[11]

The next section "Not Giving In" (18.6) begins with the argument that scholars who excel at debate and distinctions may do good or harm, depending on their motivations. It presents three stories in which Hui Shi debates with King Hui of Wei, Kuang Zhang, a student of Mengzi, and with Bai Gui, a recent acquaintance.[12]

In the first, King Hui of Wei tries to cede his kingdom to Hui Shi.

> King Hui of Liang said to Master Hui: "In former times the rulers of states were always the most worthy men. Now I am truly not your equal in worth, therefore I want to abdicate the state to you."
>
> Hui Shi refused. The king pressed him and said: "There is no state greater than this, and if I abdicate it to a worthy man, the greed and strife in the people's hearts will come to a standstill. I want you to obey me without further ado."
>
> Master Hui said: "If it is as Your Majesty says, then I cannot obey. Your Majesty is indeed a lord of 10,000 chariots, and if you elevate another by [gift of] the state, you are in a unique position to do so. I, however, am a commoner, now in a position to head a state of 10,000 chariots, but if I refuse it, then this will contribute more than ever to ending greed and jealousy among the people."
>
> Now when King Hui said to Master Hui, "In the past, the men who were in possession of states were always worthy," Shun was a case of someone who was worthy and accepted [the state]; he [King Hui] wanted Master Hui to be a Shun. Xu You was an example of someone who was worthy but refused; Master Hui wanted to be a Xu You.[13] Yao

was a case of one who was worthy but abdicated; King Hui wanted to be a Yao.

At this point, Hui Shi emerges as a worthy individual par excellence. A king tries to abdicate to him as a worthier man, he refuses, and for the best of reasons. The passage goes on to elaborate three kinds of worthy conduct in statecraft. Praise of Hui Shi, however, soon turns to censure:

> But the accomplishments of a Yao, a Shun and a Xu You did not merely consist in the fact that the one abdicated the state to Shun and that Xu You refused it, but rather that their other actions were in accord with these. Nowadays there is none of that, but people still want to be a Yao, Shun and Xu You. As a result, when King Hui of Qi was defeated, he offered subservience in Jian in cotton cloth and cap and King Wei of Qi was unwilling to accept; and Hui Shi had to leave Wei in disguise and was barely able to escape from its territory. Therefore as to one's own actions, one must not take haphazard good auspice as real merit. (*Lüshi chunqiu* 18/6/11b–12b)[14]

Hui Shi wanted to be a Xu You but was not. His conduct overall was not sufficiently virtuous, and virtue, the passage argues, cannot be reckoned by one haphazard event. Even if Hui Shi does not quite emerge as a Xu You, the passage does not dispraise him, and, on the contrary, it ascribes perfectly sensible reasons for his refusal of the throne of Wei.

In the second encounter, Hui Shi debates with Kuang Zhang, a disciple of Mengzi, who attacks Hui Shi in the following terms:

> Kuang Zhang spoke to Master Hui in the presence of King Hui of Wei: "When a farmer catches grasshoppers, he kills them, because they harm the grain. Now when you, Sir, travel about, often with many hundreds of wagons and retainers, but at least with a few dozen wagons and retainers, you eat but do not sow, and the harm to the grain is far greater."
>
> King Hui said: "Master Hui Shi will find it difficult to respond to you, but nonetheless I invite him to speak his views."
>
> Master Hui said: "Now in the construction of a city wall, some labor at beating down the top; some bear earth in baskets and go about the bottom, and yet others have the plans in their hands and oversee the construction. I am one of the overseers who hold the plans. If you change a weaver woman into silk, she can no longer manage the silk. If you change a carpenter into wood, he can no longer work the wood. If you change a wise man into a farmer, he can no longer order the farmers. Now I am an orderer of farmers; how is it that you compare me to a grasshopper?"

Hui Shi wins the argument, yet the passage rejects his self-assessment with a devastating account of Hui Shi's influence upon King Hui and his poor record as a minister of state:

Master Hui's ordering of Wei was order without order. At the time of King Hui, Wei fought fifty battles, suffered twenty defeats, and casualties beyond number or estimation. The greatest general and the beloved son of the king were taken prisoner. The stupidity of his strategy was a laughingstock for the world, and people pointed at him with avoidance. And so he requested the historian of Zhou to make his name more famous. He besieged Han Dan for three years without being able to take it. His soldiers were exhausted and the finances of the state were consumed. Then armies came from all sides, all his [King Hui's] subjects condemned him, and the lords and princes did not praise him. He apologized to Di Jian, and from then on, listened to his counsel, and as a result, the state survived. But its treasures were scattered to the four corners of the earth, and the state of Wei was diminished and went into decline. *Zhongfu* is a high title, and abdicating a state is a serious matter; his expositions that he had refused [the throne of Wei] are not credible. But since they listened to him and it came out thus, he could not be deemed skillful, and when a maladroit wants to put a state in order, there is no greater harm in the world. Fortunately, only the king of Wei had listened to him, so what he did in actuality was a general harming of the world, to which he gave the name of putting the state of Wei in order. How could Kuang Zhang's condemnation not have been entirely appropriate? (LSCQ 18/6/12b–13b)

The third encounter is with Bai Gui, a recent acquaintance of Hui Shi, who criticizes him for impropriety of speech:

When Bai Gui was newly acquainted with Master Hui, he went to see him. Master Hui advised him to be strong. Bai Gui did not reply, and Master Hui left. Bai Gui spoke to some others and said: "Someone had newly received a bride. When she arrived, she was appropriately peaceful in her demeanor and delicate and gentle in her movements. A young man had lit a torch of brushwood twigs, which burned brightly and the new bride said: 'The torch is burning too strongly.' As she entered the gate, there was a hole in the threshold and she said: 'Fill it or someone will hurt his foot.' All these things were not as they should have been, but nevertheless it [her complaint] was excessive. Master Hui also saw me today for the first time, and so his advice was excessive."

Bai Gui may have been offended by the directness of Hui Shi's remark, but his use of an analogy that put Hui Shi in the humble status of a new bride, obliged by her status to speak with the utmost of decorum, provoked offense in turn:

> When Master Hui heard this he said: "Not at all! The *Shi* says 'The joyous and pleasant lord is the father and mother of his people.'[15] Joyous means great; pleasant means longlasting. If a lord's virtue is both great and longlasting, then he is the father and mother of his people, but do fathers and mothers wait a long time before they instruct their children? Why does he compare me to a new bride? Does the *Shi* say 'the joyous and pleasant bride'?"
>
> Those who denigrate and calumnize others will be denigrated and calumnized in turn. Those who chastise others [wrongly] will be chastised in turn. The way in which he chastises others is the way in which he will in turn be chastised by them. When Bai Gui said "Master Hui had just recently gotten to know me, and gave me advice in an excessive way," and Master Hui heard it and chastised him by comparing himself to Bai Gui's parents, was this not even more excessive than Bai Gui's excess? (LSCQ 18/6/13b–14a)

Once again, the argument in the *Lüshi chunqiu* shows Hui Shi as initially acting in a reasonable manner, but eventually undercutting himself by impracticality and excess.[16] Whereas the *Zhuangzi* criticized Hui Shi's logic because it interfered with his perception of reality (variously interpreted in epistemological or mystical terms); the *Lüshi chunqiu* finds fault with his clever words because they are not matched by clever deeds, or worse, conceal incompetence and mislead those who might trust him. Both portray the problem with Hui Shi as a lack of efficacy, variously understood.

A different Hui Shi emerges when we turn to two later third-century thinkers: Xunzi and Han Fei.

THE HETERODOX PHILOSOPHER OF XUNZI

Recent scholarship has called attention to Xunzi's philosophical debts, both positive and negative. David Nivison has argued that Xunzi introduced an entirely new Confucianism, "a Confucian vision that no philosopher could have conceived until after Zhuangzi's Daoism had happened."[17] Donald Munro (who begins his study with Nivison's observation) focuses on Xunzi's discussion of Mozi as a philosophical enemy, and argues that Xunzi's interest in Mozi suggests that Xunzi's central interest is not theories of human nature or the mind, but rather "the issues of chaos and poverty, and their causes and institutional remedies."[18]

Such a view of Xunzi is particularly illuminating for his treatment of Hui Shi, whom he attacks as a heterodox thinker who propounds dangerous doctrines and neglects essentials. The first attack on Hui Shi (*Xunzi* 3), begins with this dictum: "The *junzi* [exemplary person] does not prize improper investigations or unsuitable traditions."

Xunzi gives example of six paradoxes, ascribed to Hui Shi and Deng Xi:[19]

> Mountains and abysses are level.
> Heaven and Earth are comparable.
> Qi and Qin are adjacent.
> [Mountains issue out of mouths.]
> Old women have whiskers.
> Eggs have feathers.

Of these, the first, second, and last paradox appear in *Zhuangzi* 33; the others have been emended by Tang commentators and are of uncertain origin.

> All these theories are difficult to uphold, but Hui Shi and Deng Xi were capable of it. Nevertheless, the *junzi* does not hold them in esteem *because they are contrary to the norms of ritual and morality* (非禮義之中, italics mine, *Xunzi* 6/3/3)[20]

His criticism is not the trivial one that they are silly, but the weighty one that they go against *li* and *yi*. A similar criticism appears in *Xunzi* 6, which describes doctrines of Hui Shi and Deng Xi that do not follow the models of antiquity:

> Some men do not model their doctrines after the Early Kings, and do not affirm ritual or moral principles, but are fond of treating abstruse theories and playing with shocking propositions. Although formulated with extreme exactness, their propositions concern matters of no urgency, and their theories, though defended by discriminations, are quite useless.... Such men are Hui Shi and Deng Xi. (*Xunzi* 15/6/10, trans. Knoblock 1:224)

The castigation continues in "Teachings of the Ru" (*Xunzi* 8), which describes specific aptitudes in which the *junzi* is justifiably inferior to others. After justifying the proper inferiority of the *junzi* to the farmer, the trader, and the artisan, Xunzi continues:

> He is inferior to the likes of Hui Shi and Deng Xi in being indifferent to the real nature of truth and falsity and the true nature of what is the case and what is not, so that the one blurs and confuses the other and ridicule is heaped on them both. (*Xunzi* 21/8/29–30; Knoblock 2:71–72)

The view is summarized in the chapter "Dispelling Blindness" (*Xunzi* 21), which describes the blindness of senior retainers, and disordered schools, and provides a virtual register of Xunzi's philosophical enemies:

Mo Di was blinded by utility and was insensible to the value of good form; Song Xing was blinded by desire and was insensible to satisfaction; Shen Dao was blinded by law and was insensible to worth; Shen Buhai was blinded by technique and was insensible to knowledge; Hui Shi was blinded by propositions and was insensible to realities; Zhuang Zhou was blinded by nature and was insensible to people. (*Xunzi* 79/ 21/22; Knoblock 3:102).[21]

In this perspective, Hui Shi's faults complement Mozi's: the one is blinded by utility, the other by propositions; the one disregarded good form, the other reality. Thus Xunzi, like the *Zhuangzi* and unlike the *Lüshi chunqiu* authors, directly links Hui Shi's love of argument and word play with his misreading of reality, the "reality" of Xunzi's own Confucianism. As far as Xunzi is concerned, Hui Shi's skills, real enough, are undermined by their lack of appropriate purpose.

THE SKILLFUL ANALOGIST OF THE *HAN FEIZI*

Perhaps the most sympathetic reader of Hui Shi was Xunzi's student Han Fei, who consistently portrays, not only the skill of his analogies, but their aptness. Han Fei presents any number of instances in which Hui Shi gives practical and approriate advice, typically couched in an analogy. In the first, Hui Shi's apt analogy saves a friend's life:

Tian Si had deceived the Lord of Zou, and the Lord of Zou was about to send men to kill him. Tian Si was afraid, and appealed to Master Hui. Master Hui sought an audience with the Lord of Zou and said: "Now if someone were to seek an audience with my Lord and then he were to shut one of his eyes, what would my Lord do?"
    The lord said: "I would certainly have him killed."
    Master Hui replied: "Yet a blind man shuts both his eyes; why does my Lord not kill *him*?"
    The lord said: "He cannot do otherwise than shut his eyes."
    Master Hui responded: "Tian Si has misled the Lord of Qi in the east and deceived the King of Jing [Chu] in the south; in his deception of others Si is [like] the blind man, so why is my Lord so angry at him?"
    As a result, the lord of Zou did not kill him. (*Han Feizi* 7/433)[22]

Unlike Xunzi and Hui Shi's other critics, Han Fei presents the analogy of Tian Si and the blind man as an effective strategy that saved Tian Si's life. A later passage in the same chapter also uses an analogy, this time in admonition to an acquaintance who has received royal favor:

> When Chen Xu was honored by the King of Wei, Hui Shi said: "You must on all accounts keep on good terms with the attendants. Consider the willow: plant it sidewise and it will still grow, plant it upside down and it will grow, even plant a broken branch and it will grow. But if you have ten people planting willow but one person pulling them up, no willow will manage to grow. How is it that ten people planting the easiest thing there is to grow cannot overcome one person pulling them up? Because planting is hard and pulling is easy. Although you have been adroit in planting yourself with the king, if there are many who want to pull you out, you are certain to be in danger." (*Han Feizi* 7/442)

This analogy also appears in the *Zhanguo ce* (discussed below). The analogy of the willow, like that of the blind man, is apt to the purpose, and is used to help an acquaintance. It would not appear to conform to either Zhuangzi's or Xunzi's disparaging account.

In the last argument in the chapter, Han Fei quotes the words of Hui Shi to show that human actions are not inherently good or bad, but must be judged in the context of their purposes and the motives behind them.

> Earl Tian Ding's esteem for gentlemen (*shi* 士) caused his lord to survive; Duke Bai's esteem for gentlemen caused disorder in [the state of] Jing. They were alike in their esteem for gentlemen, but different in the reasons for their actions. Gongsun Ji mutilated himself in order to recommend Bai Li; Shu Diao castrated himself in order to ingratiate himself with Duke Huan. They were alike in mutilating themselves but different in the reasons for their actions in mutilating themselves. Therefore Master Hui said: "When a madman runs east and someone pursuing [him] also runs east, they are alike in running east, but different in their reasons for running east." Thus it is said: "When people do the same thing, you cannot not make distinctions according to motive." (*Han Feizi* 7/446)

He takes the argument one step further in another passage where he contrasts the motives of a mother and an expert archer.

> Master Hui said: "If Hou Yi put the thimble on his right thumb, held the middle of the bow with his left hand, drew the bow, and then released the string, then even men of Yue would contentiously go to hold the target for him. But when a small child draws the bow, then even the compassionate mother will run into the house and shut the door."

Hence the saying: "If certain of no miss, even men of Yue would not doubt Hou Yi. If not certain of no miss, even the compassionate mother will escape her small child." (*Han Feizi* 8/456, trans. Liao 1:247)[23]

In another passage (which also occurs in the *Zhanguo ce,* discussed below), Hui Shi loses an immediate debate, but may have succeeded in making a broader argument:

Zhang Yi wanted to use alliances with Qin, Han and Wei to attack Qi and Jing, while Hui Shi wanted to use [alliances with] Qi and Jing to stop hostilities. When the two men debated, the ministers and their assistants were in favor of the words of Master Zhang, and wanted to profit by attacking Qi and Jing, and no one was in favor of the words of Master Hui, so the king in fact listened to Master Zhang and considered Master Hui's words to be impracticable. After the attack on Qi and Jing was accomplished, Master Hui went to court for an audience, and the king said: "You, Sir, should have said nothing. The attack on Qi and Jing has in fact been profitable, and the entire country expected as much."

Master Hui had the following explanation: "It was impermissible to not examine the matter! Now as for the attack on Qi and Jing, it has been profitable, as the entire country expected, but does that mean that the country is full of sages? If the attack against Qi and Jing had not been profitable and the entire country had expected that it would be, would the country be full of fools? All strategies are dubious, and a consummate doubter considers them to be half practicable and half impracticable. Now if the entire country considered it practicable, this means that Your Majesty has lost half [who did not]. A ruler who retreats [from such matters] is one who has lost the other half." (*Han Feizi* 9/530)

Hui Shi's loss of the original debate with Zhang Yi does not diminish the force of his subsequent argument. Its structure contrasts to that of most of the *Lüshi chunqiu* arguments, which portray Hui Shi as starting with a reasonable position, but ending with a ridiculous one. Here, his initial position is impracticable, but his ending defense is entirely plausible (whether or not the king listened to him).

In summary, Han Fei seems to portray both Hui Shi and his arguments in a surprisingly positive light, given his own relative lack of interest in debate. In one passage, however, Han Fei does, in passing, include Hui Shi in a series of propounders of impracticable theories, which he compares to a painting of a whip. Their words are too minute to be scrutinized and too ineffable to be carried out in practice. Like the painted whip, they cannot be used.[24]

SECOND-CENTURY ECHOES

Second-century compendia, such as the *Hanshi waizhuan* and the *Huainanzi*, seem to reflect the orthodoxy of Xunzi's new Confucianism in their treatment of Hui Shi. The passages in the *Hanshi waizhuan* are all but derived from the *Xunzi*. The *Huainanzi* retells the *Lüshi chunqiu* story of Hui Shi's law code, but ends it with a new judgment that defends the primacy of the rites over laws in ordering a state.

The Hanshi waizhuan

The *Hanshi waizhuan* gives an account of Hui Shi's paradoxes that is almost identical to Xunzi's. The passage begins with the statement that a *junzi* does not respect foolhardiness in conduct, sophistry in explanations, or a notorious reputation; he respects only what is fitting. The example of sophistry is the paradoxes of Hui Shi and Deng Xi:

> Mountains and streams are level, Heaven and Earth are comparable, Qi and Qin are adjacent, it goes in the ear and comes out the mouth, barbs have whiskers, eggs have feathers—all these theories are difficult to uphold, but Deng Xi and Hui Shi were capable of it. The *junzi* does not hold them in esteem because they are contrary to ritual and morality. (*Hanshi waizhuan* 3/29a–b)[25]

A second passage tersely summarizes the contents of Xunzi's censure of ten of the twelve philosophers attacked in *Xunzi* 6:

> Now the ignorance of the present age is due to the dressing up of heterodox theories and esteeming as cultured treacherous words that disorder the empire and confuse the common people so that in their ignorance they become so confused that they cannot tell right from wrong or order from disorder. The ones on whose account this situation persists are the likes of Fan Sui, Wei Mou, Tian Wen, Zhuang Zhou, Shen Dao, Tian Pian, Mo Di, Song Jian, Deng Xi and Hui Shi. (*Hanshi waizhuan* 4/36b–37a)[26]

The Huainanzi

The second-century *Huainanzi* (c. 140 B.C.E.) also seems to echo Xunzi's reservations about Hui Shi. *Huainanzi* 12 repeats the *Lüshi chunqiu* analogy of Hui Shi's impracticable law code. The *Huainanzi* version of the passage concludes: "For governing a state there are the rites, and it does not consist in patterns and discriminations" (*wen bian* 文辯 *Huainanzi* 12/190).[27]

So the problem with Hui Shi's law code is not that it is too nuanced or refined for the "rough" job of governing a state, but that it is the wrong kind of solution: the rites (*li* 禮), according to the *Huainanzi* and *Lüshi chunqiu* passages, are the right way to govern a state. In other words, the problem with Hui Shi may not be that he is sophistic or incompetent, but rather that, in the new Confucian discourse, he is heterodox.

FIRST-CENTURY ECHOES

The *Shuo yuan* and *Zhanguoce*, both first-century (B.C.E.) texts attributed to Liu Xiang, echo assessments of Hui Shi in earlier texts; both represent him sympathetically.

The Skillful Analogist of the Shuo yuan

The *Shuo yuan* specifically depicts Hui Shi as a propounder of analogies, and records both his skill at analogy and the discomfiture it could provoke. In the chapter "Skill at Explanation," an opponent attacks Hui Shi for using analogies, or as Christoph Harbsmeier terms them, "illustrative comparisons."[28] He defends the practice convincingly:

> A retainer said to the King of Wei: "When Master Hui speaks about affairs, he tends toward illustrative comparisons, but if Your Majesty should order him not to use illustrative comparisons, he will not be able to speak."
>
> The king agreed. The next day he gave an audience to Master Hui and said: "I wish, Sir, that when you speak about affairs, you would use straightforward language, with no illustrative comparisons."
>
> Hui Shi said: "Now if we have someone who does not know what a *dan* is, who asks 'What are the characteristics of a *dan*?' and you reply: 'The characteristics of a *dan* are like a *dan*,' then will anything have been communicated?"
>
> The king said: "It would not."
>
> "But if you were to reply instead that the characteristics of a *dan* are like a bow, but with a bamboo bowstring, then would he know?"
>
> The king said: "He would."
>
> Hui Shi said: "Now as for explanation, it consists of using the known to communicate the unknown and in that way making the person understand it. If Your Majesty now says 'No illustrative comparisons,' it cannot be done." (*Shuo yuan* 11/4a)[29]

The Strategist of the Zhanguoce

Given the *Zhanguoce*'s concern with rhetoric, we might expect a sympathetic potrayal of Hui Shi, but the picture is in fact mixed.

Some stories depict Hui Shi as an ineffectual pawn in the game of politics. In his first appearance in the text, Zhang Yi has driven Hui Shi from Wei to Chu. The king of Chu takes counsel with his ministers on his impending dilemma: How to help Hui Shi without offending Zhang Yi and the state of Qin. The proposed solution is to send Hui Shi to Song: this move avoids displeasing Zhang Yi, but also has the advantage of keeping Hui Shi indebted to the king of Chu.[30]

In another account of these shifting alliances in the story "The Five States Attack Qin," Wei wanted union with Qin and sent Hui Shi, the minister of Wei, to Chu, who was going to send him on to Qin when Du He said to Zhao Yang:[31]

> The country most responsible for the attack on Qin was Chu, but today Shi comes on behalf of Wei and you would send him to Qin. This would make it quite clear that Chu is responsible for the attack and convince Qin that Wei initiated peace [put Chu in a bad light and Wei in a good one]. You would be better advised to ignore Hui Shi and secretly send a man to Qin to offer peace terms yourself.

Zhao Yang presents the opposite of this persuasion to Hui Shi:

> Wei was first to attack Qin. If you now leave to seek peace from Chu, Chu will receive all the credit and Wei the resentment.

Zhao sent Hui Shi home to Wei and offered to send a peace envoy from Wei, but the king of Wei was unhappy. As a result, Zhao Yang made peace in Wei, to prevent Wei from joining forces with Qin and leave Chu exposed. Hui Shi comes off badly, but not because of analogies, impracticality, or heterodoxy. The hero of this persuasion is Du He, a peacemaker who speaks both for and against Wei, and persuades Zhao Yang to make peace there.

By contrast, Hui Shi is the rhetorical hero (if not the political victor) in two stories that appear in both the *Zhanguo ce* and the *Han Feizi*. The story "Zhang Yi Wants to Use Wei to Unify Qin and Wei" repeats a variation of the story of the debate between Zhang Yi and Hui Shi over whether to attack Qi and Chu.[32] "Tian Xu Honored by the King of Wei" repeats the *Han Feizi*'s account of Hui Shi's analogy between planting willow and securing political influence.[33] Other stories also show him persuading effectively.[34]

CONCLUSIONS

In summary, the received view of Hui Shi as he appears in the *Zhuangzi* and *Lüshi chunqiu* marks the earlier end of a continuum of stories which portray four fairly distinct images: (1) a sympathetic logician whose fundamental *amartia* makes the waste of his talents inevitable; (2) a maladroit sophist, more to be mocked than to be feared; (3) a dangerously heterodox philosopher who attempts to undermine the primacy of *li* and *yi*; and (4) an able strategist who uses apt analogies to give good counsel. All four images appear in third-century texts, but find their echoes in second- and first-century retellings and embellishments. All agree that Hui Shi played with words, used analogies, and was a minister in Wei. Thereafter, it becomes a matter of perspective.

One way of trying to make sense of these diverse images is suggested in a study by Christoph Harbsmeier on humor in ancient Chinese philosophy. Bearing in mind the many caveats on assessing humor across both time and place, "humor" may nevertheless provide a useful perspective to help us account for the mixed reception of Hui Shi. What sense would an author (or compiler) who had (or lacked) a sense of humor have been able to make out of the Hui Shi stories? Harbsmeier's assessment of the degree of humor (or lack thereof) in pre-Han and Han texts provides an interesting perspective on these varying assessments of Hui Shi.

The text that most strongly disparages Hui Shi is the *Xunzi*, which Harbsmeier describes as: "totally devoid of any sense of humor whatsoever," "serious and didactic throughout," and with "nothing light-hearted even in the poetic parts."[35] Harbsmeier may have underestimated Xunzi, but his account suggests an interesting rapport between Hui Shi's style and, at least, certain kinds of senses of humor. The *Lüshi chunqiu*, with its "fair share of entertaining tales" and "grotesque" and "almost surrealist black humor" provides, at least partially, a sympathetic account of Hui Shi, as does the *Zhanguoce*, which, according to Harbsmeier, "was clearly compiled by someone with a taste for the light humorous touch." Most striking, perhaps is the sympathetic account of Hui Shi in the *Han Feizi*, according to Harbsmeier, the single most important extant source of pre-Han jokes.[36]

What better foil for Zhuangzi's own edge and wit than the deliberate outrageousness of Hui Shi's puzzles, despite the poor opinion of the syncretist compiler. When Hui Shi died, Zhuangzi, by his own account, had no one with whom to talk things over, and compared Hui Shi to the man of Ying, who

> smeared the tip of his nose with plaster like a fly's wing and made Carpenter Shi slice it off. Carpenter Shi whirled up the wind with his axe, listened for the moment, and sliced. All the plaster was gone, the nose was unharmed, and the man from Ying stood perfectly still and composed. Lord Yuan of Song heard about it, summoned Carpenter Shi, and said "Now do it for me." Carpenter Shi replied, "Time was when I could do my side and do the slice, but now, my partner has been dead for some time." (*Zhuangzi* 24/843)

NOTES

1. Zz 33/1112, trans. Graham 1986, p. 285.
2. Graham 1989, p. 76.

3. Zhuangzi's own position on "logic" is not without its own debaters. For a range of views, see Graham 1970 and 1989 and responses to Hansen and Nivison in Rosemont 1991; Hansen 1983, 1991, and 1992; Ivanhoe 1992; and Raphals 1992 and 1994.

4. Both texts present complex problems of dating and authorship. For discussion see the entries on the *Zhuangzi* and *Lüshi chunqiu* in Loewe 1993. The *Zhuangzi* passages are discussed below.

5. Graham's discussion of Hui Shi (1989, pp. 76–82 and 174–83) focuses on several encounters between Hui Shi and Zhuang Zhou in the *Zhuangzi* (Zz 24/48–51, Graham 1986, p. 124; 33/81–83 Graham 1986, p. 285; 33/69–74, Graham 1986 p. 283f.; and 17/87–91, Graham 1986 p. 123) and one in the *Lüshi chunqiu* (LSCQ 18/5). He also mentions two passages in the *Shuo yuan* (SY 11/4ab, Graham 1978, p. 444f.), and *Liezi* (Lie 5.1a, Graham 1989, pp. 79–80 and 1960, pp. 94–96). For further discussion, see Hansen 1993 and Kjellberg and Ivanhoe 1996.

6. See Zz 1/36, trans. Graham 1986, pp. 46–47; Zz 1/39, trans. Graham 1986, p. 47; Zz 2/74, trans. Graham 1986, p. 54; and Zz 5/220–21, trans. Graham 1986, pp. 82–83.

7. See Zz 17/605, trans. Graham 1986, p. 123; Zz 17/606–7, trans. Graham 1986, p. 123; Zz 18/614, trans. Graham 1986, pp. 123–24; Zz 24/838–40, trans. Graham 1986, p. 101; Zz 24/843f., trans. Graham 1986, p. 124; Zz 25/891f., trans. Graham 1986, pp. 153–54; Zz 26/936, trans. Graham 1986, p. 100; Zz 27/952–53, trans. Graham 1986, p. 102; and Zz 33/74–89, trans. Graham 1986, pp. 283–85.

8. Graham dates the Hui Shi passages to the late fourth or third century, and the *Tian xia* chapter to the second (Guan 1982, pp. 61–98; Graham 1969, pp. 27–29, 1986, and 1989, pp. 172–74):

Century	Section of the *Zhuangzi*	Chapter
4th	Inner Chapters (1–7) of Zhuangzi (c. 320 B.C.E.)	1, 2, 5
3rd	"School of Zhuangzi" (17–22)	17, 18
	"Ragbag Chapters" (23–27) by or closely related to Zhuangzi	24, 25, 26, 27
2nd	"Syncretist" chapters (15, 33, parts of 11, 12, 13, 14)	33

By contrast, Liu Xiaogan has argued that the *Zhuangzi* text is far less corrupt than Graham suggests (Liu 1987). Harold Roth dates the entire compilation to the second century, at the court of Liu An at about 130 B.C.E. (Roth 1991).

9. Lin 1996, pp. 25–26.

10. The *Lüshi chunqiu* passage ends: "The state is the greatest log" (18/5/11a–b), a remark that is not in the *Huainanzi*.

11. For reference to his impracticable law code, see LSCQ 18/5/11b and 21/1/2a.

12. On the issue of actual face-to-face debate, see Lloyd 1994 and 1996. I am indebed to Nathan Sivin for discussion of this issue. I am indebted to my colleague Christopher Callanan for extensive discussion of Richard Wilhelm's translations of these passages.

13. Xu You 許由 was a legendary sage who turned down offers of rule.

14. I have consulted Richard Wilhelm's German translation of the *Lüshi chunqiu*.

15. Mao 251.

16. The next section, "Responding to Arguments" (18/7), presents six anecdotes about clever rejoinders to arguments, starting with the debate between Hui Shi and Bai Gui presented in the previous chapter (18/7/14a–b). Brief references to these debates also appear in chapter 13; as to references to Bai Gui, see (13/4/7b–8a) and Kuang Zhang (13/7/12b). In another passage, Kuang Zhang questions Hui Shi's method of study (21/5/8a–b).

17. Nivison 1991, p. 137.

18. Munro 1996, p. 193.

19. Deng Xi 鄧析 was an official in the state of Zheng during the sixth century. He developed a code of penal law, inscribed on bamboo tablets; he also had a reputation for raising objections and "turning wrong into right and right into wrong" (LSCQ 18/4/18a). According to an apocryphal story, he was executed by Prince Chan of Zheng for using his skills to undermine the law code promulgated by Prince Chan. The *Zuo zhuan* (Ding 9), however, states that he was executed some twenty years later by the minister Si Chuan 駟歂, who nevertheless continued to use the law code he developed. For discussion, see Knoblock, 1:165.

20. This translation is indebted to Knoblock 1:174.

21. 惠子蔽於辭而不知實 .

22. In preparing the following translations from the *Han Feizi* I have consulted Liao 1939 (1:236, 1:240, 1:243 and 1:287–88).

23. Han Feizi also invoked Hui Shi in an argument that a ruler must compare what he sees and hears to get the real.

> For further illustration, the men of Qi claimed to have seen the earl of the River; Master Hui remarked that the ruler had lost half the brains in the country. Its contrary is instanced by the starvation of Shu Shun by Shu Niu and the interpretation of Jing's customary law by Jiang Yi. (HF 9/518, trans. Liao 1:282)

24. HF 11/612, trans. Liao 2:27. Another passage gives an example: Mozi took three years to constuct a wooden kite, which broke on the first day. His disciples praised his skill in making it fly. He replied that he was less skillful than the maker of the cross-bar for yoking oxen, who spends less than a morning on a bar that can pull a heavy burden for a long way and lasts for many years.

Hearing about this, Master Hui said: "Mozi was exceedingly skillful, considering the construction of the cross-bar skilful and the construction of the wooden kite clumsy"(HF 11/625, trans. Liao 2:34).

25. For another translation, see Hightower 3.33, pp. 116–17.
26. Xunzi adds two more names to this list: Confucius's disciple Zi Si 子思 and Meng Ko 孟軻 (X 15/6/3–16/6/13). For another translation of this passage, see Hightower 4.22, pp. 145–46.
27. This passage is similar to LSCQ 18/5 (trans. Graham 1989, pp. 76–77). Two other references to Hui Shi appear in the *Huainanzi.* Chapter 11 describes an encounter between Hui Shi and Zhuang Zhou; chapter 19 relates Zhuangzi's mourning at the death of Hui Shi (19/342).
28. Harbsmeier 1989, p. 304.
29. A second reference to Hui Shi appears in the chapter "Miscellaneous Sayings" (SY 17), which recounts a conversation between Master Hui and a boatman who is taking Hui Shi to Liang to (he hopes) succeed the minister of Liang, who has just died (17/3b–4a).
30. ZGC 16:543, trans. Crump 1970, p. 198.
31. ZGC 16:545–46, Crump 1970, p. 190
32. ZGC 22:804, trans. Crump 1970, p. 316
33. ZGC 23:838, Crump 1970, p. 333
34. In another chapter, after the death of King Hui of Wei, heavy snow fell and the heir's ministers urged him to delay the burial. They consult Hui Shi, who persuades the heir to delay the burial accordingly (ZGC 23:826, trans. Crump 1970, p. 308).
35. Harbsmeier 1989, p. 294.
36. Milder versions of Xunzi's criticisms recur in the *Hanshi waizhuan,* a text Harbsmeier finds lacking in humor, but not without instances of sarcastic wit. Similarly, he finds the *Shuo yuan* to contain elements of "Confucian wit" (p. 294). See also pp. 298–99 (*Lüshi chunqiu*), 296–98 (*Zhanguo ce*), 299–303 (*Han Feizi*), and 303–5 (Hui Shi).

REFERENCES

Crump, James Irving, trans. 1970. *Ch'an-kuo ts'e.* Oxford: Clarendon Press.
Graham, Angus C., trans. 1960. *The Book of Lieh-Tzu: A Classic of the Tao.* Rpt., New York: Columbia University Press, 1990.
———. 1970. "Chuang-tzu's Essay on Seeing Things as Equal." *History of Religions* 9. 2–3:137–59.
———. 1978. *Later Mohist Logic, Ethics and Science.* Hong Kong: Chinese University Press, and London: School of Oriental and African Studies.
———. 1986. *Chuang-tzu: The Inner Chapters.* London: George Allen & Unwin.

———. 1986. "How Much of *Chuang Tzu* Did Chuang Tzu Write?" In *Studies in Chinese Philosophy and Philosophical Literature*. Singapore: Institute of East Asian Philosophies.

———. 1989. *Disputers of the Tao: Philosophical Argument in Ancient China*. Chicago: Open Court.

Guan Feng 關鋒. 1962. "Zhuangzi 'wai za pian' chu tan" 莊子外雜篇初探. In *Zhuangzi zhexue taolun ji* 莊子哲學討論集. Edited by Zhexue yanjiu bianjibu 哲學研究編輯部. Beijing: Zhonghua.

Han Feizi jishi (HF) 韓非子集釋. 1958. Annotated by Chen Qiyou. Beijing: Zhonghua.

Hanshi wai zhuan (HSWZ) 韓氏外傳. 1920–22. *Sibu congkan*. Beijing: Commercial Press, (hereafter SBCK).

Hansen, Chad. 1983. "A Tao of Tao in Chuang-tzu." In *Experimental Essays on Chuang-tzu*, ed. Victor H. Mair. Honolulu: University of Hawaii Press.

———. 1991. "Should the Ancient Masters Value Reason?" In *Chinese Texts and Philosophical Contexts*, ed. Henry Rosemont. Chicago: Open Court.

———. 1992. *A Daoist Theory of Chinese Thought*. Oxford: Oxofrd University Press.

Harbsmeier, Christoph. 1989. "Humor in Ancient Chinese Philosophy." *Philosophy East and West* 39.3:289–310.

Hightower, James R., trans. 1952. *Han Shih Wai Chuan, Han Ying's Illustration of the Didactic Application of the Classic of Songs*. Cambridge, Mass.: Harvard University Press.

Huainanzi (HNZ) 淮南子. 1954. *Zhuzi jicheng* 諸子集成. Beijing: Xinhua shudian.

Ivanhoe, P. J. 1992. "Zhuangzi on Skepticism, Skill and the Ineffable Dao." *Journal of the American Academy of Religions* 61.4:639–54.

Kjellberg, Paul and P. J Ivanhoe, eds. 1996. *Zhuangzi and Skepticism*. Albany: State University New York Press.

Knoblock, John. 1988, 1990, and 1994. *Xunzi: A Translation and Study of the Complete Works*. 3 volumes. Stanford, Calif.: Stanford University Press.

Liao, W. K., trans. 1939. *The Complete Works of Han Fei Tzu*. 2 vols. London: Arthur Probsthain.

Liezi 列子 (Lie). SBCK.

Lin, Shuen-fu. 1996. "Transforming the Tao: A Critique of A. C. Graham's Translation of the Inner Chapters of the *Chuang Tzu*. Ms. (Published in the symposium volume of the Second International Conference on the Translation of Chinese Literature, Taipei, December 1992. Used by permission of author.)

Liu Xiaogan 劉笑敢 41. 1987. *Zhuangzi zhexue jiqi yanbian* 莊子哲學及其演變. Beijing: Zhonguo shehui kexue chubanshe.

Lloyd, G. E. R. 1994. "Adversaries and Authorities." *Proceedings of the Cambridge Philological Society* 40:27–48.

———. 1996. *Adversaries and Authorities: Investigations into Ancient Greek and Chinese Science*. Cambridge: Cambridge University Press.

Loewe, Michael A. N., ed. 1993. *Early Chinese Texts: A Bibliographic Guide*. Berkeley: Society for the Study of Early China and The Institute of East Asian Studies, University of California.

Lüshi chunqiu (LSCQ) 呂氏春秋 [Springs and Autumns of Master Lü]. 1927–35. *Sibu Beiyao* edition. Beijing: Zhonghua.

Munro, Donald. 1996. "A Villain in the *Xunzi*." In *Chinese Language, Thought, and Culture*, ed. Philip J. Ivanhoe. Chicago: Open Court.

Nivison, David. 1991. "Hsun Tzu and Chuang Tzu." In *Chinese Texts and Philosophical Contexts*, Ed. Henry Rosemont. Chicago: Open Court.

Raphals, Lisa. 1992. *Knowing Words: Wisdom and Cunning in the Classical Traditions of China and Greece*. Ithaca, N.Y.: Cornell University Press.

———. 1994. "Skeptical Strategies in the *Zhuangzi* and *Theaetetus*." *Philosophy East and West* 44.3:501–26. Reprinted in Ivanhoe and Kjellberg 1996.

Rosemont, Henry, ed. 1991. *Chinese Texts and Philosophical Contexts*. Chicago: Open Court.

Roth, Harold. 1991. "Who Compiled the *Chuang-tzu*?" In *Chinese Texts and Philosophical Contexts*, ed. Henry Rosemont. Chicago: Open Court.

Shuo yuan (SY) 說苑. 1988. Attributed to Liu Xiang 劉向 In *Shuo yuan jinzhu jinyi* 說苑今註今譯. Taiwan: Shangwu.

Wilhelm, Richard, trans. *Früling und Herbst des Lü Bu We*. Jena, 1928.

Xunzi 荀子. 1950. Harvard-Yenching Institute Sinological Index Series, Supp. 22. Beijing: Harvard-Yenching.

Zhanguo ce (ZGC) 戰國策 [Strategies of the Warring States]. 1985. Commentary by Liu Xiang 劉向. 3 volumes. Shanghai: Guji chuban she.

Zhuangzi ji shi (Zz) 莊子集釋. 1961. Edited by Guo Qingfan 郭慶藩. Beijing: Zhonghua.

7

Transformational Humor in the *Zhuangzi*

JAMES D. SELLMANN

One would like to say: This is what took place here; laugh, when you can.

— Ludwig Wittgenstein

Rather than go toward what suits you, laugh: rather than acknowledge it with your laughter, shove it from you. Shove it from you and leave the transformations behind; then you will enter the silent oneness of nature.

— Confucius in the *Zhuangzi*

THE ROARING BUTTERFLY

In large part the history of Chinese philosophy is an interpretative tradition, and the various philosophers are basically developing different explications or radically different meanings of certain key concepts—*dao* 道, *de* 德, *yili* 義利, *liqi* 理氣. If this is not true historically, it is, at least, true today. The contemporary controversies in Chinese philosophy are primarily over matters of interpretation. Although there are numerous "camps," and at the risk of oversimplifying the profound depths of those debates, nevertheless I contend that present disputes in Chinese philosophy diverge largely between maintaining indigenous vantage points, and developing Westernized interpretations. Many of the Westernized explanations are also influenced by Christian values, introducing some concepts of the transcendent and eternal that are not part of the *sui generis* character of Chinese philosophy.[1] In a global marketplace, the unique ethnic performances become entangled in delightful conversations and the distinctions blur between indigenous, pandemic, and introduced. I want to explicate what the *Zhuangzi* is saying to, and doing to, its reader. We have all heard of "the shot heard around the world"—the American call for liberty. This essay represents the laughing roar of the butterfly heard around the world—the story of Zhuangzi's butterfly dream has been translated into numerous languages. His "dream" is even more so a symbol of freedom than the "shot" because the "dream" offers a nonviolent and humorous liberation affordable in almost any political system. The freedom of transmogrification presented in the *Zhuangzi* is not limited to freedom from political oppression, but entails freedom from social restraint and personal fears—a freedom to be spontaneous and natural.[2]

I suggest that the *Zhuangzi* is not advocating the transcendental but represents the organismic.[3] It is not dualistic but employs correlative nondual thinking.[4] It does not advocate escapism, but is antinomian and iconoclastic. It does not pursue tranquility, but *yinshi* 因是, an active participatory harmony. It is not contemplative or purposive—not rational meditation, not Buddhist meditation, not mentation. It is not mental at all, not a distant intellectual analysis, but rather the *Zhuangzi* is about living life, a co-creative life of enjoyment. "To read the *Zhuangzi* is to live it, thereby rightly living and enriching our lives."[5]

It may be tempting to interpret the story of the Peng bird as a metaphor for a transcendent sage who gets above the world. In my reading, transcendentalism in any form is not *Zhuangzi*'s perspective; it is not a view from or of a higher reality. Peng flies in this very sky; the turtle dove alights on that branch. The sagacious perspective is the awareness of the nondual bipolar interrelations of life. From the pivot of nature's creatively turning "potter's wheel," the *Zhuangzi* presents vistas of the correlative nondual, two-sided flip-flop environment in which a life is lived. With *ming* 明 (natural illumination), the correlative nondual point of view of the *zhenren* 真人—the Authentic Person—perceives the interdependency of opposites such as the Peng bird and the turtle dove, the big and the small, the right and the wrong, the conventional and the unconventional. The sage walks both ways (*liangxing* 兩行).

In anticipation of the topic of transformation, one might wonder if this essay will explore the metaphysical theories of change or if change will be limited to the physical world. Do the theories contained in the *Zhuangzi* address organic biological change or does the *Zhuangzi* propose an epistemological theory of change? Does the *Zhuangzi* disparage change like Parmenides and Plato, embrace it like Heraclitus, or does it develop a theory like Aristotle's built around causal change? As a holistic thinker, if Zhuangzi was in fact aware of metaphysics or epistemology, perhaps he too would have employed such approaches. However, his usage seems to be more deconstructive, drawing attention to the liminal concepts and propositions that support philosophical systems.

To make sense out of what is said and what is not said (the "not said" is most important in humor and irony) in the *Zhuangzi*, I approach the material with a hermeneutic sensibility. One should not only think of the way meaning and understanding are extracted from existential literature and imagery, but also one must be willing to participate in it—pulling the practical joke. In this type of literature, it is understood that the reader will take up a position in the "story" being told, where images of life forms emerge into the foreground or fade into the background, where the stories evoke an image of the creatively free, authentic life, and the reader finds herself living and transfiguring with the story. Long before Shakespeare, Zhuangzi realized that artistic play dwells in life, and life resides in the play. The *Zhuangzi* contains so many portraits of that spontaneous life—the Authentic Person (*zhenren*), the Superlative Person (*zhiren* 至人), the Spiritual Person (*shenren* 神人), the Sagacious Person (*sheng ren* 聖人).

The *Zhuangzi*'s understanding of transshaping is presented in a literary fashion that resembles existential and postmodern literature, especially Kundera, and it is representative of what might be called "liberation literature."[6] Storytelling, irony, jokes, even a simple pun—all of the elements that make up comedy, laughter, and forgetting—these are the literary devices employed in the *Zhuangzi*.

LIVING TRANSFORMATION

Consider the worlds we inhabit: cosmic, natural, social, and psychological, and how we, however minutely, contribute to their construction. Consider the rate of motion and degree of change occurring on, throughout, and among these worlds, and how their present "state" is but a passing phase in the ongoing processes of transformation. Popular comparativists have been drawing associations between contemporary science, especially general and special relativity theory, and ancient philosophies of change, such as Heraclitus, Sāṃkhya, Buddhism, and Daoism. Not wishing to jump on that bandwagon, but seeking a simple, Daoist way of getting started, allow me the freedom to give you a taste of just how radical the processes of transmogrification are in the *Zhuangzi*'s world by contrasting images from a "scientific" perspective. There are important differences; in no sense is the *Zhuangzi* concerned with hypothesis testing, or theory development, yet the text does contain some profound insights on knowledge, understanding, and wisdom.

In the *Zhuangzi*'s world anything can happen and often does. One can compare the *Zhuangzi*'s world with the "Zen effect" in quantum mechanics where particle energy is released in an apparently random manner. But the analogy is limited. In quantum mechanics the "Zen effect" is not welcome; indeterminism in physics is considered problematic in that the natural world resists the human conceptual model. That the physicists have not yet been able to provide an adequate model or theory (such as supersymmetry) of the "cosmos," leaving it a chaos, is rather unsettling to them. But it would be an utter joy for Zhuangzi's free and easy wanderings.

For the *Zhuangzi*, the "natural order of things" is NOT. Chaos and indeterminacy are not only the conditions of real life, but are also celebrated as so-of-itself (*ziran* 自然). The *Zhuangzi*'s stories present images of people and creatures who live in and delight in the fields of change. The processes of transformation are often irregular, indeterminate, ambiguous, and vague; certainly there is no abstraction of an eternal principle of change.

There are some patterns of continuity, connection, and coherence—not logical linear coherence, but disjointed ironical harmony. Zhuangzi's account depicts the correlative traits of thought; he realizes that the world is experienced and understood in terms of associations among interrelated codependent opposites: big/small; beauty/ugly; good/bad; this/that; yes/no. When an extreme of any one of the "opposites" is reached, the other is activated. This appears to be the result of correlative thought; thinking of the small converts into thinking of the big. Existentially this thought process imitates the operation of nature as well—drought will end with rain, death with life. There are numerous contrasts of this sort in the *Zhuangzi*. "There is nothing in the world larger than the tip of a new autumn hair, and Mount Tai is tiny" (5/2/52).[7] This quote expresses the *Zhuangzi*'s appreciation and appropriation of the paradoxical flip-flop of correlative thought. It also exemplifies the awareness of transformation occurring at the level of the tip of hair (micro) and mountain formation (macro). The *Zhuangzi* contains various accounts concerning the movements and alterations occurring between the sky and earth (*tian di* 天地); it depicts change on all levels from the cosmic to the personal. The text is loaded with anecdotes about all kinds of biological metamorphoses—the butterfly, a creature of holometabolism, is widely recognized as a symbol of the *Zhuangzi* because of the ample translations and often quoted story of Zhuang Zhou dreaming he is a butterfly. The text relates numerous illustrations of transmogrification within the human world. The unique contribution of the *Zhuangzi* to ancient Chinese literature is that it is the first text on self-realization that offers an unconventional "Daoist" approach without appeal to a Confucian or Mohist reliance on the social, moral, political cultivation that underlies the other philosophical trends. Even the *Daodejing* has a political focus that partly explains why the followers of Han Fei, a *Fajia* 法家 Systematizer (so-called Legalist) writer, would be interested in commentaries on it. In the *Zhuangzi*, the anecdotes about cosmic, environmental, biological, and human change and transformational growth-decay are usually exploited to illustrate personal transition, the need to accept death and regeneration, the importance of cultivating the use of the useless in the alterations of one's natural environment and one's own psycho-physical image. As Kuang-ming Wu observes it:

> Roaming in life takes on a mutual transformation of many modes of existence. Chuang Tzu shows us that we are awakened to an ever-present possibility of changing back and forth between the butterfly-world and the human-world. Such play releases us (*chieh [jie]*) from the fear of poverty and death. On the death bed we praise the "creator"-force which prepares us for a new journey.[8]

THE TEXT

The original fragments and stories that now compose the *Zhuangzi* were edited and arranged in the present order by Guo Xiang 郭象 (d. 312 C.E.). It is interesting to note that Guo Xiang retained and choose to open the collection of stories with the yarn of the mighty Kun fish undergoing a complete holometabolism, becoming the gigantic Peng bird. Do not miss the irony: "*Kun*" usually means fish roe. It is significant that the first philosophical concept to appear in the opening of this anecdote, and now the whole text, is *hua* 化 (transformation). This tale of transfiguration is also important because it depicts a radical transformation. The common place holometabolism of aquatic animalcule into land creatures (tadpole to frog), and land invertebrate into insects of flight (caterpillar to butterfly) is well known. The *Zhuangzi* contains a description of a grossly magnified transmogrification of a leviathan fish into a monster roc. This anecdote enacts a completely new, radical, metamorphosis in that it moves through all the realms of life: aquatic, terrestrial, and aerial.

THE ANATOMY OF A JOKE

> The *Chuang Tzu* describes how a mature person handles
> meaning and irony. An exhaustive elucidation is impossible
> because no one can exhaust the possibilities of play.
> —Kuang-ming Wu

The *Zhuangzi*'s presentation of transformation is contained within the humor of its literary expressions, stories, and parables. The tales are predominately about change and transubstantiation on all tiers—physical, natural, organic, and often implicitly, at the psychological level of personal renewal. It is not only a transformation of one's thinking or understanding, but also an alteration of one's embodied consciousness, and ultimately a complete metamorphosis, a holometabolism, in which the mind and body form an integrated whole wherein being, thinking, feeling, speaking, and acting are not separable in reality or in thought. The prevarications in the text attempt to activate and engender this change in the reader. And one recent literary approach to achieving this purpose is outrageous humor.

For example consider the story at the end of chapter 17, the "Autumn Floods," where Zhuangzi and Huizi are strolling along the dam on the Hao River.

> Zhuangzi said, "See how the minnows come out and dart around where they please! That's what fish really enjoy!"
>
> Huizi replied, "You're not a fish. How (or where) do you know the pleasure of fish?"

Zhuangzi said, "You are not I. How (where) do you know that I don't know the pleasure of fish?"

Huizi replied, "I am not you; so certainly I don't know you. You certainly are not a fish; so you surely cannot know the pleasure of fish."

Zhuangzi replied, "Please, let's go back to the starting point. You asked me, 'Where (how) do you know the pleasure of fish?' When you asked me, this already shows that you knew I knew. I know it here on the banks of the Hao River" (45/17/87–91)[9]

There are two different quips contained in this passage. First there is the paradoxical and humorous problem of self-referential rejection of skepticism. In doubting that Zhuangzi knows the pleasure of the fish, Huizi is in fact admitting that it is possible to know another's mental states—he knows Zhuangzi's "not knowing." This leaves open the possibility that Zhuangzi does know the pleasure of the fish. The second joke employed is a pun on the question particle "*an* 安," which acts as a general question marker, meaning "what," "where," "when," "how." Huizi asks, "how does he know," and Zhuangzi responds by telling him "where" he knows it; this underscores the perspectival and contextual dependency of knowledge. The humor in this little story is liberating in that it opens up possibilities to change one's perspective on things.

A joke not only gets one to "change one's mind," that is, to see things from a different viewpoint, but also when the joke "works," when you get the punch line, and makes one laugh, the laughter alters one's psychosomatic functions, changes body and brain chemistry, modifies one's disposition, transshaping one's outlook on life. This is to embark on an adventure into the unknown, where everything is seen afresh and new, even one's self or lack there of.

Irony and laughter loosen (*chieh [jie]*) us for such stirrings to the new. To laugh is to see beyond the transitoriness of events; laughing at oneself liberates the self into self-scrutiny, thereby allows the situation to appear meaningfully albeit often startlingly.[10]

Integrating this sense of humor into one's lifestyle is an important aspect of the Daoist teachings for personal transformation, especially in living with death.

Aside from its cost effectiveness, there are at least three good reasons to employ irony: (1) as the saying goes, the truth is told in the joke; (2) irony depicts and enacts the indescribable unexplainable truth; and (3) irony breaks down traditional habits of abstract impersonal thinking, challenging the audience to think anew. The great masters of irony, Socrates, Plato, Montaigne, Kierkegaard, and Nietzsche, to name a few, explicitly or implicitly, jest with irony's transformative ("dialectical") character. The dialectical power of a joke or piece of irony *lies* in its ability to get one to see things from "both sides" so to speak; that is, it allows one to see the conventional usage in a new unconventional (humorous) manner. This new perspective allows one to look back at the conventional usage in a new light, perceiving and feeling its limitations. It is this flip-flop of perspectives in the joke or sense of humor that drives the "dialectical" exchange and the "awakening" in and through the discourse. The *Zhuangzi*'s monkey keeper is skilled in double talk; he goes according to the circumstances (*yinshi* 因是).

> This is how the sage evens things out with his "That's it, that's not," staying at the point of rest on the potter's wheel of nature. It is this that is called "going both ways" (*liangxing* 兩行) (4/2/40).[11]

As Wu Kuang-ming observes:

> For Chuang Tzu the irony consists of a twofold built-in mutuality: (1) mutual distinction (*yu fen* [有分]) and (2) mutual interchange (*wu hua* [物化]). The ironist "double walks" (*liang hsing* [*liangxing*]), spanning his life on two roads.[12]

Hegel reflects on the dialectical interchanges and negations ultimately leading to a higher fusion. Spanning two roads steers one on to a third, the "high road" so to speak. For Hegel, the attainment of bonafide reality, through negation, contradiction and raising up (*aufheben*), driving the dialectic to continue itself becoming an idea requiring negation, and so the tour of cosmic history progresses until the Absolute Ghost (*Absolute Geist*) haunts it all—or so the schoolmasters taught. For the *Zhuangzi*, a dialectic system that leads to a "high road" (a cumulative calculus, totaling up in an absolute) would generate an alternate "low road" (say a universe of entropy, of nothing and nihilism). This illuminates Zhuangzi's use of the useless. The dialectician Huizi is on the lookout for the conventionally useful (truth) useless (lie); while Zhuangzi spins yarns concerning the use of the useless transmogrified gourds and trees.

Laughter is the *Zhuangzi*'s vehicle of transformation and liberation; laughter is the means to awaken (*jue* 覺) and loosen (*jie* 解) us from the fetters of oppression held in place by the conventions of psychosocial interaction. But laughter is not the ultimate product. One must certainly practice the method of liberation over and over again, laughing and laughing, time and time again. Eventually one can let go of the practice, let go of the laughing and simply live the life of death and generation.

So the *Zhuangzi*'s exercise in irony is not a commonly held notion of dialectics because dialectics as a "a talking through" implies a third, higher, perspective (the high road, truth, or bona fide reality) that is contradicted by a fourth alternative (the low road, falsehood, or nihilism), or the original dichotomy is simply repeated *ad infinitum, ad nauseam*. Playing on the common misconception that "dia" means "two," we can say that the *Zhuangzi*'s approach is not advocating a dialectic, a trialectic, or a quadralectic. If pressed for coinage, then because Zhuangzi enjoys the ten thousand or myriad things, "myrialectic" (the art of conversing on each and every thing) might be forged to pay that debt.[13] The irony in the *Zhuangzi* might be more fruitfully compared to a postmodernist approach. It presents a nonsystematic form of change, with a decentered, negated self, or multiple perspectives of various "selves," and a decentered sense of history. When the lines between certainty and uncertainty, dreaming and waking, right and wrong, life and death are called into question, one cannot beg that question and assume the worth of one perspective over the others. If learning is to occur, one must be able to adopt and adapt the old information in a creative manner, and not merely repeat it over and over again. If self-realization is to occur, then one must not only be able to laugh at oneself, but one must also transform—change the way one lives.

In the *Zhuangzi*'s use of irony there is (1) the naive conventional view (usually the social tradition, the Confucian approach, or the logic of the debaters), which is negated by (2) the antinomian, the bizarre, the paradoxical—the punch line. Most people, when they *get the joke or punch line*, are affected by the irony, that is, they howl with it. This laughter leads them to see through (1) and (2) toward (3) a new view that appears to be the "higher" right perspective, but this view in its turn is challenged by (4) its own negation, the "lower" wrong view. Again one cackles, and although this laughing is part of the enjoyment of life and the life-affirmative posture of the *Zhuangzi*, nevertheless it too must be snickered at and left behind. Eventually the irony and its use must be guffawed at and set aside, or else one gets trapped in an infinite meaningless cycle of laughing. So a new lived life must come out of the ironic convulsions. The hilarity teaches one to practice the life of enjoyment.[14]

THE COMEDY OF TRANSFORMATION

There is no conclusion, no end, no finish for the *Zhuangzi*. Things transpose, and keep on changing. Therefore, the compassionate meaning and empathic understanding of "transformation" as it is metaphorized in the context of the *Zhuangzi* encompasses each and every thing—in the natural world and the human world. From this perspective, transformation entails a magnitude of meaning, or "spiritual" dimension (in the sense of "high spirits" or "laughter"). Transformation is not just change of form and shape (*bian* 變) or a change of things and situations (*yi* 易), but it also entails a complete renewal of the experience of life's meaning (*hua* 化). *Hua* provides a way to move through various shapes or bodily forms within a species and across species to merge with each unique perspective, and to experience a mystical continuity with the particulars of nature. In chapter two of the *Zhuangzi*, the mystical experience is described in these terms: "heaven and earth were born together with me, and the myriad things and I are one" (5/2/52–53).

The way "*hua*" is played out in the *Zhuangzi* is very telling, especially in the context of elaborating on the mystical experience. The Daoist awareness of oneness, continuity, and, equanimity should not be interpreted as inconsistent with "parity." Every particular is of ultimate ontic significance because each has its own peculiar qualities. For example, in chapter 2, Zi Qi describes the piping of nature as: "Blowing on the myriad things in a different way, so that each can be itself—all take what they want for themselves, but who does the sounding?" (3/2/9). This passage emphasizes the difference, the unique particularity and participation of each and every instant. The rhetorical question "who does the sounding?" is the punch line. The mind imposes a gestalt or unifying image of itself in the form of a conductor or grand musician (a God or ultimate reality) to do the piping. Zi Qi hears the tone of each particular in harmony with each and every other, but not a higher melody. When the notion of "oneness" (*yi* 一) is introduced in chapter 6, we see that it entails a balancing of correlative bipolar perspectives—liking and not liking, existing and not existing, nature and man not defeating each other but acting as companions (16/6/19–20). Recognizing the correlative interdependence of life and death, the good and the bad, the sage and the tyrant, one is counseled to "forget them both and transform yourself with the way" (16/6/23).

For the *Zhuangzi*'s mystical perspective, one's awareness of the significance and joy of the ultimate change, death, is important for full participation in the processes of nature.

> If I think well of life, then for the same reason I must think well of my death. . . .
>   You . . . take on human form and are delighted. But the human form has ten thousand changes that never come to an end. (16/6/24–27)

The transformative creative power (*zaowuzhe* 造物者) of the interdependency of particulars—the *dao* as field—is the ongoing processes of the interrelated transfiguring of things. The creative changes occur and the body mutates; any kind of bizarre transmogrification can alter my arms into a rooster and a crossbow, or my legs into wheels. In death, my body and energy are merely transshaped into what? "a rat's liver; or a bug's leg?" (17/6/55).

Chapter 6 of the *Zhuangzi* gives a description of people who live and die through alterations. Then, the text breaks down the idea, telling us to forget about it, and to go on with the processes of transformation. A vivid description of a group of Daoists who, by conventional standards, are disrespectful to a corpse, is put in the mouth of Confucius. Confucius says that these men roam beyond the bounds of tradition. Because Confucius dwells within conventional strictures, he can see no way to meet with them. Then he gives the following description:

> They are at the stage of being fellow men joined with the creative process (*zaowuzhe*), and go roaming in the single breath (*yiqi* 一氣) of heaven and earth (18/6/68)

This is a form of nature mysticism; there is no transcendental element here. The mystical union is a merging with the processes of transformation which entails embracing death as a type of homecoming, or return to nature and the *dao*—fields of change.

Confucius goes on to give a description of an apparent Daoist who misbehaved at his own mother's funeral. Confucius proposes that this man views life and death from an "awakened" (*jue*) perspective that is beyond ordinary knowledge. This comes from his ability to dismantle his understanding of "*hua*" itself.

> If in transforming he has become one thing instead of another, is it required that what he does not know terminated in being transformed? Besides, at the stage of being terminated how would he know about the untransformed? At the stage of being untransformed, how would he know about the transformed? Is it just that you and I are the ones who have not yet begun to wake from our dream. (18/6/78–79; Graham 90)

Confucius continues to describe how this Daoist figure identifies with other creatures and humans, and thereby destroys the I-centered outlook. The passage "ends" with the following description of how one must awaken to "transformation," and "humor" by beginning to live the life that affirms one's own personal mutation, one's immediate experience. And ultimate meaning in life is co-created through an appreciation of one's sustained unity with each and every particular under the silent sky.

> There is no telling whether the man who speaks now is the awakener or the dreamer. Rather than go toward what suits you (*shi* 適), laugh: rather that acknowledge it with your laughter, shove it from you. Shove it from you and leave the transformations behind; then you will enter the silent oneness of nature (*liaotianyi* 寥天一). (18/6/82)[15]

The giggle and chuckle emerge from that silent void. Each and every flower petal in the valley of the lilies reverberates with the quaking butterfly's roar.

NOTES

The first draft of this paper, entitled "Transformation in the *Zhuangzi*," was presented at the Society for Asian and Comparative Philosophy panel held in conjunction with the Eastern meeting of the American Philosophical Association conference at the Washington Hilton Hotel, December 29, 1992. An earlier manuscript of this paper, entitled "Communicating with Humor in the *Zhuangzi*," was read at the East Meets West, Comparative Religion and Philosophy conference held in conjunction with the California State University, Long Beach, April 8–10, 1993.

1. David L. Hall and Roger T. Ames explicate the unique character of Chinese philosophy in contrast to Euro-American philosophy. See *Anticipating China:*

Thinking through the Narratives of Chinese and Western Culture (Albany: State University of New York Press, 1995).

2. Chen Guying, *Beiju zhexuejia Niecai* (The Tragic Philosopher Nietzsche), (Peking: Shenghua, 1987), p. 271. Chen discusses in detail how Zhuangzi seeks liberation from various forms of cultural, political and psychological oppression.

3. On the difference between organic and organismic, see Joseph Needham, *Science and Civilisation in China*, vol. 2 (Cambridge: Cambridge University Press, 1956).

4. For a discussion of these concepts, see T'ang Chün-yi, "The *T'ien Ming* (Heavenly Ordinance) in Pre-Ch'in China," *Philosophy East West*, 11.4 (1962); Angus C. Graham, *Yin-yang and the Nature of Correlative Thinking*, Monograph No. 6. (Singapore: The Institute of East Asian Philosophies, 1986), David L. Hall and Roger T. Ames, *Anticipating China*, give a detailed and historical analysis of these terms.

5. Kuang-ming Wu, *The Butterfly as Companion: Meditations on the First Three Chapters of the "Chuang tzu,"* (Albany: State University of New York Press, 1990), p. 8.

6. Liberation literature generally speaking encompasses the literature of all "liberation" approaches, such as liberation theology, liberation philosophy, liberation economics, political science, sociology, psychology. In particular, liberation literature refers to that literary genre that promotes (usually human) freedom—the religious, political, socioeconomic, psychological, spiritual liberation of a being or beings who are oppressed, alienated, or limited. For the comparison with M. Kundera, see *The Book of Laughter and Forgetting* (New York: Penguin, 1986).

7. The translations are my own; the citations give the page.chapter.line to *A Concordance to Chuang Tzu*, Harvard-Yenching Index Series No. 20 (Cambridge, Mass.: Harvard University Press, 1956). I am deeply indebted to Yang Yu-wei for teaching me how to read the *Zhuangzi*, and I have consulted the following translations: Burton Watson, *The Complete Works of Chuang Tzu* (New York: Columbia University Press, 1968), p. 43. Angus C. Graham, *Chuang-tzu: The Seven Inner Chapters and Other Writings from the Book Chuang-tzu* (London: George Allen & Unwin, 1981), p. 56.

8. Kuang-ming Wu, *The Butterfly as Companion*, p. 381.

9. *A Concordance to Chuang tzu*, Harvard-Yenching Index Series No. 20; Burton Watson, *The Complete Works of Chuang Tzu*, pp. 188–89; Angus C. Graham, *Chuang-tzu: The Seven Inner Chapters and Other Writings from the Book Chuang-tzu*, p. 123. See also the essay by Roger Ames in this volume.

10. Kuang-ming Wu, *The Butterfly as Companion*, p. 375.

11. A. C. Graham, *Chuang-tzu*, p. 54.

12. Kuang-ming Wu, *The Butterfly as Companion*, p. 376.

13. Note the irony in the term "dialectic" where it is both fallacious rhetoric (false, lie), and a rational systematic logical account of the absolute truth. Hence, I want to forge counterfeit coinage to pay my true philosophical debts.

14. This process can serve as a model for describing how learning occurs. One's naive experience is negated through a contradictory experience that leads one to have a profound unique experience, but the profound unique experience cannot be repeated because, then, it would not be unique, and so it is appropriated anew in each subsequent experience. The consummate learner comes to identify with the learning process, a process of changes, not with the cut-and-dried knowledge or outcome of the learning. Humor is the ancestral teacher, the source of all authentic learning. I call this the learning-is-a-joke theory.

15. Graham translates this passage as: "Shove it from you and leave the transformation behind; then you will enter the oneness of the featureless sky." See *Chuang-Tzu: The Seven Inner Chapters*, p. 91. This use of "featureless" should not be taken to mean that a transcendent unity is at work here; but rather a nonjudgmental parity is acknowledged. Watson translates it as: "Be content to go along and forget about change and then you can enter the mysterious oneness of Heaven." See *The Complete Works of Chuang Tzu*, p. 89. What they translate as "featureless" and "mysterious" is the character *liao*, which means "empty, solitary, silent."

8

Cook Ding's Life on the Whetstone

Contingency, Action, and Inertia in the Zhuangzi

WILLIAM A. CALLAHAN

Once Cook Ding was butchering an ox for King Wen Hui. How his hands touched it; how his shoulders leaned into it; how his foot stepped on it; how his knee dug into it—Hua! Xiang!—like playing a musical instrument, he moved his knife to make a *huo* sound; none of these actions missed a beat. They complied with the Dance of the Mulberry Forest, and accorded with the musical composition of Jing Shou.

"Oh, how wonderful!" King Wen Hui said. "How could your skill reach to such a level?"

Putting his knife aside, Cook Ding replied, "What I love is *dao*, which is more advanced than any skill. When I first started to butcher, I saw nothing but ox. After three years, I no longer perceived a whole ox. Now I don't see it with my eyes, but encounter it with my spirit. My senses' perception ceases, while my spirit and intentions proceed. I rely on the patterns of Nature in order to split into the great cavities, because this is the way the ox certainly is. Never touching the peripheral vessels, the small ganglia, the major veins, the tendons, or the tenderloins, how much less do I touch the large bones such as the femur.

"A good cook changes her cleaver every year, because she cuts with it. A common cook changes his cleaver every month because he chops with it. My cleaver is 19 years old. It has butchered several thousand oxen, but the blade is still sharp like it has been freshly whetted.

"An ox has gaps between the segments of its flesh; the blade lacks thickness. In entering into these gaps with that which lacks thickness, there is sufficient space for the blade to roam. This is why for 19 years my blade has been sharp like it has been freshly whetted.

"Even so, whenever I run into complications, I look at where the difficulty is made. With care, with concentration, my vision stops, my action is delayed—very subtly, I manipulate the knife. Huo! and the ox is already butchered. The flesh falls like dirt to the ground. I then stand up, put my cleaver at my side and look all around me. I am content and satisfied. I sheath the knife after wiping it off."

King Wen said, "Excellent! I attain the way to nourish my life by listening to my cook's words." (7/3/2)[1]

This delightful tale is the title story from the third chapter of the *Zhuangzi* 莊子—"The Mastery of Nourishing Life." It contains a basic style of life and more specifically, a style of decision-making and acting that is characteristic of the *Zhuangzi* and important for its political philosophy. As this story adequately shows, the *Zhuangzi*'s politics is not structural politics of statecraft; it is the lowly cook that knows how to live rather than the king.[2] The *Zhuangzi* has a different kind of politics, a broader notion of interrelation in personal politics. In this essay, I would like to unpack this story as a prime example of the politics of decision-making and action drawing on related concepts in the *Zhuangzi*, and in the classical Chinese tradition at large.

Conversely, many scholars criticize *Zhuangzi* as being the "relativist" of Chinese philosophy. Henry Rosemont (1988), in the first sentence of his essay entitled "Against Relativism," cites the *Zhuangzi* as a prime example of a relativist outlook, the outlook that he goes on to say plagues us all in modern times. Zhuangzi, as a relativist, is interpreted and thus portrayed as irresponsible. Lacking a solid grounding, he is not credited with a valid social and political philosophy, for in this interpretation he is seen as involved in flights of fancy that have little relation to the "real world." Indeed, this line of argument presents relativism, and thus Zhuangzi, as paralyzing purposive action. Yet throughout the *Zhuangzi*, various characters such as Cook Ding are involved in actions—actions that are "responsible" in that they respond to the situation.

In unpacking the story of Cook Ding to argue against interpretations such as Rosemont's and for a more personal politics, I will have to tell a few more tales. First, I would like to examine the social setting of this story, primarily in terms of the "Wandering at Ease" (Xiao Yao You 逍遙遊) and "Autumn Floods" (Qui Shui 秋水) chapters, for they set up the stage for "contingent action" in the *Zhuangzi*. Next, I would like to examine the linguistic setting of these actions. Then I would like to see how all these things come together in a technique characterized by the term "*ming* 明" to work to make decisions and act on them in a "contingent" way. Then I will look at the inaction that Zhuangzi's method does entail, arguing that it is related to action, containing the unlimited potential for action. Finally, I will come back to Cook Ding and his ox to suggest a method of making decisions in terms of this responsibility to the context at hand—a sort of political action for us to consider.

ZHUANGZI'S CONTINGENCY

The joy of the *Zhuangzi* comes in the reading of stories such as those found in "Wandering at Ease" and "Autumn Floods." As an enduring text, the *Zhuangzi* has survived over two thousand years as a classic because it can be read in different ways, from different perspectives, for different purposes. Following this focus on multiplicity, I choose to read the *Zhuangzi* as literature as well as philosophy. The difference between the two approaches is important—traditionally in Western scholarship, philosophy has been read for answers, for truths. Literature on the other hand, is content to provide suggestions and examples.[3]

This literary approach is particularly useful in reading Chinese literature, for the texts themselves are not stable, but corrupt from thousands of years of transmission: authorship is a problem. It is problematic to try to ascertain or reconstruct what Zhuangzi *really* meant, for the evidence to date strongly suggests that there was no one author or even editor of the text.[4] So rather than assume that meaning is created exclusively by the author, we can follow a different approach that empowers readers to create their own meanings.[5]

Furthermore, the style of the *Zhuangzi* supports this way of reading, for stories are told in terms of different characters arguing for different points—characters are rarely all right or all wrong, but take part in discourses that have their aspects of truth and falsity. The *Zhuangzi* uses many familiar characters in unfamiliar ways: for example the story in the "Ren Jian Shi" (人間世) chapter where Confucius represents a point of view that we might call "Zhuangzian" whereas the character of Confucius's favorite disciple Yan Hui speaks in a more Confucian way.[6]

Indeed, it is difficult to read the *Zhuangzi* critically because often there is no closure in the arguments and discussions reproduced in the text: each point is often supported and criticized by various characters in the text. None of the characters really seems to have the last word. So rather than engaging in a search to unearth the true meaning of Zhuang Zhou, I look to the web of arguments and seek to read the text productively to create meaning pragmatically, according to what use and relevance it has for particular projects.

Since the project of this essay concerns political and social philosophy, initially I will bracket the more mystical elements of the text. In the third section I shift gears to consider quasi-mystical circumstances, but the essay quickly down-shifts again to the examples and applications of this technique of decision-making.

STORYTELLING

The stories in the *Zhuangzi* have been read for the sheer exhilaration of exercising the imagination, flying through the skies with the magnificent bird named Peng;[7] the *Zhuangzi* has been read as a handbook for Daoist meditation;[8] Zhuangzi's stories have also inspired people to understand their worlds through the meta-phorical value of its tales.

A concept of contingency, negotiation, and interplay that calls into question universal arguments easily grows out of the "Wandering at Ease" and "Autumn Floods" chapters and is further suggested in the balance of the text. The *Zhuangzi*'s contingency is not a paralytic view of the world where all is "right" and all is "wrong," and where no action in any particular direction can be justified as better or worse. The world is not so simple. For the *Zhuangzi*, there are many "rights" and many "wrongs" that each of us judge from our own point of view.[9] We build these judgments into a system of discrimination that we use to under-stand our world. Each of us has a different point of view, and thus a different understanding of the world.

Indeed, Zhuangzi does not think in terms of a single world or order, but of many worlds and many orders each of which correspond to a perspective. These worlds overlap with each other in common experience: examine the story of the cicada and the turtledove who laugh at the huge bird Peng, saying (1/1/8):

> "I fly when I am inspired, and stop when I collide with the elm tree. Often I merely fall to the ground, not being able to reach a branch. What would anybody travel 90,000 miles to the south for?"

Or as a quail remarks in a different version of the story [1/1/15–16]:[10]

> "Why does Peng go like that? I leap and I am up in the air, landing again after merely a few dozen feet. Soaring in the midst of reeds, this is indeed the utmost of flying. In these circumstances, why does Peng go south like that?"

Being different animals, they have different perspectives, yet the cicada, turtle-dove, and quail all share the perspective of being small flying animals. The large flying animal, Peng, however, is beyond their experience and comprehension—they do not understand or appreciate its action of flying 90,000 miles to the south, for it does not fit into their view of the "utmost of flying," into their "circumstances."

It is in arguing that none of us is complete that the *Zhuangzi* criticizes the cicada, calling it "small." Smallness in Chinese literature is not just a physical quality, but a psychical one as well: *xiao ren* 小人 is usually interpreted as "small-minded person."[11]

The smallness that Zhuangzi is critical of with the cicada is being caught within a restrictive static perspective, which is taken as complete (1/1/7):

> Those whose knowledge is effective for one office, or whose conduct gets close to what is necessary to administer one district, or whose virtue complies with that of one ruler, or whose merit is verified in one state, they look at their own situation, and think that others' situations are also like it.

On the contrary, we are never complete and our experience and situation are partial. Even the cosmos is seen as partial; the *Zhuangzi* often refers to it as the "Big Piece" (*da kuai* 大塊). Rather than searching for some center, we become effective in action—wise—by looking out and enlarging our perspective.[12] Indeed, life is a process of developing our perspective in conversation, creating and expanding ourselves by experimenting with other's experiences as well.

This contingency involves neither atomized isolation, nor totalized "consensus." We are constituted by a web of relations. There are overlaps in "lifeworlds," but they are never complete; we can have communication, but never complete communication. Communication involves acts of interpretation exercised from a given perspective. Thus we must approach worlds with an appreciation of the ambiguity of these overlaps, and delight rather than despair in them.[13]

It is important for Zhuangzi that each of these perspectives is valid according to the perspective from which it arises, or else it would not have arisen. Whether we agree with a particular argument or not is another question; thus contesting perspectives must take this into account in and for communication. We are all involved in conversation, which is a process of trying to motivate others to actions that accord with what we value, while respecting that they in the end may still differ.

The crucial corollary of this point is that we should develop our perspective and life in critical contact with other influences. Following the example of Song Rongzi, a philosopher contemporary with Zhuangzi (2/1/18): "Though the whole world praised him he refused to be encouraged, or deterred, though the whole world discounted him." Song Rongzi went about his business as he saw fit. Of course, we must also respect other points of view as well, and not force ourselves on them, a mistake that Zhuangzi points out in his story of the trader from Song who tries to sell his mandarin ceremonial hats to the "barbaric" Yue tribes, whose cultural world has no use for them (2/1/34).

Zhuangzi's criticism of societal judgments leads us to another point: that there are many worlds other than the human world.

> Counting things in the world, amounts to myriads, and humans only reside in one of them.... In comparing humans with the myriad things, don't humans seem like the tip of an autumn hair on a horse's body? (42/17/11)[14]

This is where Daoism diverges from Confucianism in its most radical terms. For Daoists, the human world is interwoven with other worlds that are entertained from other perspectives—trees, animals, rocks, and so on—these worlds add up into an ever expanding composite cosmos. Zhuangzi emphasizes the existence and validity of nonhuman worlds by mixing them in his stories. He often puts both a recognizably human discourse, as well as alternatives to anthropocentrism, into the "minds and mouths" of animals and plants. In the "Wandering at Ease" chapter, Zhuangzi makes his point of the contextuality of old and young in a story mixing fungi, insects, trees, and humans:

> The mushroom of the morning does not know the old and new moon, the cricket does not know the course of seasons in a year. This is what is meant by few years. South of the Chu there is the Ming-ling tree, whose spring is five hundred years, and autumn is five hundred years. Long ago there was a huge Chun tree, with eight thousand years for its spring and eight thousand for its autumn. This is great age. Yet now, unaccountably, Peng zu is famous for his long life—all the people compare themselves with him. Isn't that a pity! (1/1/10)

It is a pity because in comparison to the Chun and Ming-ling trees, Peng zu's 800 years is not old at all. The *Zhuangzi*, thereby, opens up comparison of humans to the nonhuman as a measure of greatness. Yet in the human world we often forget this and need to be reminded. In another story, a great tree says to a carpenter: "You and I are both things; why can't we coexist as things?" (11/4/72). The project for humans is to expand the human-perspective world beyond that we each have built up in being human: "to roam beyond the four seas" and to become "selfless" (2/1/21):

> An utmost person is beyond self;
> A spiritual person is beyond merit;
> A sage is beyond reputation.

This passage conjures up images of the *Daodejing* 道德經 where subject and object blur and affairs are conducted with nonassertive action (*wuwei* 無為), unprincipled knowing (*wuzhi* 無知) and objectless desire (*wu yu* 無欲) (Hall 1983). These three concepts suggest a way in which worlds can interact without the violence of manipulation and domination, regardless of the perspective from which they are entertained. Thus Zhuangzi in the "Wandering at Ease" chapter tells us a few stories which suggest an idea of a contingent multiplicity of worlds through which we interact with humans and nonhumans, delighting in both similarities and differences in a dynamic harmony.

LANGUAGE AND ACTION

In the "Commenting on the Equality of Things" (Qi Wu Lun 齊物論) chapter, the *Zhuangzi* presents a nominal relativist theory of language that suggests how humans can relate to language and use it to act. This exposition is based on Chad Hansen's Contrast Theory of Language as found in the classical Daoist texts.[15] In this theory names are created in pairs as opposites (4/2/27):

> It is said that "that" comes out of "this," and that "this relies on "that." This is the explanation of "that" and "this" being engendered out of each other.

Examples of this as it is outlined in chapter 2 of the *Daodejing* are beautiful/ugly, good/bad, being/nonbeing, and so on. The image is of a whole that is divided by a "line" to distinguish between opposites, for example, beautiful and ugly. This is the process of distinction and naming; when we distinguish one thing, we simultaneously distinguish and name its opposite.

Now let us put the Contrast Theory of Language into the more general scheme of the relation between language and reality as found in the *Daodejing* and the *Zhuangzi*. This is a theory of prescriptive rather than descriptive language. In this theory, language is composed of names, and knowing is having the ability to manipulate and use these names toward a desired end. Thus it is "know-how" rather than "know-that." According to this Contrast Theory, names come in pairs, and thus "knowing" is knowing the distinction between them (Hansen 1983a). In making a distinction, we create desires and values, which in turn lead to actions to fulfill them. In this way the familiar "is/ought" dualism is not present, for if we distinguish and name something, we name it then because we value it over its alternative.

In the "Commenting on the Equality of Things" chapter of the *Zhuangzi*, contingency in terms of language is stressed: there is no fixed relation between the name and the object that it names: "The name is a guest of the substance" (2/1/25). The distinctions out of which names grow are not fixed, but always shifting—the line that divides the whole is not set. The "line" is shifting because Zhuangzi sees that distinctions are always made from a perspective, and since every perspective is necessarily different, the distinctions thus differ with every perspective. This is illustrated in the text's use of indexicals such as *shi/bi* 是彼 (this/that; itself/other), and especially *shi/fei* 是非 (this/not this) (4/2/29):

> "This here" (*shi*) is also "that there" (*bi*); "that there" is also "this here." There they say *shi/fei* from one point of view, here we say *shi/fei* from another point of view.

Once we divide, we are discriminating from a perspective, thus necessarily ignoring the other ways of dividing, naming, and thus knowing the world from other perspectives (5/2/57):

> To "divide," then, is to leave something undivided: to discriminate between alternatives is to leave something which is neither alternative.... Therefore, it is said that to discriminate between alternatives is to fail to see something.

The *Zhuangzi* uses both the indexical terms and the incomplete nature of dividing to remind us of the contextuality of language and the world. Thus we can only use conventional language and "usual" distinctions as a "temporary lodging place"; a system that we are not closely attached to, and are able to change when it is no longer appropriate.

Yet it is easy to forget Zhuangzi's comments on language, for once we make a *shi/fei* distinction we tend to build up a whole system of names and conventions that necessarily deny the existence of other possibilities. As Zhuangzi says (63/22/52):

> In the intercommunication of *dao*s, their division often becomes complete, and this completion becomes extermination. What goes on being hateful in this analysis is that it makes one distinction into a completed set. The reason why the completion goes on being hateful is that it makes everything there into a completed set, which once expressed cannot be contested, and then we can only see the alternative's ghost. Once the completeness is obtained, this is called committing suicide.

Yet in the face of this suicide what are we to do? Does Zhuangzi see a way to live in the changing world of conventional language and objects that avoids the construction of a static set of *shi/fei* judgments that in its "completeness" is fatal? And does it matter? What are we to do when language, "the usual," is no longer useful?

BEYOND THE "USUAL"

There is a core of intertwined passages in the "Commenting on the Equality of Things" (Qi Wu Lun) chapter and elsewhere that address these problems. A general outline of a process of decision-making and action can be fruitfully interpreted in these passages by highlighting the character *ming* 明, and two elusive pairs of concepts found exclusively in the *Zhuangzi*: (1) the whetstone of Nature (*tianni* 天倪) and the potter's wheel of Nature (*tianjun* 天均), which are equated in the "Imputed Words" (Yu Yan 寓言) chapter, and (2) the axis of the *dao*s (*dao shu* 道樞) and the Utmost Person (*zhiren* 至人). *Ming* and the whetstone/potter's wheel of Nature describe for us a technique of addressing problems when the conventional approaches (conventional language, the "usual") are no longer effective. Briefly put, my thesis is that this is done by interchanging the alternatives and harmonizing them with the situation at hand in order to make a contextual decision. There is a striking parallel in the terminology and in the technique of the *ming*/whetstone of Nature model with the second pair of concepts that deal with affairs beyond our cosmos: the axis of *dao*s and the Utmost Person.

After noting this parallel, I will relate the *ming*/whetstone of Nature model to the resulting process of decision-making and action itself, operationalizing the process to return to Cook Ding. The *ming*/whetstone model demonstrates how recognizing and developing the ability of *ming* as delineated here can help humans solve, or not solve, the problems that they encounter in their lives. In so doing, we can avoid the static system of *shi*/*fei* referred to above, and work better to solve existing problems and address new situations.

MING 明

Ming, which literally means "bright" and "to illuminate," is a common term in the *Zhuangzi*.[16] In the "Commenting on the Equality of Things" and "Imputed Words" chapters it appears eleven times in special circumstances that can be better understood if we treat *ming* as a technical term. In this context, "enlightenment" is the ability to "interchange" and to "intercommunicate," in many ways analogous with *tong* 通. *Ming* is an elaborate interchange or exchange of *shi* and *fei* judgments, and as such is a process of Daoist reversal (*fan* 反) which "illuminates" new possibilies following its literal definition (4/2/26):

> There are the *shi*/*fei* distinctions of the Confucians and the Mohists, by which what is "this" [*shi*] for one of them for the other is not [*fei*], what is not for one of them for the other is. If you wish to affirm what they deny and deny what they affirm, then there is nothing like using *ming*.

By switching *shi* and *fei* we show that they are contingent, and we are thus not bound to either one or the other. (Though we are bound in the fact that we must make *shi*/*fei* judgments to act.) In this interchanging, the *Zhuangzi* presents *ming* as a liberating skill, as shown in this passage (4/2/35):

> When deeming "that's it" to pick out a stalk from a pillar, a hag from beautiful Xi Shi, things however peculiar and incongruous. . . . Only the person who is untrammeled knows how to intercommunicate them to integrate them.

The person who is "untrammeled" is not restricted by attachment to a specific *shi* or *fei*, but can interchange *shi*s and *fei*s, and thus use *ming* to see the situation from the relevant perspectives. When we interchange *shi*/*fei*, we also interchange the perspective from which the *shi/fei* is made. Here the "untrammeled person" shifts the focus from differences to similarities (integrating the stalk/pillar and the hag/Xi Shi after separating them through distinction). It must be remembered that the untrammeled person can pursue some other axis of distinction, or shift back whenever necessary.

MING AND THE WHETSTONE OF NATURE/POTTER'S WHEEL OF NATURE

With this interpretation, *ming* is related to two central illustrations of "Commenting on the Equality of Things" chapter of Daoist methods of decision-making that result in action: the whetstone of Nature and the potter's wheel of Nature. These illustrations stress the interchange of *shi* and *fei*:

1. What is meant by "Harmonizing alternatives on the whetstone of Nature"? Treat as this [*shi*] what is not [*fei*], treat as so what is not. (7/2/90)
2. Laboring one's spirit to *ming* (i.e., illuminate) the way in which things are integrated and to fail to understand their similarities is what is called "Three in the Morning." What is "Three in the Morning"? In distributing nuts, a monkey keeper said: "Three in the morning and four in the evening." All of the monkeys were enraged. So the keeper said, "OK, if you're going to be like this, then three in the evening and four in the morning." The monkeys were all pleased.

   Without anything being missed out either in name or in substance, their pleasure and anger were put to use; this too then was "this." Therefore the sage harmonizes alternatives with his *shi/fei* while resting on the potter's wheel of Nature. It is this that is called "Letting both alternatives proceed." (5/2/37)

In each passage, the opposites—the *shi/fei*—are sharpened on a metaphorical block. This sharpening out is not a grinding down of conventional language through diurnial experience as some contend.[17] Rather it is a harmonizing that allows the diversity of the *shi/fei* distinction, for the character in question is *he* 和, which means "to harmonize" and "to mix." The sharpened *shi/fei* judgments are interchanged and equalized, and even accumulated on the whetstone of Nature. The accumulation is relative to the circumstances of the situation at hand, for we must recognize that the whetstone and the potter's wheel are not universal principles, but "tools" used in specific situations. Without *ming* we are tools of the various discourses; with *ming* they can also become our tools.

The situation for the whetstone of Nature (passage 1), comes at the end of a discussion of how to find a ground from which to judge different arguments. The narrator fails to find such a common ground between himself and the inter-locutor, much less in a third party or in something transcendent like "reason." The result is that there is no permanent ground to be found to resolve the issue, but only a pragmatic harmonizing of the contextual particulars to see which alternative works best in this situation.

In passage 2, the potter's wheel of Nature illustration concludes the "Three in the Morning" story. Here the monkey keeper solves the problem of feeding monkeys through interchange—switching from feeding them three nuts in the morning and four in the evening, to four in the morning and three in the evening. If the monkey keeper could not understand the similarities involved in the re-versal—that three/four is the same axis of discourse—then she would have been stuck at "Three in the morning." The monkey keeper succeeds because she is not attached to feeding either three or four nuts first; she can let both alternatives proceed, and see which one works for this particular group of monkeys. This is a simple illustration of the technique of *ming*, for she succeeded on the first inter-change—in reversing the feeding pattern she in turn reversed the monkeys' emo-tion from anger to pleasure.

The last part of the quotation above comments on this story, with Zhuangzi recognizing that decision-making can be more complex. A situation can have a myriad relevant distinctions involved, thus the sage must harmonize the *shi*s and *fei*s while "pausing" on the potter's wheel of Nature. We do this while "resting"; there is little sense of crisis or tension here—addressing new problems is some-thing we casually do every day.[18] We interchange both *shi* and *fei* first in the most immediate distinctions, widening the scope and accumulating the *shi/fei* and letting both proceed until an answer is found. The answer is chosen according to one's perspective—not outside conventions.

Now we can return to the central issue; the general circumstances and process of the *ming*/whetstone of Nature model is found in this passage of the *Zhuangzi*, which continues the story of the "untrammeled persons" parallel to the Cook Ding story:

> Generally speaking, things lack completion and destruction, for they are again intercommunicated and integrated. Only untrammeled persons know how to intercommunicate *shi/fei* distinctions and integrate them. Deeming "that's it" they do not use [to complete], but find for it a tem-porary lodging place in the "usual," thus the "usual" is the usable. The usable is intercommunicatable; to see as intercommunicatable is to get it; and once you get it you are almost there. *Shi* comes to an end; and when it is at an end, that of which you do not know what is so of it, you call the discourse—*dao* 道. (4/2/35)

Untrammeled persons like Cook Ding are aware of *ming* and thus do not hold on to any static names (deeming *shi*) to complete a set; for convenience they use society's names for things (the "usual") still recognizing that these names have no fixed relation to objects (only temporary lodging places). These conventional names are "usable" for communication with other people in society in normal circumstances.

At times, even untrammeled persons run into situations that are not adequately addressed by their names or their skills that are named (when the *shi*, as a system of discourse, comes to an end). Here I follow Ames (1986) in taking the *dao* as the field as opposed to the focus: the discourse is so wide that the untrammeled persons as focuses within it cannot fathom it. In these instances, they can appeal to *ming*. As the *Zhuangzi* says, "the usable is intercommunicatable (*tong*, which is indicative of *ming*)," and to see as intercommunicatable is to obtain the ability of *ming*. Once they have *ming* they are on their way to making a decision. They can sharpen the *shi/fei* on the whetstone of Nature (which follows this passage in the text), and then it is up to their particular perspective to make the decision according to the relevant circumstances.

MING AND THE AXIS OF *DAO*S

The whetstone and the potter's wheel of Nature are involved with action "in the cosmos." But throughout the text the *Zhuangzi* also refers to "outside the cosmos," "beyond the realm of things," "beyond the guidelines," and thus perhaps beyond language, knowledge, and existence as we know them. These passages in the *Zhuangzi* are certainly confusing, as well they should be, for it is impossible for a human to imagine "outside the cosmos." As Zhuangzi says: "What is outside the cosmos sages recognize, but they do not venture to comment on them" (5/2/56). Indeed, perhaps Zhuangzi's point is to metaphorically encompass processes and actions which are outside the *shi/fei* of human language and discourse. Thus following the contingency outlined above in terms of the "*Xiao Yao You*" chapter, "outside the cosmos" refers more to outside the human cosmos—what humans cannot talk about. This fits in neatly with the general Daoist concern for nonhuman worlds, in addition to human worlds.

The "axis of *dao*s" passage in the "Commenting on the Equality of Things" chapter that alludes to this problem has been a source of debate for many scholars. I would like to suggest that *ming* is related to the axis of *dao*s outside the cosmos in a similar way that it is related to the whetstone of Nature and the potter's wheel of Nature within the cosmos (4/2/30):

> Are there really "it" [*shi*] and "other" [*bi*]? Or really no "it" or "other"? Where neither "it" nor "other" finds its opposite is called the axis of *dao*s. When once the axis is found at the center of the circle there is no limit to responding with either, on the one hand it has no limit to what is "it," on the other no limit to what is not. Therefore I say "There's nothing like using *ming*."

The familiar *ming* as process is stated in the last sentence of this passage, but is it the same *ming* as we encountered with the whetstone of Nature and the potter's wheel of Nature, for there are no opposites to sharpen and interchange? Here we have an expanded prelinguistic notion of *ming* in a different context that does not contain *shi*s and *fei*s relative to a certain situation—there is no situation; there is no speech.

There is nothing. We are at the axis of *dao*s, the center of the "wheel" where the spokes of distinction converge in a lack of distinction—there "is no limit to responding with either *shi* or *fei*." There is no limit because the whole out of which distinctions are carved is still intact, thus there can be any sort of carving. The potential for all *shi* and *fei* is endless. This is a *ming* of potentiality that contains all *shi*s and *fei*s within its emptiness and inertia. The axis of *dao*s is only concerned with potential action. It is at rest, for in the action of deeming we step off of the axis of *dao*s and begin carving a path.

The axis of *dao*s should not be confused with some ultimate beginning or primeval whole—there can be a multiplicity of axes of *dao*s, each relative to a particular situation or discourse. The term "inertia" is useful in connoting this, for it refers both to a state of rest and to bodies in unchanging vector motion: for though in motion, the system is at relative rest, neither accelerating nor decelerating. The *Zhuangzi* cautions us against totalizing the *ming* process in terms of Nature, by reminding us that though using *ming* is not making distinctions, but either interchanging and harmonizing them, or leaving potential for them, the very act of using *ming* is making a distinction between "*ming*" and "not-*ming*" (4/2/29):

> This is why the wise do not follow this course [of ambiguity], but open decisions up to the *ming* of Nature; this too then is also because of a "this" distinction.

We cannot get out of discourse into any final metadiscourse. Thus the *Zhuangzi* uses language to demonstrate the limits of language.

Moreover, I would like to draw attention to the similarity between the rest taken at the potter's wheel of Nature and the inertia of the axis of *dao*s. It is in both of these "inactivities" that *ming* either (*a*) interchanges and accumulates *shi*/*fei* on the whetstone, or (*b*) creates the potential for limitless *shi*/*fei* on the axis. Because of the common relation with *ming* and the analogy of pausing, I propose that the potter's wheel/whetstone of Nature and the axis of *dao*s are parallel concepts that address different situations: (1) the world of humans and their particular interrelated discourses, and (2) the cosmos outside the discourse of humans.

MING AND THE UTMOST PERSON

Throughout the *Zhuangzi* there are references to an "Utmost Person" or an "Utmost Sage."[19] We have already encountered this personage in the "*Xiao Yao*

You" chapter. Like the axis of *dao*s, this character is paradoxical. Because of what Hansen calls the *Zhuangzi*'s "double-rhetorical" style, we can never be sure whether Zhuangzi is advocating the Utmost Person, or just presenting her for criticism.

One way to understand the concept of an Utmost Person is to see how she has the basic characteristics of the axis of *dao*s. As just stated, this is paradoxical, for it immediately contains the contradiction of a distinction: the self/other distinction. But perhaps not, for the Utmost Person could very well be a metaphor for one who has the ability to expand the ego-self to encompass all the *shi/fei*. As mentioned above, perhaps this is a metaphorical person who can expand beyond the *shi/fei* of humans to a larger composite whole or focus: the Utmost Person exercising *ming* on the axis of the *dao*s.

The main characteristic of the axis of *dao*s is the prelinguistic lack of distinctions (that is, no "it/other"). This lack of distinctions and opposites leads to two corollary characteristics: First, that the axis is at a state of rest, for there can be no action without distinctions. And second, since the axis lacks opposites and distinctions, it then lacks *shi*s and *fei*s. This means that it actually contains the composite wholes of all *shi*s and *fei*s before they are divided; it has the potential for every *shi/fei*.

The Utmost Person also has these corollary characteristics. Zhuangzi says that "The Utmost Person is beyond self" (2/1/21). Paradoxical as it may be, this gives us a basis for placing the Utmost Person on the axis of *dao*s, for there is no self/other distinction. Zhuangzi spends much time developing the idea that the Utmost Person is capable of anything, and has the potential to do anything. A passage comparing the heart-mind (*xin* 心) to a mirror illustrates this point:[20]

> Become wholly identified with the limitless and roam where there is no forboding of anything. Exhaust all that you draw from Nature and never have gain in sight; simply keep yourself tenuous. The Utmost Person uses the heart like a mirror; she does not escort things as they go nor welcome them as they come, she responds but does not store.

The Utmost Person's mirror-mind reflects the limitless potential *shi/fei* at the axis of *dao*s. As is shown in the quotation below, the *Zhuangzi* specifically identifies the mirror with *ming* (13/5/17–18): "If your mirror is bright (*ming*) the dust will not settle, if the dust settles it is your mirror that is not bright." If you can reflect the myriad *shi/fei* then your mirror is *ming*. The mirror also contains the notion of a changing world and how we cannot get attached to certain *shi/fei*, or a certain system of *shi/fei*, for a mirror only reflects, it does not hold. If we do not hold then we will be free to interchange and exercise the *ming*.

I can only provisionally offer the notion of the mind as a mirror to exemplify this relation of the Utmost Person to the axis of *dao*s, because the first "mirror" quotation also states that there is "responding." This is action of a sort as well as potential action, and as suggested above, action is not possible on the axis of *dao*s.

Elsewhere Zhuangzi delineates the Utmost Person satisfying both the conditions of inertia and of endless potential (58/22/18):

> The Utmost Person does nothing, great sages do not initiate, what is meant is that they have a full view of the universe. Now this is the essence of spiritual *ming*.

The inactivity is crucial to the fullness of potential. For as said above, once you divide something you leave other things out to start down a path of *shi/fei* that ultimately constructs a complete system. But at the axis of *dao*s there is not yet a singular path—all is present in potential. The following quotation addresses the limits of language and how the linguistic action of deeming distinguishes and grades things, and thus disrupts the harmony at the axis (75/27/5):

> Things are even when not spoken; the even with saying is uneven, all your life you refuse to say without ever failing to say.

We could say that at the axis we maintain the completeness of *shi/fei*, and the completeness of potential. But this would be ignoring that completion itself can be a finite distinction which has an end. The *Zhuangzi* illustrates this notion in the passage below (5/2/43):

> To see things as complete or lacking is to look to the Zhao clan when they play their music. To see things as neither complete nor lacking is to look to the Zhao clan when they do not play their music.

When the talented Zhao clan plays their drums and zithers, they are interpreting it according to their system of *shi/fei* and the system of the drum's and zither's construction, thus even as completely beautiful as it may sound it will have the flaw of not realizing the other possible interpretations of the music. When the Zhao are not playing the zither, the potentials of the music, the instrument, and their expertise are left intact in being at rest, for there are still the myriad of possibilities and interpretations.

TECHNIQUES OF DECISION-MAKING

To delineate the notion of decision-making in the *Zhuangzi* a few things need to be clarified. First, we must consider the difference between decision-making and problem solving. Problem solving tends to be more absolute, serving to solve the contradictions, cutting the tension once and for all. Decision-making, on the other hand, is more immanent, tentative, and pragmatic: it does not venture to break the tensions involved in the contradiction. Harmony is a relation, but not a dialectical one where thesis and antithesis are transcended by synthesis. Though cuts may occur, the tension is maintained, "Letting both alternatives proceed," although perhaps one proceeds farther than the other for the moment.

Secondly, we must consider what I mean by a situation. A situation, at the very least, includes a problem and an actor that are intertwined and thus mutually defining. The actor, strictly speaking, is a perspective. It is very difficult to specify what "perspective" is. In classical Chinese philosophy, "perspective" is seen in terms of the word *de* 德. A perspective-*de* is the unique intersection of all the lines of discourse that involve us. Along with everything else our "perspective" is always changing, as we form new discourses, enhance existing ones, and discard others in a changing interrelationship with other perspectives and *de*s (within that cosmos). According to the composite view of the cosmos that is drawn from Hansen's (1983) Mass Noun Hypothesis, a perspective can come from any space in the cosmos. But here we will focus in on the perspective of humans and the human "self" as the actor, fully recognizing that other sorts and levels of perspective are equally relevant.

Furthermore, we can explore and adopt the perspectives of other selves and societies. We employ these other perspectives (as well as our own) when we come to a problem that is not adequately addressed by our "usual" or conventional system of *shi/fei*. We use the process of *ming* to interchange the "usual" system of *shi/fei*, and also to interchange and reverse these adopted systems. In this way we can assume all the relevant perspectives from which the *shi* and *fei* of the situation were distinguished.

Here, a problem is essentially inaction. We stop action because we cannot go on with the "usual." The *Zhuangzi* illustrates this through definite localized events that are argued in terms of "temporary lodging places," and illustrated with specific stories. Zhuangzi would likely argue against drawing a situation out, for that would involve attachment, grasping and constructing a static system of *shi/fei*, which would be defied by the changing world. Hence, we can see the philosophy of the *Zhuangzi* in terms of events like butchering an ox, or more specifically, in terms of the intricacies of butchering an ox well.

The whetstone of Nature is not involved in the resulting action; it sets the stage for the *shi/fei* distinction that will be made. At the end of the *ming*/whetstone process we make our own distinctions—*de*. There are many illustrations of this in the *Zhuangzi*. The following passage stresses the action of perspective and how it is indicative of our lives (44/17/46):

> A thing's life is like a stampede, a gallop, at every prompting it alters, there is never a time when it does not shift. What should we do? What should we not do? Regardless, we will certainly continue to transform of ourselves.

Thus the action of transformation comes from the perspective, and in problem situations it comes through *ming* and the whetstone of Nature from the self. *Ming* is intimately related to this action in process: the action that comes before it and leads to it, and the action that comes after it, resulting from its use on the whetstone of Nature.

TEXTUAL EXAMPLES

There are many references in the *Zhuangzi* to the practicality of the *ming/* whetstone method. In both the potter's wheel of Nature passage and the whetstone of Nature passage, harmonizing the opposites is directly related with addressing problems, the problems of living (7/2/91):

> It makes no difference whether the voices in their transformations have each other to depend on or not. Harmonize them on the whetstone of Nature, use them to go by and let the stream find its own channel; this is the way to live out your years.

"Transformations of voices" has to do with the interchange of *shi* and *fei*. When they are sharpened on the whetstone of Nature they can be used according to our perspective to solve specific problems in the most appropriate way to *de*. Thus, the stream, our life, will find its own channel as opposed to one imposed upon us from some other oppressive perspective.

In the *Zhuangzi* there are many stories of people addressing situations and solving uncommon problems in innovative ways. *Ming* and the potter's wheel of Nature are mentioned specifically in the "Three in the Morning" passage, and there are many other stories in the text that do not mention them yet still serve as examples of this process of decision-making and action. Now let us return to the Cook Ding story. It works into our decision-making model well, for the first line states that Cook Ding was "butchering" (*jie* 解) the ox. The character *jie* is pregnant with multicoded meaning, and examining it will yield some interesting parallels. The *Shuowen* 説文 lexicon defines it with the synonym *pan* 判, which means both "to cut in two," and "to resolve." The core meaning of *jie* is "to unravel, to untie." In modern Chinese, it is found in the compound *liaojie* 了解 ("to understand"), and when we separate the characters we see that a classical reading of this compound is "to be able to unravel." Another instructive example is in the compound *jiejue* 解決 ("to resolve"), which is "to unravel to decide" with a classical reading. Hence Cook Ding is involved in a decision-making process in butchering the ox—in the end it is unraveled for the cooking. Indeed, reading the character *jie* in terms of its component parts confirms that parallel between Cook Ding and making decisions: its right side unravels into *dao*-knife 刀 and *niu*-ox 牛.

Now for the process: Cook Ding is an experienced butcher with decades of practice in his skill, so he has no problem with basic slaughtering:

> I rely on the patterns of Nature to split into the great cavities, because this is the way the ox certainly is. Never touching the peripheral vessels, the small ganglia, the major veins, the tendons, or the tenderloins, how much less do I touch the large bones such as the femur.

For this he uses the "usual," his "usual" repertoire of basic butchering skills. But when he comes to difficulties—to the end of this system of *shi/fei* that is lodged in the usual—he must call upon *ming* and the potter's wheel of Nature:

> Even so, whenever I run into complications, I look at where the dif-
> ficulty is made. With care, with concentration, my vision stops, my
> action is delayed—very subtlely, I manipulate the knife. Huo! and it is
> already butchered. The flesh falls like dirt to the ground.

When Cook Ding encounters the problem, he pauses, as at the potter's wheel of
Nature and gazes at the situation inhaling all of the *shi*s and *fei*s of this situation.
He interchanges them and sharpens them letting both *shi* and *fei* proceed until he
is satisfied with a course. Then Ding swiftly and surely makes his distinction and
acts from it, and the decision is made, a problem dealt with. The ox is prepared for
cooking.[21]

Ding is successful because he is able to hold onto his learned skills, "the
usual," but not too tightly—it is only a "temporary lodging place," for the
"usual" is just one way of naming the world. This loose grip allows Ding to move
to other lodging places, other discourses when his usual skills are not useful.
Indeed, the new skill becomes part of his "usual"—with repetition it will come to
the forefront of his shifting system of the "usual."

CONCLUSION

Understanding this process can change the way we view the world, and address
problems in it—perhaps learning from such an engagement with the issues. The
first lesson is to question any stable realistic world, or language or discourse that
we can appeal to as a grounding. Indeed, though there is an unfixed "usual" that
we normally use, it is only one among many relative sets of discourse to appeal to
at appropriate times. Education, within and without formal instruction, is the
process and practice of the gathering of discourses that facilitate conversations, be
they with other people, with problems, or with the environment.

Secondly, *ming* and the whetstone of Nature are useful for decision-making
and action beyond the "usual." The relative practice of interchanging *shi/fei* is not
obvious to those who have constructed static systems of *shi/fei*. Hence in telling us
of the contingency of language, and the necessity of interchange, the *Zhuangzi*
helps us toward realizing a simpler, perhaps enhanced, and hopefully less violent
engagement with our problems, leading to more harmonious conversations.

NOTES

I would like to thank Professor Yang Yu-wei for patiently reading the *Zhuangzi*
with me. Chad Hansen, Roger T. Ames, James D. Sellmann, and Daniel Lusthaus
made very helpful comments on earlier versions of this paper.

1. The numbers cited after each passage refer to the Harvard-Yenching Concordance edition of the *Zhuangzi*. The translations used in this article are my own, but owe a great debt to A. C. Graham's (1981) work.

2. There are numerous other examples of servants and peasants as the sages rather than a Confucian-style sage-king in the *Zhuangzi*. There are also numerous examples of how Zhuangzi repeatedly refused political office.

3. Philosophical analyses of the *Zhuangzi* often begin with this argument, but usually it is expressed as a disclaimer. Indeed, many scholars seem to just settle for a "poetic reading" since they cannot get "hard" philosophy (what Rorty calls "macho philsophy") out of the *Zhuangzi* (see Mair 1983). Conversely, I look to the strengths that literary theory can bring in addition to a philosophical reading. Actually, in Western philosophy, there is a debate going on about what, if any, distinction should be made between philosophy and literature. See Rorty 1985; Danto 1985; Barthes 1982; Kundera 1984.

4. See A. C. Graham (1986), for an analysis of the text for authorship. In "What is an Author?" Foucault (1979) goes farther to problematize authorship of writers who can be traced to one historical person.

5. Saying this, I still at times personify Zhuangzi for stylistic reasons. In these cases I am referring to the narrator character.

6. See Callahan 1994.

7. See literary translations like Burton Watson (1968), *The Complete Works of Chuang-Tzu.*

8. See Michael Saso (1983), "Chuang-tzu nei-p'ien: A Taoist Meditation."

9. See 7/2/84ff., for example.

10. This repetition is one of the many characteristics of postmodernism that the *Zhuangzi* exhibits. Its writing style is fragmentary and multiple. There is no master narrative told, but lots of little, historical stories. And many of these stories are repeated in the text with just a slight twist to show how perspective affects the telling of the tale.

11. Conversely, wise and virtuous people, e.g., sage-kings, are represented in Chinese art as much larger physically than common folk. Yet later in "Wandering at Ease" we switch perspectives and see bigness being problematized: "A yak which is huge like the clouds hanging form the sky is capable of being called 'big,' but is incapable of catching a mouse" (3/1/45).

12. This is similar to Rorty's reading of Freud, which says that "life seeks to extend its own bound rather than find its own center" by searching for the purity of our ego (Rorty 1986).

13. Politically, it is important to note that similarities also contain differences, and for the *Zhuangzi*, a community would focus on the similarities while leaving room for the differences.

14. Furthermore, the character for "things" (*wu* 物) is often interchangable with the characters for "human." See especially the *Ma Di* 馬蹄 and *Ze Yang* 則陽

chapters. Conversely, in general, Chinese landscape paintings include views of both Nature and humans.

15. See Hansen 1983a.
16. *Ming* 明 shows a curious possible parallel between Chinese philosophy and Western philosophy in the appeal to the heliotrope. See Jacques Derrida (1982) and Richard Rorty (1979) for a critical discussion of this in Western philosophy.
17. See Derrida (1982) for an argument for the effacement of language.
18. This casual attitude is also found in the Pragmatists e.g., William James's "perching," and the lack of crisis in John Dewey and Rorty.
19. This section has benefited from Lee Yearley (1983).
20. (21/7/32). I rely heavily on A. C. Graham's (1981, p. 98) translation here.
21. I benefited greatly throughout the essay by reading A. C. Graham (1983).

REFERENCES

Ames, Roger T. 1986. "Tao and the Nature of Nature." *Environmental Ethics* 8: 317–50.

Barthes, Roland. 1982. "Inaugural lecture, College de France." In *A Barthes Reader*, ed. Susan Sontag. New York: McGraw-Hill, pp. 457–478.

Burton Watson, trans. 1968. *The Complete Works of Chuang-tzu*, New York: Columbia University Press.

Callahan, William A. 1994. "Resisting the Norm: Ironic images of Marx and Confucius." *Philosophy East & West* 44.2: 279–302.

Culler, Jonathan. 1982. *On Deconstruction*. Ithaca, N.Y.: Cornell University Press.

Danto, Arthur C. 1985. "Philosophy as/and/of Literature." In *Post-Analytic Philosophy*, ed. John Rajchman and Cornel West. New York: Columbia University Press.

Derrida, Jacques. 1982. "White Mythology: Metaphor in the Text of Philosophy." In *Margins of Philosophy*. Chicago: University of Chicago Press, pp. 209–71.

Foucault, Michel. 1979. "What Is an Author?" In *Textual Strategies: Perspectives in Post-Structuralist Criticism*, ed. Josue V. Harari. Ithaca, N.Y.: Cornell University Press.

Graham, A. C. trans. 1981. *Chuang-tzu: The Seven Inner Chapters and other writings from the book Chuang-tzu*, Boston: George Allen & Unwin.

———. 1983. "Taoist Spontaneity and the Dichotomy of 'Is' and 'Ought.'" In *Experimental Essays on Chuang-tzu*, ed. Victor H. Mair. Honolulu: University of Hawaii Press, pp. 3–23.

———. 1986. *Studies in Chinese Philosophy and Philosophical Literature*. Singapore: The Institute of East Asian Philosophies.

Hall, David. 1983. "The Metaphysics of Anarchism." *Journal of Chinese Philosophy* 10.1: 49–64.

Hall, David and Roger T. Ames. 1987. *Thinking Through Confucius*. Albany: SUNY Press.

Hansen, Chad. 1983a. *Language and Logic in Ancient China*. Ann Arbor: University of Michigan Press.

———. 1983b. "A Tao of Tao in Chuang-tzu." In *Experimental Essays on Chuang-tzu*, ed. Victor H. Mair. Honolulu: University of Hawaii Press, pp. 24–55.

———. 1985. "Chinese Language, Chinese Philosophy and 'Truth.'" *Journal of Asian Studies* 44.3: 491–519.

Kundera, Milan. 1984. *The Unbearable Lightness of Being*. New York: Harper & Row.

Mair, Victor H., ed. 1983. *Experimental Essays on Chuang-tzu*. Honolulu: University of Hawaii Press.

Saso, Michael. 1983. "Chuang-tzu nei-p'ien: A Taoist Meditation." In *Experimental Essays on Chuang-tzu*, ed. Victor H. Mair. Honolulu: University of Hawaii Press, pp. 140–57.

Rorty, Richard. 1979. *Philosophy and the Mirror of Nature*, Princeton, N.J.: Princeton University Press.

———. 1985. "Habermas and Lyotard on Postmodernity." In *Habermas and Modernity*, ed. R. J. Berstein. Cambridge, Mass.: MIT Press, pp. 161–75.

———. 1989. *Contingency, Irony and Solidarity*. New York: Cambridge University Press.

———. 1986. "Freud and Moral Reflection." In *Pragmatism's Freud*, ed. Joseph H. Smith and William Kerrigan. Baltimore: Johns Hopkins University Press, pp. 1–27.

Rosemont, Henry Jr. 1988. "Against Relativism." In *Interpreting across Boundaries: New Essays in Comparative Philosophy*, ed. Gerard James Larson and Eliot Deutsch. Princeton, N.J.: Princeton University Press, pp. 36–70.

Yearley, Lee. 1983. "The Perfected Person in the Radical Chuang-tzu." In *Experimental Essays on Chuang-tzu*, ed. Victor H. Mair. Honolulu: University of Hawaii Press, pp. 125–39.

Zhuangzi. 1985. *Zhuangzi Jinshu Jinyi*, trans. and ed. Chen Guying. Beijing: Zhonghua Shuju Chuban.

9

On the *Zhenren*

DANIEL COYLE

The pages of the *Zhuangzi* 莊子 are filled with many characters: extraordinary creatures, historical sages, fantastic shamans, butchers, cripples, robbers, swordsmen, fishermen, each conveying a particular perspective or suggesting a special "knack." Yet of the many perspectives and levels of illumination within the text the most consummate Zhuangzian figure is the *zhenren* 真人, or "genuine person."[1] Of the thirty-three extant *Zhuangzi* chapters only two men are named as actual *zhenren*: Guanyin and Lao Dan (33/62),[2] two of the most obscure figures in Chinese history.[3] Although the notion of the *zhenren* is usually mentioned in Zhuangzian literature, the terms *zhen* (genuine) and *zhenren* themselves have rarely been investigated in detail.[4]

This essay will disclose the *zhenren* by presenting a full translation and explication of the first section of chapter 6, the *Dazongshi* 大宗師 or "Great Ancestral Teacher"—the *locus classicus* and only occurrence of the *zhenren* in the *Inner Chapters* (1–7)—while referencing additional explanatory chapters from the text along the way.

To begin, let us examine the term *zhen* (genuine) itself, and then *zhenren* as utilized by Zhuangzi and his school, to establish a terminological background and interpretive context for the study at hand. The earliest occurrence of the character *zhen* in extant Chinese texts appears to be in the *Laozi* and *Zhuangzi*.[5] *Zhen* only occurs three times in the *Laozi*, where it is employed as a special term to contrast with the transitoriness and superficiality of "man-made" formalities.[6] In this novel approach, "genuineness" is not understood as any sort of "unchanging reality," but rather has to do with change and "cultivation."[7] The first time we encounter *zhen* in the *Inner Chapters* is in the context of the flux and interrelatedness of life and death, where "genuineness" is something ever-present, yet without any apprehendable fixed "identity" (2/15–18). By the time of the late Han dynasty the *zhenren* must have been implicit in the term *zhen* itself, as the *Shuowen* 說文 lexicon (circa 100 C.E., surely influenced by "Daoist"[8] thought) defines *zhen* in terms of a person: "*zhen* is a 'recluse of the mountains (*xian*)'[9] changing shape and ascending into Heaven."[10] The etymological components suggest *transforming* to a *higher* level of character, thus genuineness is to be conceived as fundamentally transformational, that is, as an ongoing process of change. As Wang Bi's (226–249 C.E.) commentary to the *Yijing* suggests, *zhen* is in "constant mutation." By envisioning a new image, it appears, with *zhen*, the writers of *Laozi* and *Zhuangzi* wanted to distinguish their teaching from others. More, when the term *zhenren* occurs in a passage it usually is in the form of "definition," anticipating that the reader does not know what it means.

Many of the *Zhuangzi* chapters use *zhen* in a sort of counterculture fashion to criticize Confucius, who is seen to be a noble man but one "crippled by Heaven"—"the sort that roams within the guidelines" (6/66).[11] A classic example from the *Mixed Chapters*' (23–33), "Yangist miscellany" places Confucius and his disciples in a dialogue with a sagely "old fisherman" who has drifted upon their circle. After a bit of mockery by the stranger and a few suggestions that the whole Confucian situation is somehow lacking in "integrity," Confucius is induced to ask, "What is called *zhen*?" The stranger replies:

> "*Zhen* is the utmost of purity and sincerity. Impurity and insincerity are incapable of moving others. . . . One who is internally *zhen* moves the external daemonically.[12] . . . [Z]hen is something which is received from Heaven, it is self-so and not exchangeable. Thus the sage models Heaven, venerates *zhen*, and is not restricted by customs." (31/32–39)

The old fisherman informs us that genuine feelings move others "daemonically" or "spiritually," which in this case means spontaneously (or to invoke a Nietzschean language: by communicable natural drives[13]). The author of this passage is concerned to communicate the Yangist tenet of "protecting one's genuineness,"[14] and with upholding the ideals of *ziran* 自然 (self-so-ness) and *wuwei* 無為, which here are seen as counter to Confucian instructions. The Confucian concerns of *ren* 仁, *yi* 義, and especially *li* 禮[15] are seen as "human artificialities" that lack integrity and can endanger "heavenly" genuineness.[16] Moreover, these customs, conventions, and ritual codifications, when put into formal practice, become ossified and sometimes generate false or forced feelings that divert one from *dao* 道 (31/30f.).

The authors of the *Zhuangzi*, especially the Outer Chapters (8–22), consider Confucian thought to be somehow off course, even misunderstanding many of its own ideals. In one of the dialogues with Lao Dan (portrayed as the Zhou Archivist) Confucius begins to pontificate on the Twelve Classics. Lao Dan interrupts the "monologue," wanting Confucius to get to the simple point of it all. Finally, Confucius summarizes: "The gist lies in *ren* and *yi*." Lao Dan then asks, are these "'natural characteristics' (*xing*性)[17] of a person?" Confucius answers yes, adding: "*Ren* and *yi* are the 'natural characteristics' of the *zhenren*." Clearly, from the Zhuangzian perspective Confucius has misconceived the *zhenren*. Lao Dan responds by suggesting that this kind of conviction is dangerous and only disperses the "natural characteristics" of a person. Rather, one should trust the inner power (*de*) that accords with the cosmic processions of *dao* (13/45–53). The *zhenren*, according to a syncretist writer of chapter 15, is one who is "able to embody the pure and simple" (15/22)—one whose spirit-daemon is "unimpaired," and one who is "unmixed with anything" which means his power (*de*德) is intact (15/9f.). He is a fully integrated and spontaneous person, able to comprehend and participate in *dao* in such a way as to naturally bridge the conceptual gap between Heaven and man—a distinction that according to Graham is the "most obstinate of the dichotomies" that Zhuangzi strives to overcome.[18] The *zhenren* is human, yet as expansive as Heaven—fully embodying *dao* to the extent of "encompassing all things" (21/3f.).

Thus *zhen*, as implemented in the *Zhuangzi*, denotes "authenticity" within a transforming world, genuineness in the Nietzschean sense of being true to oneself. As a writer of one of the Outer Chapters summarizes the Zhuangzian attitudes of *wuwei*, nurturing, and keeping all the fruit for oneself: "the ancients called this the roaming in which one plucks only *zhen*" (14/44–56). This should not be understood in the conventional sense of avarice; rather, it connotes a special kind of parsimony. The focus on oneself does not involve a domination of others, but rather, the (self-)integration of one's becomings in such a way that the self is appropriated personally and socially. The *zhenren*, then, is one who can integrate (internally and externally) all the various drives that make up the person and the world in an affirmative way.

Now that we have established a context from which to interpret the terms, we are ready for the manifold difficulties of the *Dazongshi*.[19] The passage opens by framing an epistemological problem:

> Knowing the workings of Heaven and knowing the workings of man reaches to the utmost! One who knows the workings of Heaven lives by Heaven; one who knows the workings of man uses the knowledge of the known to nourish the knowledge of the unknown, completes the years given by Heaven, and is not cut off in mid-course—this is the plenum of knowledge.
>
> Even so, there are problems: Namely, knowledge has applicability only after it corresponds to something, but that which it is applicable to is particularly unstable. How do I know what is called Heaven's is not man? and what I call man's is not Heaven? Moreover, there is a *zhenren* only after there is genuine knowledge. (6/1–4)

Here we have an epitome of Zhuangzian paradox: First, the author presents a line of discourse suggesting a compromise to a presumed dichotomy, in this case that of knowing the workings of Heaven and man, and then the compromise is dismissed as inadequate.[20] Finally, the *zhenren* is introduced as somehow contingent on "genuine knowledge," yet knowledge itself has already been shown to be problematic in many ways.

After the preliminary formulation, the author straightaway calls into question the very nature of knowledge and its relation to Heaven and man. One of the *Mixed Chapters* offers a rather "mystical"[21] approach converse of the above of using "the knowledge of the known to nourish the knowledge of the unknown," suggesting that "everyone respects the knowledge of the known, but none know how to depend on the knowledge of the unknown to know how to know" (25/51–54). Together the passages impart a sort of hermeneutic circle, yet there is no closure, it is more a *correlative spiral.* Zhuangzi "shares that common and elusive feeling that the whole is more than the sum of its parts, that analysis always leaves something out, that neither side of a dichotomy is wholly true."[22] Regardless from which perspective we approach this problem of the known and unknown, ultimately, we remain in a continuum of "great uncertainty" (*dayi* 大疑). The epistemological problem is presented in a way that disables any correspondence theory of truth.

Zhuangzian thought wants to show the futility and the danger of categorizing things according to "fixed" names—deeming "that's it," and "that's not," distinguishing this's and that's—because in a continually transforming world, all things are "shifting," and our perspectives, therefore, are also "shifting" (23/58–66). Zhuangzi suggests that we practice "unlearning distinctions," for it is precisely in the act of making distinctions that *dao* is lost.[23] The "Taoist [Daoist] art of living" according to Graham, "is a supremely intelligent responsiveness which would be undermined by analyzing and choosing, and that grasping the Way is an unverbalizable 'knowing how' rather than 'knowing that'."[24] Human knowledge can never be sure about "beginnings": there are always unknown correlates, and the "embryonic beginnings" (*shi* 始) of things remain for the most part unseen. The intellect is unable to fathom the boundless depths of its own source; it can only sample perspectives of a continuum. Hence, conceptual thinking, for Zhuangzi, ends in the "tunnel-reality" of exclusion, and linear epistemology is demonstrated to be *obscurum per obscurius.*

However, all this is not to suggest a radical skepticism. As Graham notes, Zhuangzi, like Nietzsche, has "no vertigo in doubt." He emerges assured with an unconveyable knack or mystical affirmation: the sage "'assesses' actions but does not argue over them, 'sorts' events but does not assess them" with disputation; and as for that which is left over, "he 'locates' it but does not include it in the way."[25] For Zhuangzi, knowledge has to do with immediacy, circumstances, and continuity: it is always experiential and transformational. It is *gnosis* in its mystical sense—that style of thinking or style of consciousness that seeks "to destruct the very impulse to imprison reality in a system of concepts which frame it out and circumscribe it"[26]—knowledge and experience are inseparable. Theocentrism aside, Zhuangzi's language is Eckhart-like in that it cancels itself out, short-circuiting the intellect so as to open one up to spontaneity and the omnipresence of Heaven.[27]

Thus the text does not define or develop the question of "genuine knowledge" directly, even though we are told it is a proviso for the *zhenren* (6/4). Rather, it circumvents the epistemological conundrum by going into a paeanic mode, presenting the *zhenren* through the medium of "deconstructive dialectic" that moves in and out of rhyme:[28]

> What is called a *zhenren*? The *zhenren* of old did not oppose minorities, did not show off achievements, and did not scheme over affairs. One such as this could transgress and yet not be regretful, or hit the mark and not be self-satisfied. One such as this could:
>
> > ascend the heights and not feel frightened,
> > enter water and not feel wet,
> > enter fire and not feel hot.[29]
>
> Such a one whose knowledge is able to ascend to *dao* is like this. (6/4–6)

From this we can glean that the *zhenren* of old were unconcerned with the social political, indifferent to the moral, and unaffected by the physical. Epistemologically, since *dao* is omni-and-ever-present in the world as a continual oscillatory process, it should not be thought of as a "state" one "reaches." Rather, the above ability of knowledge ascending "to *dao*" refers to a broadening of one's perspectives. Recall that it was said the *zhenren* fully embodies *dao* to the extent of "encompassing all things" (21/3f.). Though modern Chinese intellectuals from 1915 to the present have been keen to compare Nietzsche's *Übermensch* to the classical Chinese *shengren* 聖人 or sage,[30] the *zhenren* is the more appropriate comparandum. The Dionysian *Übermensch* "6,000 feet beyond man and time," resonates with the *zhenren*; and recalls Zarathustra's proclamation: "I love him whose soul is overfull, so that he forgets himself, and all things are in him: thus all things become his going under."[31] The *zhenren* is impervious to the human social realm: in a passage from the *Outer Chapters* that resonates with the above description of the *zhenren*, we are told even Fu Xi and the Yellow Emperor "could not befriend him"! He is "unchanged" by life and death, and unaffected by "titles and stipends," geographical conditions and physical elements are no hindrance to him, he "completely fills Heaven and Earth," and "when he gives to others, he has more for himself" (21/66f.).

In another story that opens with an echo of the above rhyme, Liezi asks Guanyin how one attains such extraordinary feats. Guanyin replies, it is "not any kind of knowledge, skill, resolution, or daring," rather it has to do with "holding fast to pure *qi* 氣." He goes on to explain one must achieve a maximum *distance* from all things, "to roam where the myriad things end and begin," to attain the most encompassing perspective—the perspective of Heaven. Guanyin concludes his explanation with an example of a drunken man, who through his condition of "unknowing," is less likely to be injured in a fall because of his increased suppleness (19/8f.).

The point is that knowledge in the *Zhuangzi* is not knowledge of an objective world; rather it is fundamentally perspectival. The authors want to move away from a static epistemology, into a conception of knowledge that moves through experience as an unobstructed *dao*, flexibly interpreted in terms of lifestyle, attitude, aptitude, propensity, efficacy, and knack. And here (aside from the "logicians") Zhuangzi is not far away from a "classical" Chinese understanding of the process of knowing more broadly construed. As Roger Ames has suggested, knowledge in the classical Chinese model is conceived as a dynamic process of mapping and communication that aspires to a comprehensiveness—it is "'tracing' in both the sense of etching a pattern and of following it."[32] For example, a military campaign is successful insofar as the commander can *transceive* a complete circumstance. In this model, world-tracing is inseparable from world-making. "Knowing" means penetrating the various connections of phenomena so as to become aware of the possible reverberating configurations.

Having attained such a perspective, the characterizations of the *zhenren* appear less bizarre. Still, the passage continues to give itself up to speculation: The *zhenren* of old:

> He slept and did not dream,
> He woke and was without cares,[33]
> He ate and did not relish,
> He breathed deeply—from the deepest depths. (6/6)

These lines can be interpreted in a variety of ways: one might read them in terms of a particular lifestyle, symbolic language, depth psychology, yoga-like *qigong* 氣功, or mystical experience. The verse must have been puzzling even to the earliest readers, for what follows in the received text is an apparent "footnote"[34] on this practice of breathing from the "deepest depths":

> The *zhenren*'s breathing is from the heels. The multitude of men breath from the throat—cowed and submissive, they choke words as if vomiting.[35] If one's cravings and desires are deep-seated, one's Heavenly Trigger[36] will be shallow. (6/6–7)

Here, the author wants to contrast common men stuck in the realm of linguistic distinctions and worldly desire from the *zhenren* whose consciousness is open to the continuum of Heavenly spontaneity. The text continues:

> The *zhenren* of old did not know to delight in life, did not know to despise death. He sprang forth and was not cheerful; he returned and was not reluctant. He went as suddenly as he came, and that was that. Not forgetting where he originated, and not seeking where he would end, receiving things jubilantly, then forgetting and returning them: this is what is called not using the heart-and-mind to damage *dao*, and not using man to assist Heaven. This is what is called a *zhenren*. One such as this: his heart-and-mind was oblivious, his face calm, his forehead broad. Chilly like autumn, warm like spring, his jubilation and anger were communicative with the Four Seasons and fitting to things so none knew his extremities. (6/7–11)

As in the opening section of the *Dazongshi*, all dichotomization collapses. The *zhenren*'s nonchalant *wuwei* culminates in "not using the heart-and-mind to damage *dao*, and not using man to assist Heaven." The human heart-and-mind is the agent of disputation and thus dangerous to *dao*. Ultimately we cannot distinguish the work of Heaven and the work of man with our limited human intelligence, for despite the power of imagination and the manifold perspectives obtained thereby, we can never escape our own humanity.[37] Thus the "complete man" hates the question "is it in me from Heaven or man?" (23/73f.). The point is that rigid discrimination kills spontaneity, and we must abandon man's inclination to trust in "reason" if we are to become completely continuous with nature.

The *zhenren* passage continues[38] with a strange, paradoxical extended rhyme:[39]

> The *zhenren* of old,
>> He appeared appropriate but did not form a clique.[40]
>> Seemed deficient but did not accept things.
>
>> Assured, he was independent but not rigid.
>> Spread-out, he was tenuous, but not ostentatious.
>
>> Bright and radiant, he seemed jubilant.
>> High, he did not reach an end.[41]
>
>> Collected, advancing his own alluring charms.
>> Assured, gathering his own Power.[42]
>
>> Broad, he seemed like everyone.
>> Towering, he was never controllable.
>
>> Connected, he seemed to like closure.
>> Absent-minded, forgetting his words. (6/14–17)

The *zhenren* is an "adept" in every sense of the word, one who has reached a fully transceiving perspective. David McCraw notes that the conclusion here suggests forgetting any "descriptive project." Moreover, the entire *zhenren* section "proceeds with negative descriptions" that lack "positive instruction about Zhuangzi's ideals."[43] Both *Laozi* and *Zhuangzi* employ negative language because the absence of prescriptivity leaves a topic open to interpretation and keeps it personal. One cannot be told what is consistent with one's own integrity; one can only be informed of possible elements of coercion that might impede one's own spontaneity. Thus the *Zhuangzi* is concerned with diminishing conventional boundaries so as to maximize spontaneity. The Daoist seeks: to *correlate* his person with nature in such a way that his living minimizes any coercive repercussions (on himself or others), to *integrate* the various currents and polarities, internally and externally, that make up his existence, and to *affirm* his creativity in such a way that his actions are harmonious within the world.

The *zhenren* passage closes with a final paradox:[44]

> Thus his likes were one, and his dislikes were one. His "one" was one, and his "not one" was one. He became "one" as a companion of Heaven, and he became "not one" as a companion of man—Heaven and man not overcoming each other, this is what is called a *zhenren*. (6/19–20)

Comprehensive, the *zhenren* oscillates between the perspectives of Heaven and man, balancing the boundless and the conventional.[45] Of particular philosophical importance here is the complete absence of metaphysical dualism. As fantastic and enigmatic as the *zhenren* appears, there is still a *coherence* to this Zhuangzian paragon. Guo Xiang (c. 300 C.E.), the earliest known commentator and collator of the received *Zhuangzi* text, summarizes the *zhenren* passage: "The *zhenren* unifies Heaven and man, and levels the myriad extensions. The myriad extensions do not oppose each other, and Heaven and man do not overcome each other. Thus being vast he is one, being dark he is omnipresent—he mysteriously unifies the other with his own self." Guo Xiang's mystic vision resonates the ineffability of "constant *dao*" as expressed in the *Laozi*: by polarizing our perspectives between the "wonders" and "boundaries" of *dao* we are able to see how one comes to cosmographically occupy a dynamic hinge-point (or focus) within the processional continuum of *dao* where correlative opposites proceed together to form a coherency with man—how worlds and things come to be through the *polarity of diminishing limits*.

The general theme and ultimate lesson of the *Dazongshi* is "reconciliation with death,[46] conceived in terms of transformation. The *zhenren* as displayed here discloses the continuity between nature and man in all their processions, and thus reveals the culmination of the Zhuangzian attitude(s) toward death. The *zhenren* does not resist death, rather he recognizes it as a correlative of life and as one of the "natural" transformations of Heaven and Earth—that we ourselves are continuous with nature. All the characteristics of the *zhenren* are consummated in the continuity of Heaven and man.

In the *Benjing Yinfu Qishu* chapter of the *Guiguzi*[47] a writer adds to this discourse that the *zhenren* is "one whose life is received from Heaven … [he] has become one with Heaven." This calls forth an image of a "Heaven-intoxicated" person—open to Heavenly spontaneity to the point of complete saturation. There is no differentiation between Heaven and man. Moreover, this person is said to fully integrate the past and present so that there is no loss: the mysterious five *qi* of spiritual transformation "return to his body."

> The *zhenren* is unified with Heaven and connected with *dao*, holding fast to the one, he nourishes and produces the myriad kinds. He is one who: keeps the heart-and-mind of Heaven in his bosom, bestows the nourishment of Power (*de*), uses *wuwei* to envelop aspirations, worries, thoughts, and intentions—he acts with a powerful disposition.[48]

One with Heaven, the *zhenren* embodies *dao* to encompass all things, and is impervious to conventional limitations.

From the period of the Han to the Six Dynasties the *zhenren* took on a more religious significance, becoming one of the linchpins of "Daoism." Movements of alchemy, life-prolonging techniques, and the quest for "immortality" flourished, yet most mystical allusions remained firmly grounded in the *Zhuangzi*. From the Zhuangzian perspective, the *religious* experience (etymologically, that which binds together) becomes a personal rapture that elevates one from the microcosmic to an altogether macrocosmic perspective—a perspective that affirms continuity as the fabric of unity—that somehow binds one to the totality of existence in a personal integration and affirmation of all. This integration works on different levels: The individual's many drives are integrated not only into personal becoming but also into the totality of worlds. Integrity must be seen, not in the conventional social sense of outer order, that is, as a superficial affirmation of social expectations; but in a particular sense that entails the affirmation of one's own becomings, involving a balanced integration of the total self.

The message to the human multitude is that one must participate in the processes of the world, but in a way that accords with the inner power imparted to us by Heaven. As the old fisherman said: "*Zhen* is something which is received from Heaven, it is self-so and not exchangeable" (31/38). The distinction between Heaven and man remains, but only as perspectives of the "thinking man."[49] We exist in an endless continuum, and, ultimately the boundless and the conventional are subsumed by the one. The *zhenren* is presented as a model by which a person may dissolve dichotomies, and thus reach that perspective of mystical affirmation that says: "Heaven, Earth and I emerge together, and the myriad things and I are one" (2/52–53).

NOTES

1. The term *zhenren* has been translated in various ways: "Divine Man" (Balfour), "pure man" (Chan), "True Man/man" (Legge, Watson, Graham, and Schwartz), "authentic person" (Ames), "realized beings" (McCraw), just to name a few. "Authentic person" works well, conveying the idea of "authorship," but it also connotes an idea of "human agency" that Zhuangzi is trying to avoid. "Genuine person" seems to work best as it carries the least amount of "philosophical" baggage. Etymologically, "genuine" comes from the Latin *genuinus*, "natural," which is akin to *gignere*, to beget (possibly an alteration of *ingenuus*, native, or freeborn), and thus connotes a processionality necessary to any Zhuangzian interpretation.

2. All citations of the *Zhuangzi* text are from the Harvard-Yenching Sinological Index Series in the form of chapter/line number, unless otherwise noted.

3. Guanyin is the obscure "Keeper of the Pass," and supposed author of the *Guanyinzi* (now lost); Lao Dan is the "legendary instructor of Confucius" and supposed author of the *Laozi*. Graham notes that the two are in some way connected by Sima Qian's legend of Laozi disappearing forever after leaving his book with "the director of the pass," Yin Xi. See A. C. Graham's *Chuang-Tzu: The Inner Chapters* (London: Mandala, 1981), pp. 127 and 282.

4. Roger Ames has treated it briefly in his "The Common Ground of Self-Cultivation in Classical Taoism and Confucianism," *Tsinghua Journal,* 1985.

5. See ibid., p. 87. The dates and composition of these texts remain obscure, current supposition is that both emerged sometime between the fourth and second centuries B.C.E.

6. *Daodejing,* chapter 21. Wang Pang (1044–76) comments: "Once things become subject to human fabrications, they lose their reality" (Red Pine, *Lao-tzu's Taoteching* [San Francisco: Mercury House, 1996], p. 43).

7. See *Laozi*, chapters 41 and 54.

8. The title "Daoist" is a problematic term because the idea of a (consolidated) "school of Dao" (*daojia*) did not appear until the writings of Sima Tan (d. 110 B.C.E.). See Graham, *Chuang-tzu* and *Disputers of the Tao* (La Salle, Ill.: Open Court, 1989) for a detailed treatment of the problem. Moreover, by the Six Dynasties "*dao*" was also freely used to identify *xuanxue* 玄學 and certain Buddhist movements.

9. The character *xian* 仙 is usually translated "immortal," but this denotes one who is "deathless," which surely has no part in Zhuangzi's "philosophy of transformation." The theme of death is central to the *Zhuangzi*, especially the *Dazongshi* chapter, and death is usually described in terms of transformation. James Legge's terminology is adapted here for it's etymological eloquence (see *Texts of Taoism* [*Sacred Books of the East*, vols. 39, 40], vol. 1 [Oxford, 1891], p. 135). For more arguments that to define *zhen* in terms of immortal-

ity is inconsistent with Zhuangzian thought, see Ames, "Common Ground," pp. 87–88. *Xian* is composed of the graphs of a *ren* 人 (a person) and *shan* 山 (a mountain) giving the double-association of "one who dwells in the mountains" and "one who is firm or long-lasting like a mountain" (thanks to Shawn Eichman for this insight). The problem of translating *xian* warrants a study in itself beyond the scope of this paper.

10. *Tian* 天, or Heaven in a Chinese context is the interrelated correlate of Earth. It is at once: deity, celestial sphere, sky, *and* "Nature"—in no way a transcendent "kingdom."

11. Graham, *Chuang-tzu*, pp. 17, 89–90. The Zhuangzian problem of "Heaven and man" will be discussed later in the main text.

12. I am adopting Graham's translation of *shen* 神 here; see his *Chuang-tzu*.

13. Nietzsche's depth psychology is in no way directly related to Zhuangzi, yet the resonances of imagery are striking. Further affinities and justification for comparison will become apparent in the main text.

14. See *Huainanzi*, chapter 13, and Graham, *Chuang-tzu*, pp. 221, 248, and 258.

15. Graham renders these "goodwill," "duty," and "rites," respectively, but the richness of the terms is not conveyed in the English. In this particular passage, the old fisherman defines *li* as "that which has been established as the customs of the generation" (31/37). See Hall and Ames, *Thinking Through Confucius* (Albany: State University of New York Press, 1987), for the complexities involved in translating Chinese culture into the Western world.

16. This contrast between "Heaven and man" is central to the *zhenren* discourse of the *Dazongshi* that follows.

17. Graham notes that *xing* does not occur in the Inner Chapters (*Chuang-tzu*, p. 16). Benjamin Schwartz suggests that it is probably the "indeterminacy" of the human heart-and-mind, that is, that it is not the "genuine ruler" of the human organism (see 2/15–18), that leads Zhuangzi to avoid using *xing* to describe "human spiritual potential" (*The World of Thought in Ancient China* [Cambridge, Mass.: Harvard University Press, 1985], p. 234).

18. Graham, *Disputers*, p. 195. Also see James Legge, *Texts of Taoism*, 1:237.

19. The chapter is full of textual dislocations, strange verses, and oxymorons, undermining language itself and any fixity of truth. Though textually problematic, many consider the *Dazongshi* the most important chapter to understanding Zhuangzi's thought (cf. Legge, *Texts of Taoism*, 1:134).

20. Graham notes that this is a classic Zhuangzian move: Zhuangzi "will start from a preliminary formulation, either his own or quoted from some unknown source, and then raise a doubt" (*Chuang-tzu*, pp. 51 and 85).

21. We must be careful not to confuse "Chinese mysticism" with the conceptualizations of the Western mystical tradition. Graham warns that there is "no mind/body dichotomy in ancient Chinese" (*Disputers*, p. 199) and that Chinese thought lacks the metaphysical dualism on which most Western

mysticism is based (*Chuang-tzu*, p. 21). "Daoist" mysticism, as Schwartz puts it, "is a mystical outlook which remains irreducibly Chinese and entirely sui generis," and perhaps it is not so much a case of "deep mysticism as a kind of 'life attitude'" (*Would of Thought*, pp. 188, 242–43).

22. Graham, *Disputers*, p. 180.
23. See Graham, *Chuang-tzu*, pp. 54–55, 104.
24. Graham, *Disputers*, p. 186; also see Graham, *Chuang-tzu*, p. 26.
25. Graham, *Disputers*, pp. 186, 189; also see *Zhuangzi*, chapter 2, in Graham, *Chuang-tzu*, p. 57.
26. Roberts Avens, *The New Gnosis: Heidegger, Hillman, and Angels* (Dallas: Spring Publications, 1984), p. 2; cf. the final sections of *Zhuangzi* chapters 2 and 17. This mystical vision extends to the cosmological, as Seyyed Hossein Nasr (*An Introduction to Islamic Cosmological Doctrines* [Boulder, Colo.: Shambhala Publications, 1978], p. 263) writes:

> The cosmos, instead of being an exterior object, become for the gnostic (*'arif*) an interior reality; he sees all the diversities of Nature reflected in the mirror of his own being.

27. See, for example, the episode where *Ziqi* "in a trance" lost "the counterpart of his self" as well as "his own self" (2/1f. and 24/61f.).
28. I rely here on David McCraw's work on Zhuangzian rhyme. See his "Pursuing Zhuangzi as Rhymester," *Sino-Platonic Papers* 67 for a discussion of rhyme in the *Zhuangzi*.
29. This motif recurs in similar "ditties" describing "one of utmost power" (17/49), and the "utmost man" (19/7); see McCraw, "Pursuing Zhuangzi."
30. See *China Review International* 32:354.
31. *Zarathustra*, prologue 4. The resonances with Nietzsche throughout the *Zhuangzi* are remarkable, and warrant further study. For the seminal text in this area, see Graham Parkes, ed. *Nietzsche and Asian Thought* (Chicago: The University of Chicago Press, 1991).
32. Ames, *Sun-tzu: The Art of War* (New York: Ballantine Books, 1993), pp. 55–57).
33. These two lines are repeated in chapter 15 where they occur as part of a longer verse. See *Zhuangzi Duben* (Taipei, 1974), p. 192.
34. I am following Graham's punctuation, in *Chuang-tzu*, p. 84; and the apparent change in style and rhythm.
35. Most commentators interpret this clause in terms of being "defeated in debate."
36. *Tian ji* 天機. Wing-tsit Chan translates this term as "secret of Nature" and writes "by this secret is meant the secret operation of Nature, the way in which things spring forth" (*Sourcebook in Chinese Philosophy* [Princeton, N.J.:

Princeton University Press, 1963], p. 191). It is the trigger that releases the springs of Heavenly spontaneity.

37. See Graham, *Chuang-tzu*, p. 106.

38. Chen Guying and Graham agree with Wen Yiduo that the following passage is "another area of textual dislocation"; Graham suggests it may be a comment on 6/82–89 (see Chen Guying, *Zhuangzi*, p. 186f.; and Graham, *Textual Notes* (London: School of Oriental and African Studies, 1981) pp. 23–24).

> Thus when the Sage deploys troops: a kingdom may perish, but the hearts-and-minds of the people are not lost, advantages and benefits are bestowed on ten thousand generations, but not for philanthropy. Thus rejoicing in inter-penetrating things is not the practice of a Sage; having familiars is not the practice of *ren*; calculating Heavenly timing (*tianshi* 天時) is not the practice of the worthy-and-wise; communicating advantages and disadvantages is not the practice of a *junzi* 君子; pursuing fame and loosing oneself is not the practice of a *shi*; destroying the body and not being genuine (*zhen*) is not the practice of a laborer of others. Those like: Hu Buxie, Wu Guang, Bo Yi, Shu Qi, Jizi, Xu Yu, Ji Tuo, and Shen-tu Di—they were those who were suited to serving what served others, suiting what suited others and not suiting themselves. (6/11–14)

39. McCraw has noted the problematic nature of the following rhymes ("Pursuing Zhuangzi"). Extant commentaries and translations contain numerous alternate readings and suggested textual emendations for most of these verses. This translation will follow the received text, and alternate readings will be given only where significant disagreement exists. The next paragraph of the received text is almost surely misplaced and thus will not be included in the main text of this essay. See note 38.

40. Yu Yue suggests the line should be read: "He appeared lofty (*e*) but did not collapse (*beng*)."

41. This is a "literal" reading that accords with the preceding line and the apparent couplet-form of the rhyme. An alternate reading, which Graham and McCraw adopt along with many Chinese commentators, interprets *cui* to mean "to move" or "to compel," thus yielding: "Compelled, he had no choice."

42. Some read *yu* as "comfort," "to be pleased, or at ease"; thus it would read "At ease, gathering his own power."

43. McCraw, "Pursuing Zhuangzi."

44. Following the poem we encounter yet another area of textual corruption. Graham rearranges the text and inserts the following from one of the *Mixed Chapters* at 6/17:

The True Men [*zhenren*] of old used what is Heaven's to await what comes, did not let man intrude on Heaven. The True Men of old used the eye to look at the eye, the ear to look at the ear, the heart to recover the heart. Such men as that when they were level were true to the carpenter's line, when they were altering stayed on course. (replaced from 24/97f. and 24/96f., *Textual Notes*, p. 24)

The text of the *Dazongshi* continues (6/17–19) with what Burton Watson (in accord with Fukunaga) maintains is probably a later textual addition influenced by *fajia* 法家 (*Chuang-tzu*, [New York: Colombia University Press, 1968], p. 79); whereas Graham says it has become "stranded" in this chapter, and suggests it is probably an "ancient exposition" on a "mutilation" story from chapter 5 (see 5/24–31; *Textual Notes*, p. 24):

[He] took punishments as the main body, took the Rites as the wings, took knowledge as timeliness, and took power as the guide. He took punishments as the main body to be delicate in killing; took the Rites as the wings as a means to proceed in the world; took knowledge as timeliness because affairs and events are inevitable; and took power as the guide, which is to say he was one who was assured, having the sufficiency to easily reach the heights, and yet others genuinely took him as one who had to diligently march [to get there]. (6/17–19)

45. A Mixed Chapter adds "only the *zhenren* is able to escape external and internal punishments." In this passage, external punishments are interpreted in terms of conventional instruments of physical suffering, and internal punishments have to do with corroding imbalances of *yin* and *yang* (32/31).
46. See Graham, *Chuang-tzu*, pp. 76, 84.
47. The first chapter of the last *juan* of the text, generally taken to be a late Han addition to the pre-Qin *Guiguzi*.
48. See Fang Lizhong, *Guiguzi Quanshu* (Beijing: Shumu Wenxian, 1993), pp. 119–21.
49. Graham, *Chuang-tzu*, p. 20.

10

A Meditation on Friendship

BRIAN LUNDBERG

> Three men, Master Sanghu, Meng Zifan, and Master Qinzhang
> were talking to each other, "Who is able to be with others
> without being with others, be for others without being for
> others? Who is able to climb the skies, roam the mists, and
> dance in the infinite, living forgetful of each other without
> end?" The three men looked at each other and smiled, none
> opposed in his heart, and so they became friends.
>
> —*Zhuangzi*, chapter 6

The *Zhuangzi* is one of the most lyric philosophical texts of ancient China. It is filled with rhapsodic language describing the spiritual state of those who, having abandoned social conventions to pursue a quasi–nature mysticism aimed at becoming one with the world of nature or *dao*, have attuned themselves to the flow and rhythm of *dao*. As a consequence, the term "Daoist" is apt to evoke an image of the solitary hermit, living apart from society in seclusion, shunning the company of others and their state conventions. While later traditions associated with Daoism may have perpetuated the ideal of the solitary hermit, this description has little relevance to Zhuangzi himself or to the Inner Chapters of the text associated with his name.[1] In fact, the *Zhuangzi* is a text full of stories of profound friendships. In all these cases, communion among friends plays as important a role as the communion forged between an individual and the natural environment.

While the *Zhuangzi* does not speak to the topic of friendship directly, many facets of its philosophy—self-realization, realization of *dao*, and even acceptance of death—are presented in the context of intercourse among friends. Thus, the experience of friendship not only provides insight into the philosophical vision of Zhuangzi, but the human relations expressed through friendship are integral to it. This meditation is therefore devoted to exploring the experiences of friendship as they appear in the *Zhuangzi* and how befriending an *other* stimulates personal transformation. This will hopefully enrich our understanding of the *Zhuangzi*, and at the same time deepen our understanding of a topic largely neglected by philosophers—friendship, and by extension, ourselves in relation to others.

What are the parameters of friendship? Zhuangzi provides an answer in the form of a question: "Who is able to be with others without being with others, be for others without being for others? Who is able to climb the skies, roam the mists, and dance in the infinite, living forgetful of each other without end?" There are at least two points of philosophical significance. First, Zhuangzi provides a set of criteria as prerequisites for becoming friends, and second, he links the ability to *become friends* with the realization of *dao*, poetically described here as "climbing the skies, roaming the mists, and dancing in the infinite." Three conditions of friendship are delineated here: *being-with*, *being-for*, and *mutually-forgetting*. The first two conditions *being-with* and *being-for*, are somewhat self-evident aspects of friendship and should not pose any problems. It is the third feature, *mutually-forgetting*, that might require further discussion.

Generally speaking, humans are the kinds of beings that thrive in the company of others. In fact, the social nature of the human animal is a basic tenet of all early Chinese philosophy and is taken for granted in the Inner Chapters of *Zhuangzi*. The experience of *being-with* friends is an intrinsically rewarding situation, full of joy, irrespective of any benefits it may bring along with it. Most of our experience is shared with others, and the bulk of our knowledge is gained from being with others: observing, imitating, and modeling them. We learn about life through others, and thereby learn also of ourselves. Moreover, the deeper a friendship, the more one is willing to do *for* a friend, without calculation of self-gain, and often at some personal expense. In such cases, *being-for* a friend comes about naturally and spontaneously. It also seems to be self-evident that a person is more likely to forget selfish interests, whether mundane or those of a higher order, while enjoying the company of a friend. Thus, in *being-with* a friend, we forget ourselves. Forgetting oneself, however, meets Zhuangzi's third criterion of friendship only half-way. It seems that altruism is not enough for Zhuangzi. He not only requires that we forget ourselves in our concern for a friend, he also tells us that we must also forget our friend. What does this mean?

In order to address this last point, it is necessary to pause for a moment and take a look at the notions of *no-self* and *forgetting* in the *Zhuangzi*. As it turns out, forgetting is a major theme of the Inner Chapters, and is, in essence, a variation on the *no-self* theme, a thread that runs throughout the *Zhuangzi* and appears wherever discussion of spiritual achievement is found. The *Zhuangzi* states: "The utmost person is without self, the daemonic person is without merit, and the sage is without name."[2] Elsewhere, the text allows that "the great person has no self."[3] These quotes reveal an emphasis on a selfless or nonegoistic frame of reference as the key to self-realization. Only one who has forgotten personal interest, success, and reputation is qualified for praise from Zhuangzi.

In a passage from chapter 6, the "Great Ancestor Teacher," Confucius's best student, Yanhui, describes his progress as a forgetting of self and body achieved by sitting and forgetting. When Confucius asks what he means by sitting and forgetting, Yanhui replies "I drop off my limbs, drive out perception and understanding, distance myself from my physical form, get rid of knowledge, and thereby become identical with the great thoroughfare."[4] In this passage, there are at least two objects of forgetting: knowledge in the form of social conventions and formulas that limit one's vision and insight, and one's own person, more specifically, the physical body. Moreover, *dropping off* one's physical body is specifically linked to realization of *dao*, likened here to the great thoroughfare. This same motif is developed in the story of our three men who roam the mists and dance in the infinite. Zigong, outraged at the conduct of men who treat the bones of their bodies as outside themselves and sing in front of a corpse without any change in their demeanor, asks Confucius what kind of men they are. Confucius replies that these men who "forget their own liver and gall and leave behind their own ears and eyes" are the kind that are able to roam beyond the guidelines.[5] In this instance too, forgetting one's physical self is linked to going beyond the ritual guidelines, in this case, the most sacred of all—the funeral rites.

Forgetting thus functions as the technique par excellence for achieving spiritual realization and increasing awareness. Other techniques referred to include stilling the mind, and becoming empty and vacuous.[6] What all these examples have in common is an emphasis on abandoning an egoistic point of view and letting go considerations of self-interest. Only by engaging our world from a perspective of no-self can we become one with the flow and rhythm of *dao*. If the absence of self describes the spiritual condition of a fully realized person, then forgetting is its practical application.

Like most early texts in Chinese philosophy, the *Zhuangzi* is not content to describe the so-called *objective world* or the *human condition*. Rather, it aims to transform its readers and bring them to a higher state of awareness. What makes experience shared between friends especially effective for personal transformation is that genuine concern for a friend has a propensity to take one away from personal concerns and self-interest. Transactions undertaken in the spirit of friendship are important because they open the gate to an *other*, and are one of the few things in this world that can cause a person to forget and put aside self-interest. Being the object of another's concern is a moving experience, and one that transforms the way a person sees both other people and the world. By reaching out to the other and looking at the world with the interests of that person in mind, our cares are directed beyond the individual ego; connecting oneself with the outside world. In friendship, two (or more) become as one; a friend becomes an extension of oneself.

Developing a friendship is, in essence, a training in looking outward beyond and away from self-interest—only one step away from letting go of personal preconceptions, a prerequisite for the expansion of insight. Genuine friendship is therefore a highly effective source of spiritual transformation. Mystic union with the cosmos is surely a sign of spiritual awareness in the *Zhuangzi,* but mystic union between friends is equally so; the experience of cosmic oneness is not only often linked with the experience of a group of friends who are of one mind, but can be an extension of it.

It is clear that realization of *dao* requires abandoning all thought of oneself, including the way one looks at things This does not imply an absence of perspective, but actually points toward the attainment of multiple perspectives, a well-known theme of the *Zhuangzi.* Chapter 1 opens with the story of the giant *peng* bird's flight and continually contrasts its perspective with the restricted and "small" perspectives of the cicada, the turtle-dove, and the quail among others. Play on perspective is not employed to convince the reader that all perspectives are relativistic, but that we must enlarge our perspective in order to go beyond restricted *small* points of view and reach a more comprehensive vision. In this regard, the *Zhuangzi* repeatedly informs us that the differentiations we conceptualize are a "matter of the situation from which one is seeing."[7] The point is to see things from as many perspectives as possible.

Awareness is not a matter of filling our heads with more analytical knowledge, nor is it a matter of book learning, but is an abandoning and letting go of ossified conceptions. This also forms one aspect of Zhuangzi's critique of rationality. Rationality is problematic to the extent that it encourages an egocentric focus. This, in turn, has the effect of narrowing perspective, and precludes the ability to entertain the focus of the other. This is why primacy is given to intuitive feeling over against rational argument. Intuitive feeling tends to be more inclusive of the totality of a situation and is more likely to respond to the particular details of the situation in a spontaneous manner, even to the point where the doer forgets the physical self. If one can forget the needs of the physical self, then calculative rationality, prompted by self-interest, will not restrict vision to a narrow focal point but allow one to look upon the totality of the field. It is not that reason is anathema to insight, but is appropriate only where it is not the slave of self-interest. Spiritual transformation is tied to seeing things in a new light, but requires that we see the world in a non-self-centered way. In other words, there is a need to enter into other perspectives.

The *Zhuangzi,* of course, uses stories, paradox, and linguistic games to entice the reader out of sedimented perspectives and into new ones. In the context of friendship, however, dialogue is a stimulating and enjoyable prod that allows one to see through the eyes of another. Zhuangzi, through his friendship with Huishi, offers us a good example. Huishi, a representative of the "School of Names," often appears in the text of the *Zhuangzi* as an intellectual adversary, and more importantly, a companion of Zhuangzi. The friendship that these two thinkers develop is often commented upon in works on the *Zhuangzi*. However, discussion is generally limited to the intellectual influence Huishi had on the development of Zhuangzi's thought about language, logic, and rational argumentation. To be sure, when Huishi appears in the text, paradox and linguistic play is usually at issue, with Zhuangzi outdoing the master at his own game, and making a philosophical point in the process. Zhuangzi and Huishi were certainly intellectual sparring partners, yet the text itself reveals a deep and genuine friendship that goes beyond mere "professional" talk.

There is a poignant story set at the funeral of Huishi that reveals the importance of Huishi's companionship to Zhuangzi.[8] Taking part in the funeral procession, Zhuangzi turns to the other attendants and says:

> There was a man from Ying who, if plaster as thin as a fly's wing got on the end of his nose, would have carpenter Shi slice it off. Carpenter Shi, rousing the wind with his whirling hatchet, would slice it off in compliance, ridding the plaster from the nose completely and without injury, while the man from Ying stood there without losing his composure. Lord Yuan of Song heard of this, summoned Carpenter Shi and asked, "Could you try doing this for me?"
>
> Carpenter Shi replied, "I used to be able to slice like this, however, my partner is long dead." Since the death of the master, I too am without a partner. There is no one with whom I can speak to.

Carpenter Shi is not able to perform this feat of slicing off the plaster with just anybody, but requires a partner with whom he shares an intimate level of understanding and trust. While the carpenter's physical motor-skills and handling of the hatchet obviously require extreme dexterity, success ultimately depends on the calm composure of his partner, who is literally putting his life in the hands of a friend. Success requires that the two men respond to each other in attunement, and forget any fears, concerns, or thoughts of self and other that might interrupt the flow of *dao*, and result in physical harm.

By drawing this comparison, Zhuangzi intimates that his own level of success in maneuvering with *dao* is due in large measure to his companion, Huishi. Huishi certainly helped hone and sharpen Zhuangzi's wit and skill for debate, but not in a spirit of conquest. The profundity of their friendship takes them beyond mere argumentative debate and into a mode of dialogue that engenders mutual transformation and insight. As Zhuangzi laments, companions like this are hard to come by.

Bringing the discussion back to an abstract level, genuine friendship not only involves a *being-with* and *being-for*, but more importantly, requires that one *be-with others without being-with others* and *be-for others without being-for others*. Reaching a state where self-concern is completely forgotten is not easy, if even possible, but unless this state is reached, one is still in some degree trapped inside a self-made web of desires and fears that make vision *small*. As a result, this web is bound to influence one's bearing toward the world at large, and one's social interactions in particular. A person thus trapped is unable to avoid treating the other without some degree of design and expectations; there is no letting the other be the other. When this occurs, *being-with* someone is at bottom a matter of treating that person instrumentally to accommodate one's own *needs*. Likewise, *being-for* someone becomes a matter of *being-for* oneself; we do for others so that they do for us.

Genuine friendship must overcome these limited personal visions that impose constraints upon both parties in a friendship. Only by first letting the other be does one free oneself, and thereby attain that deeper and more genuine experience of enjoyment—an ecstatic enjoyment that does not constrain vision.

> Master Hui asked Zhuangzi, "Can a man really be without emotion?"
>
> Zhuangzi replied, "Yes."
>
> Master Hui probed, "But a man without emotion—how can you call him a man?"
>
> Zhuangzi responded, "*Dao* gave him a face and heaven gave him a shape. How can you not call him a man?"
>
> Master Hui continued, "Since we call him a man, how can he be without emotion?"
>
> Zhuangzi explained, "This is not what I mean by emotion. When I speak of being without emotion, what I am saying is that a man does not let likes and dislikes get in and harm his person."[9]

Zhuangzi is not advocating emotional suicide; he merely warns his readers of the dangers that emotional attachment can elicit. Emotions per se are not the problem, but attachment to them and the objects they are directed toward are. Enjoyment in the company of friends, albeit of a higher type, is something to be cultivated and achieved only after one has learned to forget both self and other. Learning to *be-with* and *be-for* a friend is dependent on giving up a reason for doing so, letting things take their course naturally and spontaneously. What Zhuangzi proposes is an emotive *wuwei*, an emotive *doing* which does so without being obtrusive.

This emotive *wuwei* confronts its biggest challenge when faced with death. Death appears frequently in the *Zhuangzi* and often in the context of friendship. The *Zhuangzi* is known for its frequent references to death and physical decay, yet as A. C. Graham makes clear, there is nothing morbid about its treatment.[10] Rather, death is looked upon as a natural part of the process of birth, growth, decay, and transformation. Whereas Zhuangzi conceptually depersonalizes the reality of death, he personalizes the experience of it, whether one's own or that of a friend. Unfortunately, fear of death and concern for life tend to drive one inward, and not only prevents the possibility of a calm detachment, but in fact, is prone to increase attachment. Detachment in the face of mortality, one's own or a friends, is the surest sign that one has mastered self-centered fears.

The type of detachment depicted in the pages of the *Zhuangzi*, moreover, does not represent pessimistic resignation in the face of the inevitability of physical demise. While resignation may earn respect and admiration for the courage and resoluteness it shows, this disposition is far from the one the *Zhuangzi* is attempting to foster—reconciliation. Numerous passages can testify to this, none better than the following:

> Master Yu suddenly became ill and Master Si went in to inquire. "Extraordinary, how that which creates things is turning me into this crooked thing. It hunches me and sticks out my back, my organs are on top, my chin hidden in my navel, my shoulders higher than my head, and my pigtail points towards the sky. The *yin* and *yang qi* are askew." His heart was at ease and unconcerned. He limped over to the well, and looking at his reflection, said "Ah! How that which creates things is turning me into this crooked thing."
>
> Master Si asked "Do you hate this?" He replied, "Why should I hate death? Suppose it transforms my left arm into a rooster, I'll keep watch on the time of night. Suppose it transforms my right arm into a crossbow, I'll look for an owl to roast.... I obtained life because the time was right. I will lose it because this is the course things take. Be at ease with your timing and live in accord with the course things take and sorrow and joy will not force their way in."

This is no expression of resignation in the face of death, but rather, conveys a sense of wonder. There is even what, to ordinary sensibilities, seems to be a "perverse" sense of enjoyment derived by Master Yu from reflecting on the part he will play in the process of ceaseless transformations. Master Yu is not emotionally dead and can still enjoy life, more profoundly than the common lot. What sets him and his companions apart is that they have let go of attachment to the emotion that binds. He and his friends have enjoyed the time they have spent together. Not only has Master Yu let go when his time has come, but so has his friend let go of that *selfish* fear when nature takes away *my* friend. Once freed from these attachments, one is then able to experience that rhapsodic mystical-like state described by Zhuangzi as climbing the skies, roaming the mists, and dancing in the infinite—hardly a description of an emotionally dead person. In Master Yu's case, all distinction between self and other is erased, enabling him to become one body with his friends, and thus, the cosmos.

NOTES

1. Questions concerning the authorship of the *Zhuangzi* constitutes its own field of research. Without delving into this matter, it is generally accepted that a single figure, assumed to be the historical Zhuangzi, penned the first seven chapters, traditionally referred to as the "Inner Chapters." The remaining chapters are either an assemblage of heterogeneous fragments, some probably by the author of the Inner Chapters, or products from the pen of later writers and added to the text as it was handed down. These writings sometimes depart from the thought of the Inner Chapters. While "hermits" do appear in the Inner Chapters, they surface with much greater frequency in the Outer Chapters, and as such, are less philosophically significant in the Inner Chapters.

2. Chapter 1, "Free and Easy Wandering."

3. Chapter 17, "Autumn Floods."

4. Chapter 6, sec. 9. The use of Confucius to expound Daoist ideas is a common feature of the *Zhuangzi*.

5. Chapter 6, sec. 6. Other well-known examples include the beginning of chapter 2 where Ziqi of South Wall "loses" himself, whose body becomes like withered wood, and mind like dead ashes. The result—he hears the pipings of Heaven.

6. In particular, see chapter 4 "The Human World," where Confucius and Yanhui are discussing the meaning of "fasting" the mind.

7. Chapter 6, "Autumn Floods."

8. Chapter 24, "Xu Wugui."

9. Chapter 5, "Sign of Full Inner Power."

10. See his *Disputers of the Tao* (La Salle, IL.: Open Court, 1989), pp. 202–4, and his partial translation of the Zhuangzi, *Chuang-Tzu: The Inner Chapters* (London: George Allen and Unwin, 1981), pp. 23–24.

11

Knowing in the *Zhuangzi*

"From Here, on the Bridge, over the River Hao"

ROGER T. AMES

The "Autumn Floods" chapter of the *Zhuangzi* concludes with a passage in which the notion of "locus" or "place" or "situation" is presented as being integral to what it means to know. Knowing, for Zhuangzi, is radically situated, and is irreducibly social:

> Zhuangzi and Hui Shi were strolling across the bridge over the Hao River. Zhuangzi observed, "The minnows swim out and about as they please—this is the way they enjoy themselves."
>
> Huizi replied, "You are not a fish—how do you know what they enjoy?"
>
> Zhuangzi returned, "You are not me—how do you know that I don't know what is enjoyable for the fish?"
>
> Huizi said, "I am not you, so I certainly don't know what you know; but it follows that, since you are certainly not the fish, you don't know what is enjoyment for the fish either."
>
> Zhuangzi said, "Let's get back to your basic question. When you asked '*How* do you know what the fish enjoy?' you already knew that I know what the fish enjoy, or you wouldn't have asked me. I know it *from here* above the Hao river."[1]

Angus Graham, in interpreting this passage, observes that the expression *anzhi* 安知 in the last lines of this exchange can mean both "*how* do you know ..." and "*from where* do you know ..."[2] But Zhuangzi is not just depending upon this linguistic ambiguity in order to win a sophistical argument. He has more philosophical fish to fry.

First, Zhuangzi wants to challenge the notions of discrete agency and the "objectivity" of knowledge—the independence of the world known, from the knower. Knowledge is always proximate as the condition of an experience rather than of an isolated experiencer. Situation has primacy, and agency is an abstraction from it. Knowledge is a tracing out and mapping of the productive patterns (*li* 理) of one's environs in such a manner as to move efficaciously and without obstruction.[3]

Secondly, for Zhuangzi, knowledge is performative, a function of fruitful correlations. Thus, it is something done—a qualitative achievement. Knowing a situation is the "realizing" of it in the sense of "making it real." Knowing is also perlocutionary in the sense of setting the affective tone of the experience. The knower and the known, the enjoyer and the enjoyment, are inseparable aspects of this same event. Agency cannot be isolated from action, and facticity cannot be separated from modality. As Zhuangzi says elsewhere, "There can only be authentic understanding when there is an authentic person."[4] One and one's posture or perspective is thus integral to and constitutive of what is known, and contributes immediately to the quality of the experience. Where you are, who you are, and what you know, are overlapping abstractions from the concrete experience itself.

The "way" in which the Daoist seeks to pursue personal "realization"—the highest quality of knowledge—is to coordinate one's conduct with the emergent cadence and regularity of the world around one, overcoming any tendencies one might have toward independence and self-sufficiency (*wu sang wo* 吾喪我),[5] and loosing oneself of any attachments that establish this discrete identity:

> Because the sage does not grab hold of anything,
> He does not lose anything.[6]

There is a caution necessary in making this point. As Chris Jochim has underscored in his contribution to this volume, it is important not to superordinate and thus naturalize an independent ego-self by making it something that we initially have, and then need to overcome. Rather, we begin as an inchoate, incipient focus of relationships, and have the opportunity to cultivate and extend these intrinsic relations, transforming them into a situated and relationally constituted "self."[7]

The point of this anecdote of Zhuangzi and Hui Shi in which Zhuangzi claims that he knows that the fish are happy *from here* on the bridge is that knowledge is always proximate, situational, participatory, and interpretative. It is because Zhuangzi is continuous with his surrounds that "knowledge" of the situation emerges, where the fishes are no less entailed in the realization of the happy experience than Zhuangzi and Hui Shi themselves. It is the situation rather than some discrete agent that is properly described (and prescribed) as happy. The reflexivity of Zhuangzi means that he is himself-in-context, where the membrane between Zhuangzi and context is porous and fluid. The event is "realized" in the doing of it. And language both articulates (*ming* 名) and commands into being (*ming* 命) the relationships that constitute Zhuangzi in his world. As the *Zhuangzi* observes,

> A path (*dao*) becomes a path by people walking it.
> A thing being called something becomes it.
> Why is it so?
> It is so because it is so.
> Why is it not something other than what it is?
> It is not because it is not.[8]

Zhuangzi's experience with the fishes entails a continuity between his world and the world of the fishes, and as such, his claim to knowledge is a claim to having been there. However, being continuous with the fishes and collaborating with them in the experience, does not deny the fishes their difference. The absence of a discrete and individuated self and the attachments that define it, does not discount the importance given to the particular, and to the uniqueness of its perspective. In fact, it is only through Zhuangzi's deference to their difference—by allowing them to be what they are—that the experience can be optimally fruitful and "enjoyable" for all concerned.

This notion of what we might call "proximate knowing" can be reinforced by rehearsing what the twentieth-century comparative philosopher Zhang Dongsun 張東蓀 takes to be the distinguishing characteristics of Chinese epistemology. When the knower and the known establish a relationship, according to Zhang, there are three conditions:

1. They are intrinsically related such that each relationship influences the other, the relationships are intricate and complex, and each member of the relationship is different after the relationship has been established, and changes with it.
2. All relationships are mediated by layer after layer of intervening experience, rather than being unmediated and direct.
3. Knowledge is always a kind of interpretation rather than a copy or representation.[9]

In reflecting on an important transformation that occurs when moving between European sources and its Chinese version, An Yanming observes that there is a "priority of ethics over epistemology" such that epistemological concepts in

their European version often become "a source of ethical standards rather than . . .
a key to reality" when removed to China.[10] Applying this insight to Zhang
Dongsun's characterization of Chinese epistemology, we would have to allow that
he is not only reflecting on epistemic assumptions characteristic of the Chinese
tradition, but more fundamentally and importantly, on how personal, communal,
and political relationships are formed and develop. The epistemic commitment lies
in "realizing" a viable community rather than "knowing" the truth about the world.

This is where Zhuangzi's analytic "sidekick," Hui Shi, comes in. His is a
unique perspective that is illustrative of the importance of the particular. He is an
important element in the anecdote, and contributes directly to the quality of the
experience. As we learn from Lisa Raphal's essay in this volume, the portraits of
the sophistical Hui Shi in the classical corpus are many and varied, and yet there is
no disputing the fact that Zhuangzi loved this man dearly, and credited him with
being the occasion on which Zhuangzi himself was able to turn his best ideas. The
emptiness left by Hui Shi's passing is told with some poignancy after Zhuangzi's
favorite interlocutor has left this life:

> Zhuangzi was in a burial procession when he passed the tomb of
> Huizi. Turning around to address those following him, he said to them:
> "There was a man of Ying who, when finding a piece of mortar on the
> tip of his nose as thick as a fly's wing, would get Carpenter Rock to
> swipe it off with his blade. Carpenter Rock wielded his axe like the
> wind, and doing as he was told, would cut the bit of mortar away
> cleanly without injury to the nose. And the whole time the man of Ying
> would stand there without batting an eye.
>
> Lord Yuan of Song heard of this, and summoning Carpenter Rock
> to him, said, 'Try to do this on me.'
>
> Carpenter Rock replied, 'As for me, I once was able to swipe the
> mortar off with my blade, but it has been some time now since my
> target died.'
>
> Since Huizi died, I too have had no one as a target, no one to really
> talk with!"[11]

Huizi, a philosopher of an analytical, positivistic bent, appears in several anecdotes
throughout the *Zhuangzi* as the rather straight and humorless target of Zhuangzi's
many ripostes. In this particular reverie, Zhuangzi acknowledges that his own
repartee—his ability to wield his wit like the wind—has been dependent upon his
relationship with Huizi who could stand his impeccably logical ground without
batting an eye. Death has made Huizi one of a kind, because in Huizi's absence,
there is no one who can take his place in a relationship that has made these rich
philosophical experiences possible. Zhuangzi cannot carry the conversation on
alone, and the quality of his experience in the world is diminished with the demise
of this particular interlocutor.

"Proximate knowing" is entailed by the way in which *xin* 心, conventionally translated as "heart-and-mind," is understood within the culture. First, and most obviously, the heart-and-mind does the work of both cognizing and feeling, there is no dichotomous relationship between intellection and sensation, between thinking and living. Secondly, taking our cue from Chinese medicine, we have to think physiologically rather than anatomically. The term *zhen mo* 診脈 means "to take a pulse" rather than "to locate and examine a blood vessel or artery," and as such, has systemic reference. Similarly, *xin* is, first and foremost, the systemic function of thinking and feeling, and only derivatively, an organ that represents this function.

We can further illustrate this notion of "proximate knowing" by appealing to the classical Chinese language in which the cultural experience is embedded. There are some usually unannounced features of the classical Chinese language (in addition to the absence of the copula verb explored below) that are illustrative of a situational, rather than agency-centered, conception of experience. To begin with, Chinese terms often, much to the perplexity of the English translator, entail both the subject and the object of understanding. For example, *ming* 明, "bright," can refer derivitively to the perspicacity of the subject, or to the or brilliance of the object, but more fundamentally, to both at the same time. That is, it is an illumined situation. Conversely, *bi* 蔽 can mean derivitively obscured vision on the part of the subject, or something covering the object of one's vision, but more fundamentally, to both at the same time. That is, it is an obscure situation. And *de* 德 can refer derivatively to the beneficence of the ruler, or derivatively to the gratitude of the people, but more fundamentally, to both at the same time. That is, it is a situation of giving and getting.[12]

A second revealing feature of the classical Chinese language is paronomastic definition. When we consult the dictionary which seeks to explain the Chinese world, we discover that terms are not defined by appeal to essential, literal meanings, but rather are brought into focus paronomastically by semantic and phonetic associations. "Exemplary person" (*junzi* 君子), for example, is defined by its cognate and phonetically similar, "to gather, to assemble" (*qun* 群), with the assumption that "people gather round and defer to exemplary persons."[13] "Mirror" (*jing* 鏡) is defined as "radiant" (*jing* 景): a mirror is a source of illumination. "Battle formation" (*zhen* 陣) is defined as "to display" (*chen* 陳). The "achieved person" (*ren* 仁) is defined as someone "who is slow to speak" (*ren* 訒).[14]

What is remarkable about this sense of meaning is that a term is defined nonreferentially by mining relevant and yet seemingly random associations implicated in the terms themselves. Further, erstwhile nominal expressions ("things") usually default to verbal expressions ("events")—for example, "mirror" to "brilliance"—underscoring the primacy of process over form, and situation over agency, as grounding presuppositions in this tradition.

There is a recurrent expression in the *Daodejing* that makes a point similar to the *Zhuangzi*'s River Hao anecdote in a refrain that ends several of the verses:

"From this (*yici* 以此)." For example, posing the question: "How do I know that the world is so?" the text answers, "From this."[15] The question rephrased is: What is your perspective on this? So the question "how?" also means "whence?" And the answer is not only "thusly," but also "from here." Knowing can only be "here" and thus can only be "from this," which is inclusive of one's perspective, as opposed to "from that," which would exclude it. The focus, then, is not upon the external environs as an object of knowledge, but upon the perspective where the act of knowing takes place.

As we saw in the *Zhuangzi* anecdote, also implicit in this question, "how?" is "how well?" That is, how much influence do you have in the shaping of this world qualitatively? The expression "this (*shi* 是)" functions both descriptively and normatively, identifying the place and affirming it qualitatively.

A familiar pattern in the *Daodejing* is for a particular verse to end with "this is what is meant by ..." (*shi wei* ... 是謂 ...). This refrain is not simply a descriptive claim; it is prescriptive and affirming: "correct is what is meant by ...." This is how things are; and this is desirably so.

The dictionary tells us that *shi* 是 sometimes means "this" as in the phrase, "that (*bi*) comes from this (*shi*) 彼出於是,"[16] and sometimes means "right" as in "what is right (*shi*) for one, is wrong (*fei*) for the other" 欲是其所非而非其 所是.[17] In fact, *shi* is both an indication and an affirmation of what is so—it is an *amor fati*, the affirmation of the particular details of this situation. And since affirming something commands it to be so, it is an effort to construe the world in a particular way with the authority that, from one's perspective, this is the way it ought to be: "This is so (and that is not), and I affirm it so."

The Daoist tradition is critical of the Confucian willingness to limit its concerns to the human world alone. It does not reject the "extension" of oneself in the development of one's humanity (*ren* 仁).[18] But the Daoists seek to go further in extending oneself to all things by "acting authentically and without coercion" (*wuwei* 無為). The Daoist texts, like their Confucian counterparts, see resistance to the emergence of a discriminating self, as a precondition for integrative natural action and the extension of one's *de* 德 that follows from it. In a *Zhuangzi* parody on Confucius:

> Yan Hui said, "I have made progress."
> "How so?" inquired Confucius.
> "I have sat and forgotten (*zuowang* 坐忘)."
> Confucius, noticeably flustered, inquired: "What do you mean by 'sitting and forgetting?'"
> "I have demolished my appendages and body, gotten rid of my keenness of sight and hearing, abandoned my physical form, and cast off knowledge, and in so doing, have joined the Great Thoroughfare." said Yan Hui.
> "This is what I call 'sitting and forgetting.'"[19]

Perhaps the most helpful metaphor available in the Daoist texts to elucidate the notion of "interpenetration" achieved in joining "the Great Thoroughfare" (*datong* 大通) is that of the tally. The *Daodejing* states:

> The sage, holding onto the left half of the tally
> Does not demand payment from others;
> The person with potency (*de*) takes charge of the tally;
> The person without potency looks to collecting on it.[20]

The meaning of this rather obscure passage is made clear in the fifth chapter of the *Zhuangzi*, the title of which is "*De* Satisfies the Tally" (*dechongfu* 德充符). This chapter is a series of anecdotes about a motley series of mutilated cripples who, under normal circumstances and under the sway of conventional values, would be ostracized from their communities. Their crippled physical forms, often the result of amputatory punishment, would be certain grounds for societal rejection. Having overcome discreteness by extending their *de* to contribute to and integrate themselves with the community, however, they "satisfy the tally" with their *de* and not only blend harmoniously with their societies, but further come to exercise considerable influence in establishing the importances of their respective worlds. The extent and quality of their *de* is such that they are important factors in the on-going process of defining values and establishing an aesthetic and moral order.

In the Daoist tradition, the extension of one's *de* is described in more pervasive terms than in the Confucian literature. As in the Confucian tradition, at times such a person becomes the embodiment and protector of the human order, a styler of new culture, and a source of new meaning. But the Daoists take it beyond this into the natural world.[21] The "authentic person"—*zhenren* 真人 the Daoist version of the consummating person—embraces the *de* of the natural as well as the human environment. By becoming coextensive with the *de* of the ox, for example, Cook Ding in butchering its carcass is able to penetrate and interpret its natural lineaments and interstices without distraction, and hence is able to become an efficacious butcher;[22] by becoming coextensive with the *de* of the wood, Carpenter Qing is sensitive to the quality and potential of his materials without distraction, and hence is able to become an efficacious craftsman.[23] The absence of a "dis-integrating" discrete self and the cultivation of an open, situated presence, makes these exemplars open to the *de* of their natural environments, so that the environment contributes to them, making them potent and productive, and they contribute to their environments, interpreting and maximizing the possibilities of those things which constitute their world.

The dynamic nature of this process of extending one's *de* is underscored in the vocabulary that defines the Daoist tradition. The person of pervasive *de*, for example, is called *zhenren*—"the authentic person."[24] The character, *zhen* 真, meaning "authentic" or "genuine," is classified under the radical *bi* 匕, which means "to transform" (*hua* 化). In the *Zhuangzi*, the process of existence itself is referred to as the "transformation of things" (*wuhua* 物化). As the Daoist *zhenren* extends himself to become one with his natural environment, he becomes increasingly deferential to the transformation of things. To the extent that he embraces the *de* of his totality within his particularity, he is integrated and efficacious at whatever he does. What might be perceived as his interface with "other" is in fact coincident *de*, enabling him to facilitate and interpret the natural expression of whatever he encounters. His hands express the clay, and the clay expresses his hands.

This situational self stands in stark contrast to the familiar notion of discrete agency. The importance invested in the notion of discrete human agency in the Western tradition derives arguably from an historical analogy between the human being's essential self (*psyche*), and Deity. The essentializing copula verb ("is" from L. *esse*) establishes the static agent, separating and superordinating one's unitary self from one's actions, one's attributes, and one's modalities. The copula verb "copulates"—it joins what is originally two, into one. In the Judaeo-Christian tradition, God is the primary causal agent—perfect and unchanging—existing independent of His actions. And human beings are shaped by Him in His own image. Just as this unitary God originates activity and orders the universe purposefully, so the unitary human being as microcosm acts from design to shape the world. The perfection of the universe and the unity of the Logos or knowledge that defines it is guaranteed by the unchanging perfection of its Maker. To know is *gnosis*: to know the One behind the many.

By contrast with this familiar classical Western model of knowing, classical Chinese philosophy, exemplified by this River Hao passage in the *Zhuangzi*, has a fundamental commitment to the process, the motion, and the change, integral to all experience. To begin with, the classical Chinese language has no copula verb that would entail an assumed separation of agent from action, self from context, essence from attribute.[25] It is this appeal to the copula verb—"he *is* ..."—that attempts to join the originally separate agent to everything else.

The classical Chinese language, operating without the copula verb, then, leaves the whole process intact without assuming an abstracted agent. In fact, agent, action, attribute, and modality are all included in what are fundamentally "events" rather than "things." Thus, in classical China, a human being is not what one *is*; it is the compounding narrative of what one *does*—an always unique field of experiences, beliefs, and feelings.

In the absence of a discrete and independent agency, knowing is the unraveling and the coordinating of the patterns (*li* 理) of continuity that emerge and persist in the natural, social, and cultural flux in which we are radically and resolutely embedded. These patterned regularities give life coherence and make it more and sometimes less predictable. Pattern is not imposed upon the world by some external agency, but rather, resides within the world as the rhythm and cadence of a living stream. And any particular human being is simply one impulse integral to this continually unfolding process.

In a world where process and change are deemed prior to form and rest, there can be little incentive to develop notions of discrete agency. From the classical Chinese perspective, agents cannot be decontextualized and superordinated; to identify and isolate an agent is an abstraction that removes a person from the concrete reality of flux, exaggerating this person's continuity at the expense of the ongoing transformative process. Since change is interior to all situations, human beings cannot act upon a world that stands independent of them. Rather, they are interdependent with the world in which they reside, simultaneously shaping and being shaped by it. Order is always reflexive, entailing the agent within the action itself. Agency and action, subject and object, are not contraries, but interchangeable aspects of a single category: experience. Thus, the distinction between the agent and the action, between subject and object, between what does and what is done, is simply a matter of perspective. We read and interpret *Zhuangzi*, and *Zhuangzi* shapes and thus expresses us.

The classical Western model of order invests a great deal in causal explanations—especially efficient causes—that attempt to identify and isolate the discrete agent responsible for an event. By contrast, the Chinese model is situational, seeking to understand the whole range of relevant causal conditions and the relations that obtain among them as they come to sponsor any given occurrence.

Instead of causal agency, the Chinese notion of "situationality" is captured in *shi* 勢, which, as an ongoing process that includes agency within it, means at once "situation," "momentum," and "manipulation." *Shi* includes all of the conditions that collaborate to produce a particular situation, including place, agencies, and actions.

The classical Western search for order is ambitious; its goal is the clear, the exact, the comprehensive knowledge of the unitary cosmic design and the forces that drive it—those natural and moral "laws" that structure and regulate the natural and human universe. The classical Chinese approach is much more modest; it seeks to understand the always novel continuities that define and give meaning to *this* particular moment and *this* particular place in life's ongoing process.

The classical Western metaphysical model is based on the concept of a universal blueprint made up of unchanging formal principles that, once understood, make change predictable and logarithmic. The Chinese model allows that regularity is always attended by change, and this makes order dynamic, site-specific, and provisional. Given that the patterned regularity is never decontextualized or detemporalized, the rhythm of life is indefatigable and irreversible, and is evident in the configuration of each snowflake, the grain of each piece of wood, the aura of each sunset, the complexity of each personality, as these always unique phenomena, emerge in the temporal flow only to recede into it again.

Because this classical Chinese sense of order entails a thoroughly symbiotic relationship between its formal and its fluid aspects, every situation is necessarily unique, making globalizing and essentializing generalizations problematic. In fact, in a Borgesian sense, every "event" should have a proper name to underscore its singularity, and this proper name should be continually updated to respect the ongoing transformation of its referent.

In classical Western theology, shaped and given definition by Greek metaphysical assumptions, the equivocation between "unity" and "uniqueness" is resolved in favor of "unity": the One True God, a knowledge of which makes all things intelligible. Thus, in any of the various conceptions of a single-ordered universe assumed by the early systematic philosophers, the many phenomena comprising the world are defined in accordance with unifying principles that determine the essential reality of the things of the world.

But this term "one" is ambiguous. This single world of classical China is "one" in the sense that it is a continuous plenum, so that everything is related to and dependent upon everything else. It is also "one" in the sense that everything in it is unique, *one* of a kind (rather than one of a *kind*). Again, it is one in the sense of being resolutely hierarchical and centripetal, with overlapping patterns of deference ultimately (and ideally) generating only one center. In fact, beginning from the assumption that all of the myriad things which constitute the world are unique, the philosophical problem that has dominated Chinese thinking across the centuries is how do we coordinate all of the unique particulars of our world to maintain a centered and a productive continuity? How do we achieve harmony (*he* 和) here and now? It is this sense in which China strives to be truly "*Zhongguo*" 中國—the centered kingdom. Centripetal harmony and continuity are grounding cultural values in the Chinese tradition which, in both the classical and modern world, explain phenomena such as the drive toward one China, commentarial deference to canonical orthodoxy, religious sensibilities grounded in ancestor worship and locality (*zongjiao* 宗教), rationality defined in terms of unbroken and coherent patterns (*ho li* 合理), the persistence of government through a pyramidal and centralized bureaucracy, and so on.

The Chinese world is not "one" in the classical Greek sense of a single-ordered "*uni*"-verse where some external, independent, and determinative principle provides unity and order to something other than itself. It is not "one" in the sense that would make it a closed system, defined in terms of abstract, universal, necessary, and unchanging natural and moral laws. Rather, the boundary of Chinese world is the family lineage, the local county line, a shared past, the Great Wall—the advancing line that divides "inside" from "outside," making what lies beyond peripheral and only marginally relevant.

Returning from these more abstract observations to Zhuangzi, Hui Shi, and the happy fishes, this anecdote has now become part of our experiential repertoire, and to the extent that we can play with it to get on the "inside" of the *Zhuangzi*, we too can know the enjoyment of the fishes from the bridge over the River Hao.

NOTES

In this essay, I have appropriated and elaborated upon a few pages of chapter 1 in David L. Hall and Roger T. Ames, *Thinking from the Han: Self, Truth, and Transcendence in Chinese and Western Culture* (Albany: State University of New York Press, 1998).

1. *Zhuangzi* 45/17/87. All references are to *Chuang Tzu* (Peking: Harvard-Yenching Institute Sinological Index Series, Supplement 20, 1947). Cf. A. C. Graham, p. 123. All references are to A. C. Graham (trans.), *Chuang-tzu: The Inner Chapters* (London: George Allen & Unwin, 1981).

2. Graham, p. 123.

3. This definition of "experience" in the *Zhuangzi* has an analog in John Dewey who says:

> Intelligence ... is not ours originally or by production. "It thinks" is a truer psychological statement than "I think." Thoughts sprout and vegetate; ideas proliferate. They come from deep unconscious sources. "I think" is a statement about voluntary action. Some suggestion surges from the unknown. Our active body of habits appropriates it. The suggestion then becomes an assertion.... The stuff of belief and proposition is not originated by us. It comes to us from others, by education, tradition, and the suggestion of the environment. Our intelligence is bound up, as far as its materials are concerned, with the community life of which we are a part. We know what it communicates to us, and know according to the habits it forms in us. Science is an affair of civilization not of individual intellects.

See John Dewey, *The Philosophy of John Dewey*, ed. John J. McDermott (Chicago: University of Chicago Press, 1973), p. 713.

4. *Zhuangzi* 15/6/4; cf. Graham, p. 84.

5. *Zhuangzi* 3/2/3; cf. Graham, p. 48.

6. *Daodejing* 64.

7. This notion of the extension of proximate knowledge is also found in the *Analects*; see 14/35:

> The Master said, "I study what is near at hand and aspire to what is lofty."

8. *Zhuangzi* 4/2/33; cf. Graham, p. 53.

9. See Zhang Dongsun, *Zhishi yu wenhua: Zhang Dongsun wenhua lunzhu jiyao*, ed. Zhang Huinan (Beijing: Zhongguo Guangbo dianshi chubanshe, 1995), p. 172ff.

10. See An Yanming, "Liang Shuming and Henri Bergson on Intuition," in *Philosophy East & West* 47.3:337.

11. *Zhuangzi* 66/24/48; Graham, p. 124.

12. The passage in *Analects* 14/34, echoing perhaps *Daodejing* 63, requires this understanding of the language to be intelligible:

> Someone asked, "What do you think about the saying: 'Repay ill-will with beneficence (*de*)'?"
>
> The Master replied, "Then how would one repay beneficence? Repay ill-will by remaining true. Repay beneficence (*de*) with gratitude (*de*)."

13. As it insists in the *Analects* 4/24: "Excellent persons do not live alone; they are sure to have neighbors."

14. See *Analects* 12/3.

15. *Daodejing* 54. See also 21 and 57. Another repeated expression that has the same import is "Therefore discarding that he takes this. (*gu qubi quci* 故去彼取此)." See 12, 38, and 72.

16. *Zhuangzi* 4/2/27; cf. Graham, p. 52.

17. *Zhuangzi* 4/2/26; cf. Graham, p. 52.

18. This point is made in the Brian Lundberg piece on Daoist "friendship" in this volume.

19. *Zhuangzi* 19/6/89; cf. Graham, p. 92.

20. *Daodejing* 79.

21. Kirill Thompson and his fisherman have suggested as much in his essay in this volume.

22. *Zhuangzi* 7/3/2; cf. Graham, pp. 63–64.

23. *Zhuangzi* 50/19/54; cf. Graham, p. 135.

24. For a fuller discussion, see Danny Coyle's analysis of *zhenren* in this volume.

25. It is interesting, and not surprising, that under the influence of Western languages, the modern Chinese language has introduced *shi* 是 as the copula verb. As we have seen, this is a term which in the classical language serves as a demonstrative pronoun and a definite article—"this," as well as an expression of affirmation—"right." So when the copula is used in modern Chinese, it is not conjoining two things, but pointing at and affirming something on a single plenum from a particular perspective. "*Ta shi Meiguoren*"

About the Contributors

ROGER T. AMES is Professor of Philosophy and Director of the Center for Chinese Studies at the University of Hawai'i. He is editor of *Philosophy East & West* and *China Review International*. His recent publications include translations of Chinese classics: *Sun-Tzu: The Art of Warfare* (1993); *Sun Pin: The Art of Warfare* (1996) and Yuan Dao: *Tracing Dao to Its Source* (1998) (both with D. C. Lau); and the *Analects of Confucius* (with H. Rosemont) (1998). He has also authored several interpretative studies of Chinese philosophy and culture: *Thinking Through Confucius* (1987), *Anticipating China: Thinking Through the Narratives of Chinese and Western Culture* (1995), and *Thinking From the Han: Self, Truth, and Transcendence in Chinese and Western Culture* (1998) (all with D. L. Hall).

WILLIAM A. CALLAHAN is a Lecturer in the Department of Politics at the University of Durham, England. He received his Ph.D. in Political Science and M.A. in Chinese Studies from the University of Hawai'i at Mānoa. His research interests include Chinese philosophy, the cultural politics of East Asia, and international relations. At present, he is writing a book entitled *Confucianism, Greater China and East Asian International Relations* and has published articles in *Philosophy East & West*, *East West Film Journal*, *Pacific Review*, *Asian Review*, *Boundary 2*, and *Alternatives* as well as chapters in numerous edited volumes.

DANIEL COYLE received a B.S. in Physics from Birmingham Southern College and a M.A. in Comparative Philosophy from the University of Hawai'i. He has studied at Taiwan Normal University, Peking University, and has reviewed for *China Review International*. He is currently writing his dissertation at the University of Hawai'i.

CHRIS JOCHIM is Professor and Program Coordinator, Comparative Religious Studies Program, San Jose State University, where he has taught since 1985. He is the author of *Chinese Religions: A Cultural Perspective*, which holds a prominent place in the Prentice-Hall Series in World Religions. He has also published articles on various aspects of Chinese religion and philosophy in such journals as the *Journal of Chinese Religions, Journal of Religions Ethics,* and *Philosophy East & West.* Currently, he is engaged in research on the nature and development of Confucian traditions in contemporary Taiwan.

BRIAN LUNDBERG is a Ph.D. candidate in the Philosophy Department at the University of Hawai'i completing his dissertation entitled, "Musical and Ritual Therapeutics in the *Xunzi*: The Psychophysical Dynamics of Self-Crafting." He has worked with Professor Yang Yu-wei for three years reading the classics of Confucianism and Daoism, and has published "Aesthetic Dimensions in the Confucian Project of Cultivating One's Person" in *Asian Culture Quarterly.*

JOHN MAKEHAM is a senior lecturer in Chinese studies at the Centre for Asian Studies, University of Adelaide, Australia. Since publication of his *Name and Actuality in Early Chinese Thought* (SUNY Press, 1994) he has been working on a long-term research project on the Chinese commentarial tradition of the *Analects* and has recently published studies from this project in *Monumenta Serica* and *T'oung Pao.*

RANDALL PEERENBOOM, having accepted a post of Acting Professor of Law at UCLA School of Law, is currently practicing law in Beijing with the international firm Freshfields. His recent academic works include *Law and Morality in Ancient China: The Silk Manuscripts of Huang-lao* (SUNY Press, 1993); "Confucian Harmony and Freedom of Thought: Right Thinking Versus the Right to Think," in *Confucianism and Human Rights,* ed. Wm. de Bary (Columbia University Press, 1998); "Right, Interests and the Interest in Rights in China," *Stanford Journal of International Law;* Law and Ritual in Chinese Philosophy, in *Routledge Encyclopaedia of Philosophy* (1998) and "The Limits of Irony: Rorty and the China Challenge" in *Philosophy East & West* (2000).

LISA RAPHALS is author of *Knowing Words: Wisdom and Cunning in the Classical Traditions of China and Greece* (Cornell University Press, 1992) and *Sharing the Light: Representations of Women and Virtue in Early China* (SUNY Press, 1998). She has published chapters in collected volumes on Confucius, *Zhuangzi,* and the *Shiji* and a range of articles and book reviews (*Bulletin of the School of Oriental and African Studies, CLEAR, Routledge Encyclopedia of Philosophy, Journal of Chinese Religions, The Journal of Religion, Philosophy East & West, Taoist Resources*). She teaches in the Comparative Literature program at UC Riverside.

JAMES D. SELLMANN holds two Bachelor of Arts degrees in Philosophy, and Psychology from the University of Nevada, Las Vegas, 1979; and two Master of Arts degrees in Asian Religions, 1981, and Asian Philosophy, 1983, and the Doctorate in Chinese Philosophy, 1990, from the University of Hawai'i. As Associate Professor of Philosophy at the University of Guam, he also coordinates the honors program. He has published in *Philosophy East & West, Asian Culture Quarterly, Indian Philosophical Quarterly,* and various anthologies and reference works and is currently working on a book concerning the role of time in the political philosophy of *Master Lu's Spring and Autumn Annals (Lüshi chunqiu).* He also has been reconstructing the philosophical thought of Pacific Islanders in Micronesia.

HENRY G. SKAJA received his B.A. in philosophy from San Francisco State University, and his Ph.D. in philosophy from the University of Hawai'i. He is currently a lecturer in philosophy at Chaminade University of Honolulu, and at Leeward Community College. He has also taught for a number of years in Taiwan. His publications include articles and reviews in *Chinese Culture* (The China Academy, Taipei) and *Philosophy East & West.*

KIRILL O. THOMPSON, Ph.D., Hawai'i 1985, teaches at National Taiwan University. He is an active member of the American Philosophical Association, the Society for Asian and Comparative Philosophy, and the Society for the Study of Chinese Religions. His principal publications on Taoism and Neo-Confucianism have appeared in *Philosophy East & West* and the *Journal of Chinese Philosophy.* Professor Thompson has been concerned to explicate the original "applied" attitude of Chinese philosophy as well as to bring insights from Chinese philosophy to bear on problems in Western philosophy. He also enjoys the intersection between philosophy and literature.

Index

A

agency, 220, 226
alchemy, Daoist, 205
Allinson, Robert, 44–45
Ames, Roger T., 40, 46, 112, 186, 202
An Yanming, 221–222
Analects, The, 10, 75–94
anātman, (no self), 45
artist, as Daoist sage, 125–140

B

Berling, Judith, 43–44, 60–61
Book of Changes, (Yi Jing), 111, 198
Buddha nature, (*tatathagarbha*), 42
Buddhism, and Daoism, 8, 45

C

Campbell, James, 102–103
Chan Buddhism, (Zen), 29, 42
chang xin, (constant heart-mind), 53
Confucian, social virtues, 103–116
Confucianism, and Daoism, 5–6, 10–11,
    103–116, 131, 148, 180, 225
Confucius, stories of, 22, 23–25, 26–27,
    75–94, 171–172, 177, 198–199, 224
contingency, 177–179
copula, absence in classical Chinese, 223,
    226
correlative thinking, 166
cripples, significance of, 225
Csikszentmihalyi, Mihaly, 62–65

D

dao, (Tao; way), 18, 21, 24–25, 28–30,
    44–45, 52, 101–102, 104–105, 107,
    112–114, 171, 186, 201, 220; *dao
    shu*, (axis of daos), 186–188, 204;
    daode, (field-focus), 2–7, 199
Daodejing, (Laozi), 1, 3, 21, 25–2 6, 180,
    197, 223–224; and image of water
    16–20
Daxue, (Great Learning), 47
de, (Te; virtue; potency), 101–102, 103,
    106, 107, 190, 225–226
death, 13, 166, 171, 204–205, 213, 216–
    217, 222
decision-making, 176–192, esp. 189–190
deeming, *(wei shi)*, 185–186, 200
definition, paranomastic, 223
Descartes, René, 38
detachment, 217
Dewey, John, 10, 14, 102–109, 113–114
dialectic, 169
Ding, Cook, 12, 47, 66, 134, 175–192,
    225
distinction-making, 181–182, 200, 203
Dobson, W. A. C., 47
drives, Nietzschean, 199
dualistic thinking, 38–39, 41, 181
Durell, Lawrence, 129

E

eccentricity of Daoist sage, 125–140

ecstatic experience, 61–62
Elvin, Mark, 40, 46
emergent order, 227–228
emotion, (*qing*), 216
emptiness, (*xu*), 52
Eno, Robert, 66
eremitism, 88–91, 105–106, *see also*
    hermitism
ethics, Daoist, 4–5, 65–68; and episte-
    mology 221–222

F
fantastic tales, 60–61
Fingarette, Herbert, 46
fish, symbolism, 17–19
fishermen, significance in the Zhuangzi, 9,
    15–30
flow, 36, 56–65
flux, 226–228
forgetting, (*wang*), 44–45, 49–50, 55, 60,
    212–213
freedom, 163–172
friendship, 13, 14, 19, 211–217; as *being-
    with, being-for* and *mutually-forgetting*,
    212–213, 215–216
Fukunaga, Mitsuji, 111

G
Gaozi, 110
gnosis, 200–201
God, 226
Graham, Angus Charles, 1, 25–26, 36, 53–
    54, 59, 65–66, 75, 86, 101–109, 144,
    200
Guan Feng, 1, 144
Guiguzi, 205
Guo Xiang, 57–58, 62, 167, 204

H
Hall, David L., 45–46
Han Feizi, 11, 143–144, 150–153, 155
Hansen, Chad, 181, 188
Hanshi waizhuan, 153
Harbsmeier, Christoph, 154

harmony, 228
Hegel, G. W. F., 169
Heraclitus, 19
hermitism, 15–30, 211, *see also* eremitism
Homer, 66–67
horizontal and vertical alliances, 152
hua, (transformation), 170–172, 225–226
Huainanzi, 1, 8, 25, 143–144, 145, 153–
    154
Hui Shi, (Huizi/Master Hui), 11–12, 13–
    14, 49, 143–156, 169, 220–221;
    friendship with Zhuangzi, 214–215,
    222
humor, 12, 14, 163–172

I
individualism, 39
indeterminacy, 165–166
integration, 205
irony, 168–170
Ivanhoe, P. J., 66

J
ji, (self), 9, 35–68, esp. 46–56
jie, (understand; cut up), 91, 168–169
Johnson, Frank, 38–39
Jung, Carl, 21–22

K
Kjellberg, Paul, 43, 57, 66
knack stories, 59–60, 63–64, 175–192
knowing, proximate, 221–223
knowledge, as knowing, 2–3, 13–14, 200–
    202; as unlearning, 21; as situated,
    219–228
Kohn, Livia, 62
Kun (fish), 17–18, 167

L
language, and action, 181–182
Lao Dan, 198–199
Lao Siguang, 41
Laozi. See Daodejing
Lau, D. C., 109

li, (pattern), 3, 220, 226
li, (ritual), 131, 198
li yi, (ritual and morality), 149
Liezi, 1
Liezi, (Master Lie), 60–61
Lin Ji, 42
Lin Tongqi, 40
Liu Guangyi, 42
Liu Zongyuan, 28–29
Lo Genze, 1
Locke, John, 38
locus, (situation), 219
Loy, David, 45
Lüshi chunqiu, (*The Springs and Autumns of Lü*), 11, 82, 86–88, 143, 144–148, 152

M
Mair, Victor, 36
Mauss, Marcel, 37
McCraw, David, 204
Mencius, 10–11, 75–94
Mencius, 101–102, 104–105, 112–114
metamorphosis, 17–18, 167
Miller, Henry, 11, 14, 125–140
ming, (command; destiny), 10, 111–112, 221
ming, (illumination), 12, 164, 177–192, esp. 183–184
mirror, 188
Mozi, 81
Mozi, 148
Munro, Donald, 148
mysticism, 56–65

N
nature, human, 101–105
Nietzsche, Friedrich, 13, 39, 127, 200–201
Nin, Anaïs, 129
Nivison, David, 148
no-self, 9–10, 35–68, 212

O
oneness, as unity *vs.* uniqueness and continuity, 228
order, 227–228

P
Paper, Jordan, 61
paradox, 143–144, 170, 199–200, 203–204, 215
paranomasia, 223
particularity, 221, 226–227
Peng (bird), 164, 178, 214
personhood, 17–18, 46–56, 64–65; pluralistic conception of, 67–68
perspective, 181, 200, 205, 214
Pindar, 18
poetry, 27–30
politics, 176
postmodernism, 170
process, 226–228

Q
qi, (breath; energy), 17–18, 52
Qian Mu, 58
Qing, Carpenter, 225

R
realization, stages of, 20–26
relativism, 66, 176
ren, (others), self and, 53
ren yi, (humaneness/kindness and rightness/propriety), 87–91, 103, 110, 198
renxing, (human nature), 101–105, 110
Rosemont, Henry, 40, 176
Roth, Harold, 1, 62

S
sage, Daoist as unconventional, 125–140
sagehood, levels of 20–27, 43–44; as social, 211–217
self, 2–3, 9–10, 14, 35–68; modern concept of, 37–40; as analytic, 39; as monotheistic, 39; as individualistic, 39; as materialistic-rationalistic, 40; as physical, cognitive, moral and aesthetic, 41; (*wu; wo*), 42–43, 55–56; postmodern, 45–46; Confucian, 46; and ethics, 65–68
self-transformation, 44–45
sex, dao of, 131–133
shamanism, 61

shan, (good; desirable; excellent), 108–110

shen, (person; body), 9, 47–51

shen, (spirit), 44

Shen Dao, 55

shengren, (sage), 2

shi, (situation; circumstances), 227

shi, (this; affirm), 224

shi/fei, (this/not this; systems of judgment), 181–192

Shuen-fu Lin, 144

Shuo yuan, 143, 154

Sikong Shu, 29–30

Sima Qian, 76–78

skill. *See* knack stories

St. Augustine, 38

St. Francis, of Assissi, 18

subjectivity, 40–46

T

Tao Yuanming, 21

Taylor, Charles, 37, 40

Thales, 18

Thoreau, Henry, 127

tian, (heaven; nature), 85

tianjun, (potter's wheel of nature), 12

tianni, (whetstone of nature), 12, 175–192, esp. 184–186

timeliness, (*shi*), 79–80, 88–90

transformation, 163–172, 226–228

Truth, 24–26

U

untrammeled persons, 185–186

usual, (*yong*), 182–183, 191–192

Übermensch, as *zhenren*, 201

W

Waley, Arthur, 104

Wang Bi, 198

Wang Pengling, 40

Wang Shumin, 58

Wang Wei, 29

Watanabe, Takashi, 83–84

water, significance in Daoism, 16–20, 60

Watson, Burton, 36, 101, 111

Way, as social, 102–111, 112–114

wei, (artifice), 102

whetstone of nature (*tian ni*), 175–192, esp. 184–186

wildness, 21, 22, 125–140

Williams, Bernard, 66–67

wo, (self), 46–56

worldhood, 227–228

worlds, pluralism of, 178–181

writing, dao of, 129–131

wu, (nothing; no): *wu ji*, (no self; selfless), 35–68; *wu xin*, (mindlessness), 52; *wuwei*, (anarchy; nonassertive activity), 4, 7–8, 10, 103, 106–107, 112, 180; *wuyu*, (objectless desire), 4, 180; *wuzhi*, (nonpincipled knowing), 4, 180

Wu Kuang-ming, 35, 42–43, 166, 169

Wu Yi, 41–42

Wu Zhen, 27

X

xin, (heart-mind), 9, 50–53, 105, 223

xing, (nature), 57, 105

xinzhai, (mind-fasting), 51, 52, 62

Xunzi, 10, 11, 75–94, 143–144

Xunzi, 101–102, 148–150

Y

Yang Xiong, 58

Yang Yu-wei, 11, 14, 138–140

Yi Jing. See Book of Changes

yinshi, (the deeming that goes by circumstance), 164, 169

yin-yang, 17–18

you, (wandering), 35, 63–64

youxin, (letting ones heart wander), 51–52

Z

Zhang Dongsun, 221–222

Zhang Zhihe, 27–28

Zhanguoce, (*Intrigues of the Warring States*), 25, 143, 151, 152, 154–155

zhen, (genuine), 197–199

zhenren, (authentic person), 2–4, 12–13, 14, 164–165, 197–205, 225–226

zhi, (knowledge; cooperative intelligence), 103–108, 112

zhiren, (perfected self; ultimate man; utmost person), 43–44, 53, 61, 187–189

Zhong Kui the Demon-Queller, 11, 14

Zhu, Yang, 25

Zhu Xi, 18–19, 58

Zhuangzi, 1

ziran, (self-disclosure; spontaneity), 2–3, 198

zuo wang, (sitting and forgetting), 62

Zuozhuan, 77

DATE DUE
